HANDS ON
Chicago

D1317718

Kenan Heise

and

Mark Frazel

BONUS BOOKS, CHICAGO

04 03 02 01 00   10 9 8 7 6

Library of Congress Catalog Card Number: 86-72778

International Standard Book Number: 0-933893-28-0

Bonus Books, Inc.
160 East Illinois Street
Chicago, Illinois 60611
www.bonus-books.com

Printed in the United States of America

To the librarians and teachers whose wits and resources
help make Chicago a livable city

Contents

Foreword

Kenan Heise and his colleague Mark Frazel know as much about Chicago as anybody around. Let's say they know enough about it to explain its reputation. Let's say they're up on its history from the pre-Fire to the post-Daley days. That's, give or take a year or two, a century and a half. Let's say there's no better way to celebrate this city's sesquicentennial than by having this book in hand.

Heise runs a bookstore like none other. All the works on all the shelves of his Evanston shop deal with one subject only: Chicago. Naturally. It's the man's obsession. And our good fortune.

The neighborhoods that make up Chicago and their multi-cultured, multi-colored and multi-lingo peoples are also the subjects (and the objects) of Kenan Heise's obsession.

If you want to call it a mini-encyclopedia, it's okay; though I'd go easy on the modifying prefix. Compact may be a better word.

I've lost count of the number of times I've called on him to help me out with a date, long forgotten, or with a place (yes, Bryan made his Cross of Gold speech at the Coliseum), or with some arcane weather fact (yes, it was over 100 degress Fahrenheit the day Harding was nominated.)

When it comes to finding out all sorts of things about this town's past and much of its present, Kenan Heise is my man. And, I trust, yours.

STUDS TERKEL

ACKNOWLEDGMENTS

This book has benefited greatly from the generous care and concern shown to it by the following people: Anne Coyne, whose last-minute contributions made it a much better work; Mary Jo Doyle, who encouraged the authors to do some additional brewing; as well as John Lux, Richard Bridis and Michael Emmerich, who did some very good editing.

Very special thanks go to artist Scott Holingue for his fine, original artwork in this book.

The authors are also indebted to both the writing and personal encouragement of Chicago writers Herman Kogan, Lloyd Wendt, Bob Cromie, the late Emmett Dedmon, Allan Eckert, Edith Freund, Mary Craig, Anita Gold, David Mamet, Mike Royko and Studs Terkel.

For help in compiling the pictures for this book, we particularly wish to thank: Grant B. Schmalgemeier for the use of his photo-postcard collection; Riverview historian Chuck Wlodarczyk; Marty Schmidt, who found a better way to recopy historic photo postcards; photographers Ovie Carter, Karen Engstrom, Carol Heise, William M. Scott, and Mati Maldre; the staffs of the Chicago Tribune reference room, the CTA, the Chicago South Shore & South Bend Railroad, the Chicago & North Western Railroad, Northwestern Memorial Hospital Archives, Historic Pictures Service, Inc. and the Art Institute.

BIBLIOGRAPHICAL RECOGNITION

The authors made use of a personal library on Chicago of over 9,000 titles in writing the book. Still, certain books were more helpful than others and we would like to acknowledge some of them. These include:

Chicago and Its Suburbs (1874); *The Fergus Historical Series* (1876 to 1890); *The History of Cook County* (1884) and *The History of Chicago* 3 vol. (1884-85-86) both by A.T. Andreas; *The Jungle* (1906); *A History of Chicago* 3 vol. (1937-40-47) by Bessie Louise Pierce; *Chicago and Its Makers* (1929); *Forty-Four Cities in the City of Chicago* (1942); *Black Metropolis* (1945); *Chicago: Growth of a Metropolis* (1969); *Lost Chicago* (1975); *Chicago: A Historical Guide* (1979); *The Local Community Fact Book* (especially the ones for 1960 and 1980); *Gateway to Empire* (1983); The series of brochures on Chicago historical and architectural landmark sites produced and published by the staff of the Commission on Chicago Historical and Architectural Landmarks (1970s and 1980s); *A Guide to Chicago's Public Sculpture* (1983); *Chicago: A City of Neighborhoods* (1986); *Back of the Yards: The Making of a Local Democracy* (1986); *Haymarket Scrapbook* (1986); *Chicago* by Studs Terkel (1986); and *Swift Walker* by Lloyd Wendt (1986).

Put Your Hands On Chicago

"There are two kinds of people in this country. There are the ones who love Chicago and the ones who think it is unmitigated hell. I love it. If the world has been my oyster, Chicago has been my cocktail sauce."

—Louella Parsons

PART ONE

Previous page: Michigan Avenue and Monroe Street.

Sarah Bernhardt called Chicago "The pulse of America."

"Most fantastic and folksy of great cities. . . She is unruly at heart; more than a little goofy; she will be one of the last to be tamed by the slow frost of correctness," said Christopher Morley in *Old Loopy.*

At the turn of the century, Chicago Symphony Orchestra founder Theodore Thomas explained: "One reason I came to Chicago was that I understood the excitement and nervous strain that everyone, more or less, suffered who lived there, and realized the consequent need of establishing a permanent musical institution in such a community."

All of these individuals got involved with Chicago, put their hands on it and learned by doing this, it becomes almost manageable.

This book is meant to be a guide to the pulse of Chicago rather than to all its sites and trendy places. We have attempted, in the first part, to compile a mini-encyclopedia of the city, its characters, events, traditions, foibles, buildings, sculptures and legends. The second half describes its community areas, all seventy-seven of them. The two sections are threaded together with a time-line that gives a quick history of Chicago from the visit of Jolliet and Marquette in 1673 to the city's 150th anniversary in 1987.

We have not trimmed thorns to create our portrait of this rose. We present Chicago as described by G.W. Stevens in 1898: "Queen and guttersnipe of cities, cynosure and cesspool of the world: Not if I had a hundred tongues, everyone shouting a different language in a different key, could I do justice to her splendid chaos. The most beautiful and the most squalid, girdled with a twofold zone of parks and slums; where the keen air from the lake and prairie is ever in the nostrils and the stench of foul smoke is never out of the throat; the great port a thousand miles from the sea; the great mart which gathers up with one hand the corn and the cattle of the West and deals out with the other the merchandise of the East; widely and generously planned with streets of twenty miles (in length), where it is not safe to walk at night; the chosen seat of cutthroat commerce and munificent patronage of art; the most American of American cities and yet the most mongrel; the second American city of the globe, the fifth German city, the third Swedish, the second Polish, the first and only Babel of the age. Where in all the world can words be found for this miracle of paradox and incongruity?''

Chicago is a mystery that you can probe armed with facts and we have packed this book with them. But you encounter the city's soul only through its feelings and we have also attempted to record them.

Chicago is coming on strong in the 1980s. You can sense vitality in the Loop, on Michigan Avenue, in River City and Dearborn Park, in suburban shopping centers and industrial complexes, and even in the poorest, most crime-ridden neighborhoods.

One hundred years ago Mayor Carter Harrison I said of Chicago: "The young city is not only vigorous but she laves her beautiful limbs daily in Lake Michigan and comes out clean and pure every morning." It is the same town that Nelson Algren called "Hustletown." Although it is not as young as when Carter Harrison knew it or as much on the make as Algren described it, Chicago is every bit as vigorous.

O'Hare International Airport—which many visitors notice first—has new terminals. The Chicago Historical Society has expanded. The Shedd Aquarium is going to develop out into the lake. Through vagaries of political manipulations, McCormick Place has struggled to construct an enormous exhibition hall annex. The Chicago Theater has been refurbished and reopened. There will be a new Chicago Public Library.

The most dazzling new look is in the excitingly tall glass architecture of the Loop. It has acquired at least a hundred new skyscrapers in the last three decades, in an area where not one went up between 1935 and 1955.

The theaters in Chicago are jumping as in no other city. They have produced Pulitzer Prize winner David Mamet, ex-Goodman Theater now Lincoln Center director Gregory Mosher, actor John Malkovich, the extraordinarily successful Second City graduates such as the Belushi brothers, Mike Nichols, Elaine May and a whole new world of traditional, experimental or unpeggable drama.

Chicago's writers are thriving. They include not only Nobel Prize winning novelist Saul Bellow, Pulitzer Prize winners poet Gwendolyn Brooks, chronicler Studs Terkel and columnist Mike Royko, but also a long list of artisans with something to say: Edith Freund, Bill Granger, Stuart Dybek, Harry Mark Petrakis, Bette Howland, Stuart Kaminsky, Mary Craig, Cyrus Coulter, Leon Forrest, Laurence Gonzales, A.J. Budrys, William Brashler, Jack Fuller, Eugene Kennedy, Walter Olesky, June Brindel and the highly popular Andrew Greeley.

In the 1980 census, for the first time the suburban population outstripped Chicago's. But most suburbs are newer than the city's neighborhoods and lack their character. Many, however, seek an identity to avoid becoming just a couple of housing developments adjacent to fast-food strips.

Chicago is being tested. It wanted a World Fair in 1992 and cheered when the Bureau of International Expositions selected Chicago to be its site. But citizens also demanded an Environmental Impact Study to gauge the long-range effect on the environment. Questions about its economic feasibility also surfaced. Recent fairs in New Orleans and Knoxville did little to help these cities, especially their neighborhoods. They were economic disasters. Ultimately, funding was denied for the 1992 fair. The feeling existed that—like the 1893 World's Columbian Exposition, which was a beachhead of eastern culture on Chicago's shore—it would not represent Chicago or be good for the people of the city.

The city's Hispanic population has at last won a fistful of political power and elected Latino aldermen to represent them. It is the fastest growing ethnic group in Chicago but until recently its people had no political spokesperson to represent their interests or broker their assimilation and needs.

Geographically, Chicago remains the center, the hub of

America, the heart of the heartland. It is in the so-called Rust Belt, a geographic area suffering the loss of heavy manufacturing jobs that are flowing steadily to the South. Those who in the past frequently spoke of the Rust Belt don't seem to be complaining about it as much anymore. The city has strong natural resources, ones that helped build it.

Recent changeovers in Chicago have been dramatic. Empty factories north and south of the Loop have become need-filling residential lofts or shopping malls. Heavy industry sites have become light industry facilities. Rehabilitation and renovation are big industries in the city.

One good example of new commercial restructuring is the city's wholesale produce market, the South Water Market. In the 1930s and 1940s, before refrigerated trailer trucks, train shipments of fresh fruits and vegetables were broken down in Chicago for shipment to the Midwest, East and South. This era is over. The piggyback trucks still go to these areas, but a revolution in American eating habits has created a new taste for fresh fruits and vegetables. Currently, Chicago's produce merchants sell more to their Midwest customers than they formerly did to half of the nation.

Chicago remains a very popular place to visit. New hotels on the Near North Side stand beside refurbished ones welcoming conventioneers and other visitors. In 1985, the Conrad Hilton at 720 South Michigan Avenue—long the world's largest hotel—was renovated for $150 million and reopened as the luxurious Chicago Hilton and Towers.

But it is not the Loop and North Michigan Avenue that register the most critical improvement in Chicago's vital signs. It is in the neighborhoods, especially ones that have been on the decline. Communities that had been inundated by a dismal hopelessness have started to show some of the strongest signs of new vitality. Here are a few examples:

—Healthy supermarkets and retail establishments are critical to restoring neighborhoods, just as they are often the first institutions to abandon declining ones. Uptown, a few years ago, was one of the first down-and-out communities to get a new supermarket and shopping mall. It worked.

—In 1986, Matanky Realty and a group representing the Third Ward combined to develop a $10 million shopping mall in one of the poorest neighborhoods in Chicago. It will be along the Dan Ryan Expressway at Garfield Boulevard (5500 south), next to the Robert Taylor Homes. The center will include a supermarket, discount store and drugstore. It will mean jobs for the neighborhood as well as generally lower prices for those who need them most.

—For several decades in Chicago, rehabilitation usually meant gentrification—taking away basically sound housing from the poor and the middle classes by wealthier persons. Despite a dire lack of federal funds with which to reverse the slum-making process and benefit the poor, the 65th Development Corporation has rehabbed some of Woodlawn's most run-down buildings into decent housing for community members. This corporation—made up of a crossing-guard, an assistant pastor, housewives and several widows from the area—exemplifies Chicago's new self-determined spirit as much as any real estate cartel building a Loop skyscraper.

—With even fewer resources, a group in North Lawndale—a particularly destitute neighborhood—calls itself "Slum Busters." They have taken it upon themselves to sweep streets, clean alleys and vacant lots, and plant flowers in a neighborhood many outsiders have written off.

The city has initiated a vitally important boulevard improvement plan called "Boulevard Restoration: A Catalyst for Neighborhood Improvement." It started with South King Drive (once known as Grand Boulevard) from 43rd to 59th streets. The hope is that the improvements on the boulevard strips will favorably affect adjoining neighborhoods.

In the early 1970s, there was a Top-40 hit song, "The Night Chicago Died." Chicago didn't die. It didn't even come close. But its pulse did slow down a little.

The 1980s present a new time of challenge and hope.

When you get your hands on it, Chicago can be a user-friendly city. It will also be a rewarding place, people, experience and idea.

a
b
c

Abattoir by the Lake

"Abattoir by the Lake" was a name for Chicago coined by H. L. Mencken, employing the French word for "slaughterhouse." Far from intending to be derogatory, Mencken saluted the city he called "the literary capital of America." The acknowledged genius of the American language described the city in a 1917 *Chicago Tribune Magazine* article: "In Chicago, there is the mysterious something that makes for individuality, personality and charm. In Chicago, a spirit broods upon the face of the waters. Find a writer who is indubitably an American in every pulse-beat, who has something new and peculiarly American to say and who says it in an unmistakably American way and nine times out of ten you will find that he has some sort of connection with the gargantuan and inordinate abattoir by Lake Michigan—that he was bred there or passed through there in the days when he was young and tender. . . I give you Chicago. It is not London-and-Harvard. It is not Paris-and-buttermilk. It is American in every chitling and sparerib, and it is alive from snout to tail." On April 17, 1920, Mencken published another version of this article in the London *Nation,* adding: "Chicago has drawn them (writers) in from their remote wheat towns and far-flung railroad junctions, and it has given them an impulse that New York simply cannot match—an impulse toward independence, toward honesty, toward a peculiar vividness and naivete—in brief, toward the unaffected self-expression that is at the bottom of sound art. New York, when it lures such a recruit eastward, makes a compliant conformist of him, and so ruins him out of hand. But Chicago, however short the time it has him, leaves him inevocably his own man, with a pride sufficient to carry through a decisive trail of his talents. Witness Anderson, Dreiser, Masters, Sandburg and Ade."

Abra

The great granddaughter of John D. Rockefeller, Abra Prentice Anderson Wilkin, has parlayed this heritage and a fortune inherited from the artificial insemination business of her father (J. Rockefeller Prentice) into a permanent ticket on Chicago's front row. She wrote a gossip column for the *Chicago Daily News* with her ex-husband Jon Anderson (a former *Time* and now *Chicago Tribune* writer). Abra also published a short-lived magazine *The Chicagoan* with him. Glossy magazines love to feature photo-essays of her East Lake Shore Drive penthouse apartment. Her numerous social credentials include serving as co-chair of the Passavant Hospital Cotillion.

Addams, Jane (1860-1935)

Born in Cedarville, Illinois, on September 6, 1860, Jane Addams—one of the most famous women in U.S. history—seems a figure larger than life. Founder of Hull House, author, woman suffrage advocate, and tireless worker for international peace, Addams became in her time the symbolic representative of what a woman could achieve. Her popular sanctification and image as humble and self-sacrificing obscure the fact she was a shrewd businesswoman and organizer. Her most famous book, *Twenty Years At Hull House,* must be

---

TIMELINE of CHICAGO HISTORY

1674 Marquette returns to site of present-day Chicago and winters on the South Branch.

1682 French explorer Robert Cavelier, Sieur de La Salle, for first recorded time uses name "Checagou."

1779 Jean Baptiste Point du Sable, first recorded settler of the region, trades with Indians.

1800 Du Sable sells his "mansion" and leaves.

1803 Fort Dearborn founded.

1804 John Kinzie, an Indian trader and silver maker, buys Du Sable's outpost.

---

read critically now. She lived in the era when people with "new money" tried to create good with it. Critical of their efforts, she hung between radical and band-aid solutions. Author Christopher Lasch said: "She was 'natural' indeed, gentle and compassionate—the very model of Christian charity. And because of this, many people forget that Jane Addams wrote some of the most discerning studies of industrial society to be found in the literature of social criticism." Her reputation reached its peak before World War I. An outspoken critic of United States' entry into the war, Addams was shocked when popular opinion turned violently against her. Not until she shared the Nobel Peace Prize in 1931 did her popularity return. When Jane Addams died in Chicago on May 21, 1935, the public acclaim given her compared to anyone of her time. Her major books are: *Democracy and Social Ethics* (1902); *Newer Ideals of Peace* (1907); *The Spirit of Youth and the City Streets* (1910); *Twenty Years at Hull House: with Autobiographical Notes* (1910); *A New Conscience and an Ancient Evil* (1912); *The Long Road of A Woman's Memory* (1916); *Peace and Bread in Time of War* (1922); *The Second Twenty Years at Hull House: September 1909 to September 1929* (1930); *The Excellent Becomes the Permanent* (1932).

Algren, Nelson (1909-1981)

Born March 28, 1909, in Detroit, Michigan, Nelson Algren, to use his own words, was as Chicago as "a crosstown transfer out of the Armitage Avenue barns." Tough, iconoclastic, hard drinking and brawling, Algren was a perpetual outsider in Chicago's literary world. His most famous words of wisdom are: "Never play cards with a guy named Doc. Never eat at a place called Mom's. And never sleep with someone whose problems are greater than your own." In March 1975 Algren left Chicago for good, disenchanted with the city he had written about for so long. "It's a good city now for insurance people," was his bitter analysis, "But it's not a good place for people in the arts—writers, artists, actors. It's a very poor city for that. Giants lived here once. It was the kind of town, thirty years gone, that made big men out of little ones. It was geared for great deeds then, as it is geared for small deeds now." Algren died on May 9, 1981, in Sag Harbor, New York. His important books are: *Somebody in Boots* (1935); *Never Come Morning* (1942); *The Neon Wilderness* (1947); *The Man with the Golden Arm: A Novel* (1949); *Chicago: City on the Make* (1951); *A Walk on the Wild Side* (1956); *Who Lost an American? Being a Guide to the Seamier Side of New York City, Inner London, Paris, Dublin, Barcelona, Seville, Almeria, Istanbul, Crete, and Chicago, Illinois* (1963); *Notes from a Sea Diary: Hemingway All the Way* (1965); *The Last Carousel* (1973); *The Devil's Stocking* (1983).

Alinsky, Saul David (1909-1972)

Saul Alinsky, someone once said, "is to community organizers what Freud was to psychoanalysis." In 1939, with Joseph Meegan, he founded the Back of the Yards Council. Meegan directed the Davis Square Park but was, according to his wife in the book *Back of the Yards: The Making of a Social Democracy,* "very parochial." Alinsky, by contrast, graduated in 1930 with a degree in sociology from the University of Chicago. He had worked in the labor movement and had a knack for social work. Alinsky thought of himself as a radical, which he defined as someone "who helps his fellow man." He describes liberals as "the kind of guys who walk out of the room when

TIMELINE of CHICAGO HISTORY

1812 On August 15, Indians massacre troops and their families leaving Fort Dearborn.

1816 On July 4, Fort Dearborn resettled by garrison of 112 soldiers under command of Captain

Hezekiah Bradley. Kinzie returns to settlement.

1818 Illinois receives statehood on December 4. Fur-trader Gurdon S. Hubbard, whom the Indians call "Swift Walker," first visits area.

1820 Writer Henry R. Schoolcraft visits the five-family Chicago settlement.

1823 Major Stephen H. Long leads government exploring expedition through Chicago.

the argument turns into a fight." (This quote has also been attributed to Heywood Hale Broun.) He believed staunchly in grassroots agitation. "People don't get an opportunity or freedom or equality or dignity as an act of charity," he claimed. "You need organizations to make the other side deliver." The Back of the Yards Council tried to mobilize unemployed stockyards workers into building an indigenous neighborhood coalition that would get adequate city services for their area, stop crime, and develop community resources. In 1940 Alinsky started the Industrial Areas Foundation to fund his by then nationwide organizing activities. He also had a hand in beginning The Woodlawn Organization (TWO) and the Northwest Community Council. Organizers all over the world have avidly studied Alinsky's 1946 *Reveille for Radicals,* a book the French philosopher Jacques Maritain called "epoch-making." Another critic, Wilton Krogman, added: "I venture to assert that the book is the product, not the cause, of an epoch. In fullest measure, the author has faith, hope and charity. Not the charity that patronizes, but the understanding that dignifies. He has a surging hope that people can and will work out their salvation." Alinsky died at age sixty-three on June 12, 1972, in Carmel, California.

Altgeld, John Peter (1847-1902)

In *Profiles in Courage* John F. Kennedy wrote with admiration of John Peter Altgeld, governor of Illinois from 1892 to 1896: "Warned by Democratic leaders that he must forget those convicts (three men unfairly imprisoned as a result of the 1886 Haymarket bombing) if he still looked toward the Senate, Altgeld replied, 'No man's ambition has the right to stand in the way of performing a simple act of justice.' " Clarence Darrow eulogized Altgeld, his spiritual father, as "always and at all times a lover of his fellow man." Altgeld was a Civil War veteran, a lawyer concerned with the plight of the poor and immigrants, a judge who crusaded against the unfairness of the criminal "justice" system, and a governor who was derided after pardoning the Haymarket prisoners as "John Pardon Altgeld" and vilified as a bomb-throwing anarchist himself. His aggressive campaigning on behalf of the poor and his utter seriousness displeased his enemies and all they could sway. President Grover Cleveland, a Democrat like Altgeld, used his office for the benefit of the wealthy and the trusts. During the infamous Pullman strike, Cleveland used an injunction and troops to break it. Altgeld, as astute politically as he was dedicated to humanitarian beliefs, reorganized the Democratic Party, writing the crucial 1896 party platform that transformed the Democrats into champions of the masses. The 1896 Democratic Convention decisively repudiated President Cleveland. Altgeld might have received the nomination instead of William Jennings Bryan had he been born in the United States and therefore constitutionally eligible.

Andreas, A. T.

The fiftieth anniversary of Chicago's incorporation as a village was in 1883. Its original population of three hundred had swelled to well over half a million. The celebration focused attention on the startling fact that the young, exploding city had a history—and a few of the early residents were still around to tell it. A. T. Andreas took on the daunting task of recording Chicago's past. The Fire of 1871 had destroyed a large portion of city documents, manuscripts, records, books, and all records of the fledgling Chicago Historical Society (founded 1856). Despite this, Andreas created a superb work. He discovered materials believed burnt, transcribed oral histories, contacted early settlers who had moved away from Chicago and

---

*T*IMELINE *of* CHICAGO HISTORY

1826 Mark Beaubien opens hotel on corner of Lake and Market streets; it will burn down in 1851.

1827 Winnebago war scare. Congress authorizes building of Illinois and Michigan Canal. Archibald

Clybourne builds first slaughterhouse in area.

1828 John Kinzie dies.

1829 Ferry service crosses river at Lake Street.

1830 On August 4, James Thompson files plat for 267-acre portion which will become town of Chicago.

collected old maps. Andreas produced a three-volume *History of Chicago* as well as a companion volume tracing the history of Cook County. To this day, Andreas' books—issued in 1884, 1885 and 1886—remain the motherlode of early Chicago history. His focus is on the native Indians and early explorers, the municipal history of the city, industry, medicine, military, railroads, theater, the Fire of 1871, architecture, religion, sports and people. Volume one alone has twenty-eight maps in it. Many of his sources had never received critical scrutiny before Andreas drew on them, so errors and rough spots dot his otherwise masterful narrative. Andreas' style, writing and perspective are those of an accomplished historian.

Archer Avenue

This street was called "Archey Road" by Finley Peter Dunne's character, Mr. Dooley. Archer Avenue is an artery across the heart of Chicago. It cuts southwest through the city and suburbs, parallel to the old Illinois and Michigan Canal where the Stevenson Expressway now runs. Among other things, it served as a personal highway to the farm of William B. Archer, a canal commissioner in the 1830s.

Armstrong, Louis "Satchmo" (1900-1971)

Louis Armstrong was born on July 4, 1900, in a poor section of New Orleans. After shooting off a gun, he spent a stretch in the Colored Waifs Home for Boys. He learned how to play various instruments, then took up the cornet in the Waifs Band. He marched in New Orleans' famed street parades. According to his guitarist, Danny Barker, Armstrong came out "blowing sounds no one had ever heard before." His reputation reached Chicago where "King" Joe Oliver (also from New Orleans) was playing the Lincoln Gardens. Oliver invited Armstrong to come up the river and join him. In Chicago, Oliver's band was becoming a crucial catalyst in the development of jazz. Often criticized as "sloppy" and "New Orleans hokum," this music was exciting, strange and new. Oliver's musical style has

14

been described as "predictable, positive and consistent," whereas Armstrong's style was more relaxed. Armstrong flourished under Oliver's discipline, and in time replaced his tutor as "King." His raspy voice became almost as famous as his cornet. Armstrong moved to New York, but he returned to Chicago during the Twenties—an era he later described as his happiest. Other black musicians tried to blow him down, and white musicians tried to imitate him, but none were as relaxed or mellow. Armstrong toured the world, recorded dozens of albums and kept playing up until two years before his death.

Art Institute of Chicago

The Art Institute of Chicago, on the east side of Michigan Avenue at Adams Street, occupies the former site of the Interstate Industrial Building, a large ornate Victorian building that housed commercial shows and national political conventions. In a change from commerce to culture on the city's front lawn, this structure was torn down in 1891 to make way for the Art Institute, built in time for the 1893 World's Columbian Exposition. Chicagoans, such as Bertha Palmer and other "new money" types, were among the first to collect the radical French painters known as Impressionists. Andrew Carnegie and eastern millionaries tried to stop people from purchasing these works and called for the repudiation of this new fashion in French art. Chicagoans traveled to Europe and acquired the paint-

---

TIMELINE of CHICAGO HISTORY

1831 On January 15, Cook County created by state legislature. On March 31, a post office opens in Chicago. First two tavern licenses awarded to Elijah Wentworth and Samuel Miller.

1832 New floating bridge at Lake Street becomes diving board for local Indians. In July, 58 soldiers die of cholera on their way to fight the Black Hawk War.

1833 On August 10, town of Chicago incorporated. All 28 legal voters cast their ballots for town trustees. Treaty of Chicago signed with Indian tribes to remove themselves west of Mississippi. On November 26, John Calhoun founds *The Chicago Democrat.*

ings anyway. Today a priceless collection of Impressionist paintings hangs on the Art Institute's walls. Other highlights on display include El Greco's *Assumption of the Virgin* and *St. Francis,* Rubens' *Holy Family with the Infant St. John and Elizabeth.* During the 1933 A Century of Progress Exhibition, a radically different painting in the Art Institute blazed a trail in the country's artistic consciousness: Grant Wood's *American Gothic.* The Art Institute's vast collections contain more than a hundred of Toulouse-Lautrec's most famous works, and priceless paintings by Cezanne, Renoir, Degas, Manet, Picasso, Monet, Van Gogh and Gauguin. Its primitive, Pre-Columbian and Oriental collections are among the world's finest; as are its Ryerson and Burnham libraries of art and architecture. The painting that probably best represents the Art Institute to the world is Seurat's *Sunday Afternoon on the Island of La Grande Jatte.*

Atom, First Controlled Splitting of

At 3:25 p.m., on December 2, 1942, scientists led by Italian physicist Enrico Fermi achieved the first controlled atomic reaction or release of nuclear energy. It occurred in a supervened laboratory built in a converted squash court beneath the stands at Stagg Field on the campus of the University of Chicago. Fermi had been invited by the Metallurgical Laboratory of the Manhattan Project to come to Chicago and try to create, using uranium 235, a controlled nuclear reaction. The ultimate goal was to build an atomic bomb. There were no guarantees the reaction, once set off, could be stopped or that Chicago would be left afterwards. After Stagg Field was torn down, "Nuclear Energy," a sculpture by Henry Moore, was installed on the spot where this perhaps most significant and terrifying event of the twentieth century took place. Fermi continued to teach at the University of Chicago until his death in 1954. After World War II, the university built a twelve million dollar atomic research center named in his honor the Fermi Institute for Nuclear Studies.

Auditorium Theater Building

On Congress Street between South Michigan Avenue and Wabash Avenue, the Auditorium Theater Building is one of the finest products of the fruitful collaboration of Dankmar Adler and Louis Sullivan. This multi-use building housed an acoustically perfect theater, hotel and office space. In *Lost Chicago,* David Lowe described the impact of Sullivan and Adler's Auditorium on those attending its December 9, 1889, opening night dedication ceremonies, presided over by President Benjamin Harrison: "There was another word heard that December night: Beautiful. In the decoration of the interior, Sullivan proved beyond doubt that architects need not look to Greece or Rome or the Middle Ages to create beauty. The forms, based on nature, that he created were more than sufficient. In the Auditorium's long bar, Sullivan surpassed himself and in so doing he made architectural history. Here he gave his theories of decoration untrammeled play and enriched the room's ceilings and columns with a wondrous foliate flowing like nothing the world had ever seen. By that act Louis Sullivan's fertile imagination had created Art Nouveau, the style that was to dominate the end of the century." Not all art historians agree with Lowe's attribution, however. In 1946 Roosevelt University purchased the building. The theater was restored and reopened in 1968.

TIMELINE of CHICAGO HISTORY

1834 In October, $60 borrowed to drain State Street. Stagecoach service to St. Louis inaugurated. *Chicago American* established. First large vessel, *The Illinois,* enters river under full sail on July 12. Fire Warden empowered October 13 to employ bystanders to fight fires.

1835 First Tremont House erected. In December fire engine purchased for $896.38. John S. Wright, wealthy at age 19 from Chicago land boom, donates first regular school building to city. Potawatomies stage a violent, disturbing dance the night before their migration west. First city graveyard opens. On November 4, first volunteer fire department, The Pioneer Hook and Ladder Co., organized.

St. Mary's Catholic Church, erected in 1833 on the southwest corner of State and Lake, is sometimes credited as being the first full balloon frame building. This drawing is from E. O. Gale's book, *Reminiscences of Early Chicago*, an excellent source for details of life in Chicago during the 1830s.

Baha'i House of Worship

The Baha'i House of Worship, in the northern suburb of Wilmette, was completed in 1953. Chicago has two interesting connections with the Baha'i faith. Its first mention in the United States occurred during a Presbyterian minister's presentation at the World Parliament of Religions at the 1893 World's Columbian Exposition. As a result, the first American (Chicago insurance salesman Thorton Chase) joined the Baha'i religion. Often called the world's fourth major religion, the Baha'i faith began in Persia in 1848. Its prophet-founder, Baha'u'llah, whose name means the "Glory of God," spent many years in prison because of his religious beliefs. He died in 1892. This faith—thousands of whose members have been slaughtered by the reactionary Islamic government of Iran—stresses the oneness of God, humanity and religions. Temples such as the one in Wilmette have been built around the world because the founder asked for beautiful houses of worship open to all for meditation and prayer. The extraordinarily beautiful Baha'i Temple on Sheridan Road at Linden Avenue is a popular tourist site and place for worship, meditation and study. Architect Louis Bourgeois designed the 191-foot tall, nine-sided temple. Lace-like concrete, tall and elaborately carved windows create a serene impression. Visiting hours at Baha'i House of Worship are from 10 a.m. to 5 p.m. daily in the winter and 10 a.m. to 10 p.m. in the summer.

Balloon Frame

In the first half of the nineteenth century, urban growth in America was generally a slow affair. Chicago, however, grew more quickly than any other city in the nineteenth century. One reason was its location along the trade route between the East Coast and rich prairie land of the Mississippi River Valley. Geology played an important role. Iron mines lay to the north, coal mines to the south. Human resources were crucial too. Its initial mixture of Yankees, Virginians, Germans and Irish was followed by other immigrants who arrived, settled and thrived in Chicago. But the city's phenomenal physical growth may partially be attributed to a unique invention credited to Chicago builder George Washington Snow: the balloon frame. The simple log cabin was the most frequently constructed type of building in the "West," as Chicago was called. Although not difficult to erect, log cabins could not easily be adapted for many uses. Buildings, whether for commercial or residential use, often took months and years to construct. In 1833, builder Augustine Taylor erected St. Mary Catholic Church at Lake and State streets with G. W. Snow's revolutionary form of construction—the balloon frame. This style became known as "Chicago construction." Siegfried Giedion defined it as a replacement "of thin plates and studs—running the entire height of the building and held together only by nails—for the ancient and expensive method of construction with mortised and tenoned joints." With enough lumber and nails, which Chicago had in abundance, a balloon frame building could go up in a week.

Bauler, Mathias "Paddy" (1890-1977)

More than one reform mayor has come and gone in the city since the colorful saloonkeeper and 43rd Ward Alderman Paddy Bauler opined "Chicago ain't ready for reform." His saloon at 403 West North Avenue was the fiefdom from which he dispensed political favors and patronage. And no one threw a better beer and bratwurst party than Paddy. The 43rd, a Near North Side ward that he ruled for nearly five decades, encompassed extremes of both poor and rich precincts. Lake Shore Drive reformers were constantly certain they had Paddy on the run. He started his career in politics driving a garbage truck. Garbage pickup has continually been a treacherous issue for reformers. Voters have thrown out otherwise successful reformers who failed to get the garbage picked up or were sabotaged by a ward superintendent who controlled pick-up. Bauler loved to tell a probably apocryphal story about how he used this issue to retaliate against his opponents. When Mayor Edward Kelly mentioned a garbage pickup complaint by an irate Gold Coast resident, Paddy asked the mayor how many votes he thought he'd received in her precinct. "You got one," Paddy growled, "Let the lady pick up her own garbage." Bauler retired in 1967 and spent the rest of his days pursuing his famous hobby—world travel, frequently to Paris, Hong Kong and Munich where he developed a fondness for its beer. Bauler died August 20, 1977. The fortune he had supposedly amassed was never found. This did not surprise one acquaintance who said, "Everything he had was in cash. He never even had a checking account. And he spent it faster than any man I ever saw. He had a hell of a life."

Beaubien, Mark (1800-1881)

Ferryman, fiddler and tavernkeeper in the 1830s, Mark Beaubien made a lasting contribution to early Chicago: he fathered (by two wives) twenty-three children (three more than his brother Jean Baptiste Beaubien). His nickname was "Jolly Mark." He arrived from Detroit in 1826 when the settlement had fourteen taxpayers and thirty-five voters. In 1831, for fifty dollars a year, Beaubien purchased the right to ferry Chicagoans across the river. From John Kinzie, Beaubien bought a one-room log cabin on the southeast corner of what is now

Lake Street and Wacker Drive. In 1831 he added a two story addition that was the first frame structure in Chicago. He opened this as the Sauganash hotel after the Potawatomi Indian name of his friend Billy Caldwell. When Caldwell asked him what he intended to call the hotel, Beaubien replied, "I'm going to name it after a famous man." By no means a luxury hotel, the Sauganash was described by English visitor Charles Latrobe in 1833 as "a vile two-story barrack," adding "all was in a state of most appalling confusion, filth and racket." After retiring from the ferry business, Beaubien sat on his front porch, shooting ducks and other water fowl in the Chicago River. He also raced horses and played the fiddle for dances at the Sauganash. He sold the hotel in 1834 and built another, the Coffee Exchange House. Jolly Mark died in Kankakee.

Beef Trust

In 1930, Chicago was entertained by a vaudeville act—consisting of young women under twenty-one and each weighing over 200 pounds—billed as "The Beef Trust." Their name was a take-off on the cartel that controlled meat prices, except in their case "beef" meant avoirdupois. For their most outrageous stunt, a public relations man had the eight, with their combined weight of over two thousand pounds, climb aboard the supposed last hansom cab in Chicago. Its horse suffered a fatal heart attack. They don't make vaudeville acts, or p.r. agents, like they used to!

TIMELINE of CHICAGO HISTORY

1836 Galena and Chicago Union Railroad granted charter. "Long John" Wentworth arrives in city. On July 4, ground broken for Illinois and Michigan Canal. Four hundred and fifty vessels carrying 60,000 tons dock at city. A "liberty" newspaper, *Chicago Commercial Advertiser,* first published.

1837 Town becomes city of Chicago on March 4; William B. Ogden elected first mayor of Chicago, defeating John Kinzie 469 votes to 237. In March, motto "Urbs in Horto"—a city set in a garden—adopted. Population of city is 4,117. Six wards laid out.

Bellow, Saul (born 1915)

The 1976 Nobel Prize for Literature winner Saul Bellow has been for three decades the pre-eminent figure on Chicago's literary landscape. His nine novels are the product of a refined mind that grapples resolutely with the complexities and disappointments of our modern era. Bellow's art represents a triumph of will over intractable matter. The critic Irving Howe wrote, "Bellow has not only become a master of his own special idiom, that verbal impasto which mixes vernacular richness with mandarin eloquence, racy-tough street Jewishness with high-flown intellectual display; he has also found his place, no longer a dangling man, as a person and a writer." Bellow was born June 10, 1915, in Lachine, Quebec. He attended the University of Chicago, received his bachelor's degree from Northwestern in 1937 and did graduate work on anthropology at the University of Wisconsin. Of his Nobel, Bellow told the *New York Times* in 1981, "I don't intend to let this laurel wreath of heavy metal sink me. I know people like John Steinbeck thought it was the kiss of death, but I've decided to choose my own death kiss. No one's going to lay it on me." His major works are: *Dangling Man* (1944); *The Victim* (1947); *The Adventures of Augie March* (1953), Winner of the National Book Award for fiction; *Seize the Day* (1956); *Henderson the Rain King* (1959); *Herzog* (1964); *Mosby's Memoirs and Other Stories* (1968); *Mr. Sammler's Planet* (1970); *Humboldt's Gift* (1975); *To Jerusalem and Back: A Personal Account* (1976); *The Dean's December* (1982); *Him with His Foot in His Mouth* (1984).

Billy Goat Tavern

Located across the street from Tribune Tower on the lower level of Michigan Avenue, the entrance to the Billy Goat is around the corner on Hubbard Street. It was originally across from Chicago Stadium on West Madison Street on the West Side. In 1945 its proprietor, the late Sam "Billy Goat" Sianis, placed a terrible and long-lasting curse on the Cubs after he and his famous pet billy goat were ejected from Wrigley Field during a Cubs World Series game. The Billy Goat's fast-moving hamburger line inspired John Belushi's famous "Saturday Night Live" skit: "cheese-booga cheese-booga, Pepsi no Coke." As a restaurant, the Billy Goat probably deserves minus stars—its hamburgers and egg sandwiches are barely edible—but, along with Riccardo's around the corner at 437 North Rush, it remains a legendary hangout and colorful place to visit. The Billy Goat's cast of characters often includes *Tribune* columnist Mike Royko, known to have a quiet beer in this unpretentious setting.

Black Hawks

Tribune sportswriter Bernie Lincicome once described hockey as "an alley fight on skates where it is easy to lose sight of both the object of the game and the puck." Without doubt, hockey is the only sport where disgruntled spectators throw everything from heated pennies to octupi onto the ice. Hockey aficionados know and love their sport as few sports fans do. The Black Hawks have imported from Canada heroes as rugged, physically determined and brutal as any professional athletes. The Black Hawks consistently make the Stanley Cup playoffs and occasionally win their division but tend to be disappointing in the playoffs. Fans who throw octupi are more concerned with the show than the win.

*T*IMELINE *of CHICAGO HISTORY*

1838 Buckner S. Morris elected mayor. On June 1, city council issues scrip in $1, $2 and $3 denominations. First regular theater, the Rialto, opens on Dearborn Street between Lake and South Water streets.

1839 Benjamin W. Raymond elected mayor.

1840 (Population: 4,470) Alexander Lloyd elected mayor. On July 10, John Stone, first murderer convicted in Cook County, is hung. Regular steamboat service to Buffalo, New York, begins.

1841 Francis C. Sherman elected mayor. The *Prairie Farmer* first published

as *The Union Agriculturist.*

1842 Raymond elected mayor again. On May 2, first waterworks of pipes made from hollowed-out logs begin pumping "pure" water throughout the city.

1843 (Population: 7,580) Augustus Garrett elected mayor.

The Blues

Chicago has long been the capital of indigenous urban black music—electrified blues. The blues grew out of jazz, gospel and rural acoustic folk song traditions brought to the "bright lights, big city" by poor black musicians who migrated here throughout the 1920s and 1930s. Chicago has supported famous blues bars, such as Theresa's basement at 4801 South Indiana (now closed) and the Checker Board Lounge, street-corner jam sessions, successful record companies (Chess Records that was on south Michigan Avenue and currently Alligator Records) and a yearly Blues Festival in Grant Park. Blues greats such as Muddy Waters (McKinley Morganfield) and Howlin' Wolf (Chester Burnett) have died, but their music lives on old 78 r.p.m. records and new re-releases. A new generation of blues musicians such as B. B. King, Buddy Guy, Junior Wells and Koko Taylor still earn respect, if not much money. On Sunday morning, Maxwell Street is a great place to hear raw street blues. Musicians here are hard-driving, raucous and always electrically amplified. The wholesale appropriation of Chicago's electric blues by white rock stars in itself constitutes a tribute to the importance of this musical style. Elvis Presley, the Rolling Stones, Eric Clapton and Led Zeppelin are only more famous examples of white musicians who built careers pilfering every lick they could from Chicago blues musicians.

Brach, Helen Vorhees (1911-1977?)

A sixty-five year old widow and heiress to the E. J. Brach & Sons candy company fortune, Helen Vorhees Brach disappeared on February 17, 1977. She left behind myriad clues and suspects, but no solution. The police never decided—if indeed Brach was done in—who her killer was. Suspects included the chauffeur and caretaker Jack Matlick, her brother Charles Vorhees and a favorite horsetrader Richard Bailey. In 1950 multi-millionaire Frank Brach was on his second marriage when he met Helen Vorhees, a widow and hatcheck girl from Hopedale, Ohio. Frank died twenty years later leaving his $20 million estate to her. A staunch animal lover, Helen buried a pet dog Candy in a satin-lined coffin after an elaborate wake in a local funeral

Maxwell Street on Sunday mornings offers unmistakable scenery and the sounds of the Blues.

Photo, Carol Heise

home. Helen Brach herself got neither coffin nor wake. She was last reported seen alive by the chauffeur Matlick when he allegedly drove her to O'Hare Airport to catch a flight to Fort Lauderdale. In a study of this mysterious case, *Thin Air,* Pat Colander pointed out Brach only carried an overnight case, instead of her usual forty pieces of luggage. Many theories have been posited to explain the disappearance. Surely the most grisly suggested one suspect ground up her body in a meat grinder purchased at Marshall Field and fed the pieces to her three pet dogs.

Bradley, Dr. Preston (1889-1983)

Dr. Preston Bradley was a stalwart of the optimistic and progressive movement that flourished in pre-World War I Chicago. This movement articulated the city's spirit, affecting poets, novelists, social workers, educators, unionists and ministers. Its adherents believed the world was getting better, and human nature was perfecting itself as knowledge and democracy grew. A native of Linden, Michigan, Bradley was student pastor in Grand Blanc, Michigan. Assigned in 1911 to the Presbyterian Church of Providence in Chicago, Bradley's liberal views clashed with the church when he said in a sermon, "I can't believe God would damn a little child to eternal hell because it had died without being baptized." Bradley started his own congregation and subsequently aligned with the independent People's Church founded in 1880 in Chicago. His brief, nondogmatic sermons became immensely popular. His Uptown congregation, which had first met at the Wilson Avenue Theater, built the People's Church at 941 West Lawrence Avenue in 1926. Bradley began to broadcast sermons over the radio. His pithy vignettes attracted listeners and he was dubbed the "Aesop of the Airwaves." They continued to be aired after his death. After 1925 he served for five decades on the Chicago Public Library Board, leading the fight against Mayor "Big Bill" Thompson and his board appointee J. "Sport" Herrman's proposed book burning. A life-long liberal, Bradley was a theist rather than a humanist. The grand hall in the Cultural Center—the site of musical performances and literary discussions—is fittingly named after him.

Brooks, Gwendolyn (born 1917)

The unique flavor of Chicago poet Gwendolyn Brooks is apparent in the titles of her books: *A Street in Bronzeville, The Bean-Eaters, Annie Allen, Riot,* and *Family Pictures.* Brooks is black, a woman, eloquent and anchored in the things immediately around her. In 1945 she published a slender volume of poetry, *A Street in Bronzeville,* that rare book dealers appraise between $300 and $500, a range normal for first books by great writers but unusual for a living author. In an era when poetry books are rarely purchased, the startling fact is her books sell. In 1949 for *Annie Allen,* Brooks became the first black to be awarded a Pulitzer Prize. Her intention as a poet, in her own words, is "to vivify the universal fact, but the universal wears contemporary clothing very well." Brooks is poet laureate of Illinois and wrote an often quoted poem in honor of Harold Washington's election as mayor of Chicago.

Bubbly Creek

Before World War I when the stock yards were at their busiest, the herculean task of carrying away slaughterhouse sewage was borne by a small branch of the Chicago River. Known as Bubbly Creek, this waterway percolated, fermented and stank. When a *Tribune* reporter tried to row across in 1915, a six foot bubble arose, enveloping the boat. Later "Duchess of Bubbly Creek" Mary McDowell succeeded in rowing across the creek. She proved it navigable and, therefore, eligible for federal clean-up funds. Meat packer Gustavus Swift often visited Bubbly Creek to make sure no usable slaughterhouse by-products were being wasted. *The Jungle* describes Bubbly Creek: "The grease and chemicals that are poured into it undergo all sorts of strange transformations, which are the cause of its name; it is constantly in motion, as if huge fish were feeding in it, or great leviathans disporting themselves in its depth. Bubbles of carbonic acid gas will rise to the surface and burst, and make rings two or three feet wide. Here and there the grease and filth have caked solid, and the creek looks like a bed of lava." Today the creek is truncated, rather hard to find and has lost its stink, but it is still known as Bubbly Creek. It is now a mile and a half long, running into the South Branch just east of Ashland Avenue.

*T*IMELINE *of CHICAGO HISTORY*

1844 Alson S. Sherman elected mayor.

1845 Garrett elected mayor again. Immigration of Jews to Chicago.

1846 John P. Chapin elected mayor. *Western Herald* begins as temperance and anti-slavery news-paper. First celebration of St. Patrick's Day.

1847 James Curtiss elected mayor. On June 10, *Chicago Tribune* founded. Cyrus H. McCormick moves to Chicago and founds a factory to manufacture reapers.

1848 (Population: 20,023) James H. Woodworth elected mayor. First railroad operates in city. On April 3, Chicago Board of Trade opens. City limits pushed to North Avenue on the north, Wood Street on the west and 22nd Street (now Cermak Road) on the south. First message by telegraph received from Milwaukee on January 15. First plank road, Ogden Avenue, completed.

Buckingham Fountain (1927)

One of the largest in the world, Buckingham Fountain provides its visitors for 10½ hours a day from Memorial Day to Labor Day with a symphonic display of water. Located in Grant Park at Congress Parkway, its dancing water is orchestrated by computer from Atlanta, Georgia. Its basin, when filled, contains one and a half million gallons of water. Depending on wind conditions, major displays use approximately fourteen thousand gallons a minute through 133 jets. Dedicated on August 26, 1927, Kate Buckingham donated the fountain in memory of her brother Clarence. It was designed by Jacques Lambert after a similar fountain at Versailles. The fountain operates from 11:30 a.m. to 9 p.m. and then the color display from 9 p.m. to 10 p.m. During July and August, a noon-time display (not in color) is presented daily from 12:30 p.m. to 1:00 p.m.

Burnham, Daniel (1846-1912)

Architect Daniel Burnham, co-author of the Chicago Plan and chief architect of the 1893 World's Columbian Exposition, is probably best known for the often-repeated quote: "Make no little plans. They have no magic to strike man's blood and probably will themselves not be realized." Historians believe this statement is apocryphal. In an effort to tie it to Burnham, his biographer Thomas Hines wrote: "The origins of the 'make no little plans' motto are ambiguous and difficult to document. Burnham apparently never wrote out or delivered the piece in the exact now famous sequence quoted by Charlie Moore. . . the additional lines (in the quote) were probably drawn by Willis Polk from conversations or correspondence with Burnham that are now lost." In an excellent summary of Burnham's greatness, Hines wrote, "Obviously and admittedly, Burnham became the public relations partner, sniffing the Chicago air for new jobs and clients: meeting, greeting, shaking hands, talking, lunching, explaining, convincing and reassuring." Burnham was a shrewd businessman, consummate back-slapper and expert at obtaining architectural commissions. Without Burnham's inveigling skills, the firm of Burnham & Root, Architects, would never have been able to showcase the stupendous and innovative designs of John Wellborn Root. In 1892, after Root died, Daniel

Jane Byrne: Chicago's first woman mayor ran against and beat the invincible Democratic Machine.

Courtesy, the *Chicago Tribune*

Burnham was short-sighted, however, in his work on the World's Columbian Exposition. He turned to an imitative style of architecture and a whitewashed look. Burnham also failed to envision the greatest dreams that could have come out of the Chicago Plan, which in 1909 he authored with Edward Bennett. The plan failed to embrace the city's neighborhoods. With its ambitious proposals for development of the lakefront and river, the Chicago Plan captured the city's imagination. This has rightly earned Burnham a memorable spot in Chicago's history. After his death on June 1, 1912, Burnham's ashes were buried on the wooded island in Graceland Cemetery.

Byrne, Jane (born 1934)

Feisty in time-tested Chicago style, combative, and war-chest building mayor from 1979 to 1983, Jane Byrne ran against and humbled the supposedly invincible Democratic Machine. Under Mayor Richard Daley, she had served as co-chairman of the Cook County Democratic Party and as his Consumer Affairs Commissioner. After her election, Byrne often bestowed considerable power on people whom she had earlier condemned as members of an "evil cabal." Her successor, Mayor Washington, avoided such a policy with a vengeance, preferring to build his own powerbase with workers loyal to him. The imaginative highlight of her administration was when Byrne moved into the Cabrini-Green housing project to draw attention to its severe problems. She lost in the 1987 Democratic mayoral primary to Harold Washington.

Cabrini-Green

A public housing project on the Near North Side at Division and Halsted Streets, Cabrini-Green has the highest visibility but not highest crime rate of the city's crowded high rise projects. It is named after Saint Frances Cabrini, an immigrant nun who ministered to the needs of the original Italian neighborhood that it replaced. The evolution of this now-massive housing project reveals Chicago's lack of comprehensive urban planning. In August 1942, the 586 rowhouses of the original Cabrini project opened. In 1958, the Cabrini Extension added 1,925 more units in fifteen high-rise buildings. Finally in 1962, the Chicago Housing Authority built the William Green Homes. Today, the total number of public housing units concentrated at Cabrini-Green is 3,600—six times more than it had in 1942. The cold and monolithic appearance of the later highrises symbolizes Chicago's unwillingness to provide adequate and decent housing for its poor. Cabrini-Green, plagued with continual elevator failures and numerous other problems, is a monument to thoughtless urban planning and forced ghettoization.

Camp Douglas

Named after Senator Stephen A. Douglas, Camp Douglas was a large prisoner of war camp that from 1862 to 1865 existed along the lake on the South Side of Chicago. This military prison covered sixty acres from 31st to 33rd Street and from Cottage Grove Avenue east to Giles Avenue west. During the Civil War, approximately 30,000 Confederate soldiers were incarcerated here. These prisoners lived in 156 roughly–built wooden barracks facing a large open yard and surrounded by a twelve-foot stockade fence. Prior to 1862, Camp Douglas had been a Union Army base where arms were collected and recruits trained. After Ulysses S. Grant led the capture of Fort Donelson in Tennessee on February 16, 1862, almost nine thousand Rebel prisoners were sent north to Camp Douglas. Deplorable health and sanitary conditions at the camp were somewhat alleviated when a citizens' relief committee collected and distributed supplies. Before the Civil War ended in April, 1865, more than one thousand prisoners died at Camp Douglas and are buried in Oak Woods Cemetery. A high-rise apartment, shopping center and school occupy the site of the camp today.

Capone, Alphonse "Scarface" (1899-1947)

The name most commonly associated with Chicago all over the world is Al Capone's. A rebel against the establishment and its rules during national Prohibition, Capone led the underworld that carved out territories in Chicago to sell illegal booze. Capone ran his organization on the belief that a strong man at the top (himself) could best divide up all proceeds. In the popular imagination, Capone symbolized a daring and successful outlaw. He was considered by the people harmless, a mere supplier of booze to a thirsty population who "rubbed out" only other gangsters. Capone corrupted many levels of society with favors, payoffs, violence, prostitution, gambling and labor racketeering. The effects of his many-tentacled empire were anything but innocuous. He hurt small businessmen, young girls forced into prostitution, union members and the occasional unlucky bystander caught in a machine gun cross-fire. He was born January 17, 1899, in Brooklyn, New York. Originally a member of the Five Pointers gang, in 1919 Capone was brought to Chicago by Johnny Torrio, a nephew of Big Jim Colosimo. Torrio had Big Jim shot—allegedly by Capone—and he took over control of the mob. Little Hymie Weiss then filled Torrio full of bullets, but Torrio survived. He handed the reins of the underworld over to Capone. Attempting to wipe out a rival gang in one stroke, Capone masterminded the infamous St. Valentine's Day Massacre of February 14, 1929. Ironically, his downfall did not come violently but through charges of income tax evasion. On October 11, 1931, Capone was sentenced to eleven years in prison, aggregate fines of $50,000 and court costs of $30,000. At Alcatraz, his health broke down from tertiary syphilis. Released after serving eight years, Capone died at his palatial estate in Palm Island, Florida, on January 25, 1947. He is buried at Mount Carmel Cemetery in Hillside.

A Century of Progress

In 1933 a world's fair was erected along Burnham Harbor and on Northerly Island. A Century of Progress commemorated a hundred years of Chicago's growth and the fortieth anniversary of the World's Columbian Exposition, the city's previous fair. Its most famous attractions were the Sky Ride, numerous pavilions celebrating American businesses and dancer Sally Rand's then risque "fan dance." Even though it took place during the middle of the Depression, A Century of Progress was a big enough success to be extended until 1934—and it made a profit. In contrast to the World's Columbian Exposition, its architecture blended modern and art deco styles.

Ceres

The six-ton, 31-foot 6-inch aluminum statue of Ceres, Roman goddess of grain, stands proudly at the top of the Board of Trade Building at 141 West Jackson Boulevard at the south end of LaSalle Street. Sculptor John H. Stoors designed *Ceres*. The statue was erected in 1930. *Ceres* originally looked down on the Loop but in a change since 1930 surrounding buildings now tower above it.

"Checagou"

Chicago is a corruption of an Indian word "checagou." The most respected authority on the origin of the word, historian Milo Quaife, wrote: "Over the significance of the name of the city much ink has been spilled. It is obvious that the admiring natives who called La Salle's Fort Crevecoeur, doubtless the only structure more substantial than an Indian hut or wigwam they had ever seen, 'Checagou,' were thinking neither of polecats nor wild onions, but rather of the size and appearance of the structure. 'Checagou' was a word signifying great or powerful; as such, it might be applied to the polecat, the wild onion, a fort, or river, or any other thing having the quality of bigness or strength." Determining how La Salle or early native Indians pronounced the name is impossible. If someone claims to be from Chicago, it is easy to tell if he or she ever spent time here. Outsiders enunciate the name differently. For example, in some of his movies John Wayne pronounced it, "Shicahgo." Local residents pronounce it, "Shi-caw-go." Mayor Daley a lifelong Chicagoan, used a Bridgeport variant "Shi-caw-ga."

Chicago Board of Trade

Chicago had a population of less than 20,000 in 1848 when eighty-two men banded together above the Gage and Haines' flour store to form the Chicago Board of Trade. From this humble beginning came a worldwide computerized com-

---

*T*IMELINE *of* CHICAGO HISTORY

1849 Cholera epidemic claims almost 3 percent of population. First synagogue, KAM, which stands for the "Men of the West," erected on Clark Street. Major Chicago River flood.

1850 (Population: 28,269) James Curtiss elected mayor again. Allan Pinkerton establishes Pinkerton's Detective Agency to help the "underground railroad." City lit by gas for first time on September 4. Council, on October 21, resolves Fugitive Slave Law is cruel and unusual punishment and ought not to be respected by any intelligent community. Congress approves land grants to establish Illinois Central Railroad.

---

munications network. It ties hand-signaled bidding on the 32,000 square foot trading floor together with international grain sellers and speculators. It is now the world's most active commodity market handling annually over ten million contracts. In the early days, farmers went from merchant to merchant to get the best grain price. Unsold grain was sometimes towed into the lake and dumped. The Board of Trade and new grain elevators for storage eased discrepancies in supply and demand. Speculators today buy futures (agreements to buy grain at a fixed price on a certain date), reducing risks for both merchants and farmers. The "pit," as the floor is known, has seen many an ambitious speculator attempt to take the risk out of the future by cornering the market. Some such as Benjamin P. "Old Hutch" Hutchinson succeeded. Others such as Joseph Leiter lost millions of dollars trying. Shoving and pushing help traders make themselves noticed on the crowded trading floor.

Chicago Defender

The northern newspaper that informed southern blacks for several generations that there was another world, that there were voices attacking lynching and that the Ku Klux Klan was vulnerable was the *Chicago Defender,* founded in 1905 by Robert S. Abbott. During the World War I era, the paper was distributed nationally and, in the South, often surreptitiously. Today its circulation is one-tenth what it was then, but it is a solid force in Chicago's black community. The Bud Billiken Day parade was one of the paper's inventions in an effort to give black children a fun hero figure and to build circulation.

Chicago Fire of 1871

Well over a hundred years afterwards, the Chicago Fire dominates the history of the city. The one event almost

There are no photographs of the Chicago Fire of 1871, although the city had many professional photographers at that time. This sketch appearing in London's *Graphic* showed the first building going up while the city was still smouldering.
KH collection

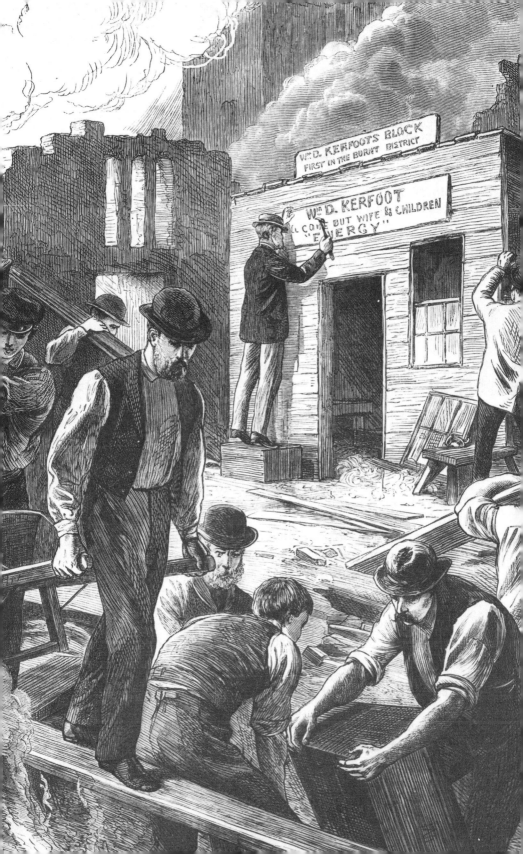

everyone knows about the city's past, the great fire of 1871 has been memorialized in books, dioramas, Chicago Historical Society exhibits, plays, prints and movies. From approximately 9 p.m on Sunday, October 8, until Tuesday, October 10, 1871, the holocaust destroyed the Near Southwest Side, what is today the Loop and the North Side (east of the Chicago River northward to Fullerton Avenue). This includes what is now Sandburg Village, Old Town and the Gold Coast. Fanned by immensely hot winds, the fire melted almost everything in its path. The death toll could only be approximated because the flames burned many bodies beyond recognition and in the aftermath uncounted numbers of people simply left the city. Here are some facts about the Fire:

■ A death-toll of 200 to 300 is sometimes given, but this figure is the accepted guess because there is no certain way of knowing whether people died or moved.

■ An estimated 94,000 were left homeless after 15,768 mostly wooden buildings on 2,200 acres burned.

■ The fire's cost was estimated at $175 million to $300 million. A third of Chicago's buildings were insured, but not all claims were paid because some insurance companies were destroyed too.

■ It possibly did start when a cow kicked over a lantern in Patrick and Kate O'Leary's barn at 550 West DeKoven Street on the Southwest Side.

■ The Fire Academy of Chicago presently stands on this site. A sculpture by Egon Weiner, *Pillar of Fire,* which shows three intertwined bronze flames, commemorates this historic place.

■ Another blaze in Peshtigo, Wisconsin, on the same day was upstaged by the Chicago Fire. More than a thousand people died and thousands of acres burned near the southern tip of Green Bay.

■ The total rainfall in the summer of 1871 was two and a half inches instead of the usual nine inches.

■ During the two-day inferno, people took refuge in Lake Michigan, and in empty graves at the City Cemetery, which had not yet been converted into Lincoln Park.

■ The glow of the fire could easily be seen across Lake Michigan and as far away as Lake Geneva, Wisconsin.

■ In the months afterwards, more people died in Chicago due to overcrowded conditions during re-construction than had died during the Fire.

■ In 1874, Chicago suffered another fire that burned a section of the Loop.

■ The most recent big fire was the burning of McCormick Place in 1967.

Chicago Historical Society

The city was only nineteen years old when the Chicago Historical Society was founded in 1856. Materials it gathered and protected in the subsequent fifteen years were destroyed in the Chicago Fire of 1871. While the fire wreaked havoc on the ambitious young society, in the aftermath it made the group's mission all the more crucial because so many books, records and documents of Chicago had been lost. With difficulties caused by diversion of contributions, construction and constant space problems, the society's collecting has fluctuated over recent years. The need to sort and catalogue exists whether or not the society is acquiring items aggressively. Collecting includes not only books and papers. A South Side woman, for example, recently responded to a request for the donation of her mint condition Schwinn bicycle from the 1950s. Its library represents a small part of the society's holdings. Shelves of books, including city directories, line its walls. Helpful librarians,who can find

*T*IMELINE *of* CHICAGO HISTORY

1851 Walter S. Gurnee elected mayor. City receives charter from legislature on February 10. North-western University founded June 14. On June 3, Moses Johnson, an escaped slave, arrested and later freed by the crowd.

1852 First passenger train from east arrives May 22 over Michigan Southern and Indiana Northern Railroad. On February 24, David Kennison, Boston Tea Party participant and Fort Dearborn survivor, dies at age 115 and is buried in Lincoln Park.

1853 Charles M. Gray elected mayor. On February 12, legislature passes act setting city limits as Western Avenue, 22nd Street, North Avenue east to Sedgewick, north to Fullerton, east to the lake.

37

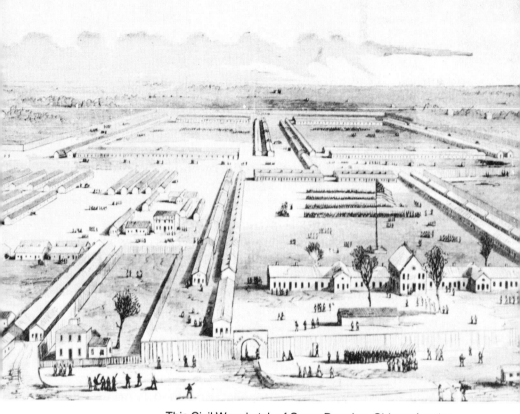

This Civil War sketch of Camp Douglas, Chicago's prison camp for Confederate soldiers, was done by F. Munson and appeared in *Harper's Weekly.*
KH collection

out what Chicagoans need to know, make it researcher-friendly. The society's publication activities unfortunately no longer include book publishing. Sixty to a hundred years ago, it produced excellent books such as *The Location of the Chicago Portage.* But its quarterly magazine *Chicago History* is particularly readable in the new larger format adopted in 1969 and regularly contains articles about little-known facets of Chicago's history. The society's exhibits usually receive rave reviews. Among many others, it has mounted exhibits on Chicago's music, the city's furniture-making industry, Maxwell Street, the history of costume design in Chicago, and a celebration of Louis Sullivan's ornamental architecture. Its permanent exhibit includes dioramas depicting the Chicago Fire of 1871 that especially fascinate the many school children who visit the museum. The programs the society sponsors, often in conjunction with exhibits, draw full

abc

houses because the Chicago Historical Society has built a substantial following reflecting its long-time efforts to expand the interest in Chicago history.

Chicago Mercantile Exchange

The words in its name don't explain much about what goes on at the "Merc," as it is known colloquially. An analogy with the Chicago Water Tower may help. The water tower encases a standpipe that in the nineteenth century eased fluctuations of water usage. Similarly, the Merc—with its traders, hedgers and speculators—provides an outlet for fluctuations of supply and demand in such commodities as pork bellies, live cattle, live hogs, Standard & Poor's 500 stocks, gold bullion, three-month certificates of deposit and Eurodollars, other foreign currencies and energy futures. The Merc is located on a 40,000 square-foot trading floor in twin towers between Wacker Drive and the Chicago River and Madison and Monroe Streets. Predecessors of the Merc were the Chicago Produce Exchange (opened 1874) and the Chicago Butter and Egg Board (begun 1895). The Mercantile Exchange opened December 1, 1919. Butter and eggs are no longer staples of the Merc—its last butter future was traded in 1976 and eggs are perhaps the least traded item.

Chicago Public Library

Chicago's first free library, the Mechanic's Institute, was actually privately owned. In the mid-1800s, mechanics were the heroes of a newly industrialized society. They were educated, inventors and liberals who spread through meetings and the free library their ideals. After the Fire of 1871, however, the city needed a new library. Twelve thousand books were donated by the people of Great Britain. These formed the core of the new Chicago Public Library's collection. On January 1, 1873, it opened in a large iron former water tank at LaSalle and Adams called The Rookery. In 1897 a new central library building was constructed on a plot at Michigan Avenue and Randolph Street formerly called Dearborn Park. This building—totally unlike the straightforward style of the Chicago School of Architecture—is a combination of Renaissance, Neo-Greek and Roman forms that overawes with its grand marble and mosaic decorations. But by 1922 Chicago Public Library head Carl B. Roden called for construction of a new library. However, it was not until the 1970s—five decades later—that the Chicago Public Library moved out of the old building. After first-class renovation it was renamed the Cultural Center. The library was stored in the Mandel Building, an old warehouse behind the Equitable Insurance Building at 425 North Michigan Avenue. Controversy over a central library dragged on until a new site, across from the Goldblatt Store Building on South State Street, was finally chosen in 1986. Despite the furor over the main library's location, Chicago has long been a good book town and the Chicago Public Library reflects the city's love for reading, especially in the number and quality of its neighborhood branches and the general helpfulness of its staff.

Chicago School of Architecture

Blossoming in the 1880s and 1890s, the Chicago School of Architecture was made up of a group of architects who were more interested in their American roots than in traditional classical styles espoused by East Coast architects. Louis Sullivan, Dankmar Adler, John Wellborn Root, and to a lesser degree his partner Daniel Burnham, were the mainstays of the school. William Lebaron Jenney and Frank Lloyd Wright are also associated with it. These architects were inventive, adding salt to mortar so brick could still be laid during the winter and developing the floating concrete caisson structure. Iron and later steel skeleton frames opened wide floor spaces. The Chicago architects wished to create buildings in tune with the spirit of America. The hallowed Greek and Roman models were discarded. Their greatest structures celebrated American design, not psuedo-Gothic or ersatz Renaissance styles. The deeply democratic architecture of Sullivan and Root represent the true heritage from which modern twentieth-century American architecture evolved.

Chicago School of Television

In the late 1950s, a number of live television shows emanating from the studios of the National Broadcasting Company in Chicago became known as "The Chicago School of Television." Under the direction of station manager Jules Herbuveau, a lively and laid-back style of memorable programming flourished. Among the now classic shows of this era were Burr Tilstrom's "Kukla, Fran and Ollie," "Garroway At Large," "Studs' Place," "Ding Dong School," and "Walt's Workshop." Historians consider these programs the golden era of live television.

Chicago Seven Conspiracy Trial of 1969

It ranks second in importance only to the Haymarket trial in terms of the upheaval caused and devisive impact on Chicago's history. The 1969 trial of eight radicals and youth-movement figureheads for an alleged conspiracy to incite riots during the disastrous 1968 Democratic National Convention marked a watershed in American political life. The movement confronted a graven establishment willing to go to any lengths to crush dissent. The defendants were the flamboyant Yippies Abbie Hoffman and Jerry Rubin, anti-Vietnam war organizers David Dellinger and Tom Hayden, Rennie Davis, Lee Weiner, John Froines and militant black activist Bobby Seale,

*T*IMELINE of CHICAGO HISTORY

1854 Isaac L. Milliken elected mayor. Of 65,782 residents, 35,857 are foreign born.

1855 Levi D. Boone elected mayor. Germans riot over Sunday closings of saloons. Raising of street grades begins. Carter H. Harrison, Sr., arrives in city. Cyrus B. Bradley, first Chief of Police, reorganizes force.

1856 Population of Chicago is more than 84,000. Thomas Dyer elected mayor. Mapmaking company Rand McNally founded. Juliette Kinzie publishes *Wau-Bun: The "Early Day" in the Northwest.* Chicago Historical Society founded.

The era of the streetcar has become both nostalgic and romantic, even though—for lack of money—the city's streetcars were not often repaired and even less frequently modernized. This last ride was June 21, 1958.

Courtesy, the CTA

who later was separated from the proceedings. This unlikely group was defended by a latter-day Darrow, William M. Kunstler, whose acerbic courtroom style earned him contempt citations from the judge, Julius J. Hoffman. A bound and gagged Bobby Seale was the image seared into the nation's conscience during the trial. In the words of one juror, "For the first time in my life I was afraid of my government." The parade of witnesses included Mayor Daley, Dick Gregory, Norman Mailer, Timothy Leary and cops who had impersonated hippies. The spectacle resembled both a circus and pogrom. Ultimately the first guilty verdicts were overturned.

Chicago Sun-Times

The *Chicago Sun-Times* of today is the surviving combination of three earlier daily newspapers in the city: the *Chicago Daily News* (founded by Melvin Stone in 1876, closed 1978), The *Chicago Times* (founded in 1929) and The *Chicago Sun* (founded by Marshall Field III in 1941, the week before the attack on Pearl Harbor). The *Times* survived through the Depression and World War II until it was purchased by Marshall Field IV and merged into The *Sun,* creating The *Sun-Times.* Field humorously referred to his newspaper as the "McCormick Reaper" because he wanted to provide an alternative morning voice to Colonel Robert R. McCormick's archconservative *Tribune.* In tabloid format, the *Sun-Times* survived the glitzy image many other similar tabloids have, the ownership of Australian media magnate Rupert Murdoch and several journalistic faux pas after ownership was transferred from Field Communications to Murdoch. In a leveraged buy-out, publisher Robert Page purchased The *Sun-Times* from Murdoch in 1986 and publishes a healthy independent newspaper that competes daily with the larger-staffed and technologically advanced *Tribune.*

Chicago Theater

The Chicago Theater at 162 North State Street opened October 26, 1921, with what an over-enthusiastic *Chicago Evening American* reporter called "the greatest presentation ever attempted." Norma Talmage starred in "The Sign of the Door." Buster Keaton kept them laughing. Charles M. Wacker, beer baron and Chicago Plan Commission chairman, was master of ceremonies. The *Tribune* praised the Chicago Theater as Balaban & Katz's "flagship," a title that the firm used from then on for the Chicago Theater, where both live stage performances and motion pictures were shown. In 1925 the chief of police tried to close the theater down after the showing of the film, *My Sister from Paris.* On August 3, 1933, fan dancer Sally Rand was arrested for failing to wear the bits of gauze a policewoman had added to her skimpy costume. A comedian opening the show, Johnny Perkins, tried to get arrested too, but the police said they were not looking for "publicity seekers." Among countless famous acts that have appeared at the Chicago Theater were Will Rogers, Al Jolson, Eddie Cantor, Sophie Tucker, Bob Hope, Jack Benny, Sid Caesar, Milton Berle, Martin and Lewis and Bo Diddley. Through the 1960s and 1970s, the theater slowly fell into disrepair and was finally closed. Completely restored and refurbished to its original splendor at a cost of $4 million, the Chicago Theater reopened on September 10, 1986. Frank Sinatra headlined the gala reopening.

Chicago Transit Authority (C.T.A.) *and* Regional Transportation Authority (R.T.A.)

The C.T.A. is responsible for Chicago public bus, "L" and all of the subway transportation lines. The R.T.A. oversees bus and train lines running through most suburban areas. Established by legislation passed on April 2, 1945, the C.T.A. was granted a fifty-year franchise to operate local transit in the city. On June 4, 1945, popular approval was given when voters of Chicago and Elmwood Park passed a referendum. On October 1, 1947, the C.T.A. officially began operation by purchasing the rolling stock and facilities of the Chicago Surface Line and Chicago Rapid Transit Company. A third previous local transit system—the Chicago Motor Coach Company—was acquired by the C.T.A. five years to the day later. In 1953, the C.T.A. bought the elevated facilities and right-of-way from Montrose Avenue to Linden in Wilmette. The R.T.A. officially came into existence in the late 1960s.

Chicago Tribune

Chicago's oldest daily newspaper, the *Chicago Tribune,* was founded in 1847. It thrived during the Lincoln-for-President campaign and Civil War and shepherded the infancy of the Republican Party. Since then—through publishers Joseph Medill and his grandson, Colonel Robert R. McCormick—the *Tribune* as a rule adhered slavishly to its principles. A diversified media conglomerate today, the Tribune Company owns paper mills, a chain of radio and television stations and other newspapers, including the *New York Daily News.* As a newspaper, the *Tribune* ranks among the top five (according to *Editor & Publisher,* in 1983 the top five were the *New York Times, Wall Street Journal, Washington Post, Los Angeles Times,* and the *Tribune*) in the nation and has won a fistful of Pulitzer Prizes. The paper is credited with excellent coverage in all its sections.

Clout

"Clout," perhaps the most unusual term that Chicago has contributed to modern political discourse, describes a curious concept. Under Mayor Richard J. Daley (1955 to 1976), many mayors before and a couple after him, political authority in Chicago—the power to get things done—was distributed in the way a corporation's shares are. One share meant some say, a block of shares meant power and a majority of shares meant control. In political terms, this power—no matter what the amount—was transferable. A precinct captain had one share. He could obtain garbage cans for his neighbors, get a building inspected, street-light repaired, or gain entree to his ward committeeman to get a traffic ticket "taken care of." A ward committeeman or alderman had control of a certain number of patronage jobs to be doled out to allies (five laborer jobs equaled a judgeship), preferential treatment in getting potholes filled or

TIMELINE of CHICAGO HISTORY

1857 "Long John" Wentworth elected mayor. Merchants Savings Loan and Trust Co. (now Continental Bank) opens. Episcopal Church of St. James opens.

1858 John C. Haines elected mayor. First

steam fire engine arrives in February, nicknamed "Ye Great Skwirt Long John" after mayor. On July 9 and 11, candidates for U.S. Senate, Stephen A. Douglas and Abraham Lincoln, address partisan crowds from balcony of Tremont House.

1859 On April 25, four horse-drawn streetcars travel rails on State Street from Lake to 12th streets. Dwight L. Moody organizes his first mission Sunday school.

curbs fixed and a voice to support his side in community disputes. An alderman, such as Thomas Keane (the City Council manager later convicted of bribery), decided who received lucrative city contracts and who was appointed assistant department head. The mayor oversaw the distribution of this power and had the final word on its use. These shares of power—small or large—were informally but everywhere known in Chicago as "clout." By investing in or supporting the Democratic organization—through position, contributions or in certain outside roles such as religious leader, newspaper editor or ethnic leader—one accumulated this invisible but very real clout. In Chicago clout meant the ability to get things taken care of, often the little things. It was a well-run, albeit feudal, political system.

Colosimo, Big Jim (Died 1920)

Big Jim Colosimo was the first kingpin of Chicago bootlegging. He came to Chicago from Consenza, Italy, in 1887. In pre-World War I days, Colosimo distributed carloads of grapes to Sicilian families on the Near West Side and then sold the wine they made without paying taxes. Big Jim operated Colosimo's Cafe at 2126 South Wabash, a fashionable Levee district nightclub. After receiving several threats against his life from Black Hand extortionists, he imported a New York bodyguard, Johnny Torrio, credited with starting the Chicago syndicate and responsible for bringing Al Capone to the city. Colosimo fell in love with Dale Winter, a popular singer from his club. Torrio ordered him assassinated because Colosimo stopped paying attention to running the crime empire. On May 11, 1920, Colosimo was murdered in the lobby of his cafe. Some historians contend Al Capone shot Colosimo. Because he had divorced his wife to marry the singer, the Catholic Church refused Colosimo a religious burial.

Cook, Daniel (1794-1827)

Tradition says Daniel Cook, an early U.S. Representative from Illinois, neither set foot nor rode a horse in the county now named after him. As chairman of the House Ways and Means Committee, he played a significant part in getting Congress to fund the Illinois and Michigan Canal. This was a crucial development for the future greatness of the county that would bear his name. Cook died in his early thirties.

Couch, Ira (1806-1857)

In the 1830s, Ira Couch, an early Chicago hotel-keeper and realtor, started the Tremont House. He amassed a $5 million estate at his death. Couch is most famous for being buried in a Lincoln Park mausoleum that stands behind the Chicago Historical Society. Some contend other members of the Couch family lie here too. The Couch burial vault is the only relic of the years when Lincoln Park south of Armitage Avenue was the city's public cemetery. The reason the vault has never been removed is because its massive size makes it too expensive to move. The only other person still thought to be buried in Lincoln Park is Boston Tea Party survivor David Kennison, who died at age 116 in 1852. In the summer of 1986, however, approximately fifteen more bodies were uncovered during construction in Lincoln Park.

*T*IMELINE *of* CHICAGO HISTORY

1860 (Population: 109,206) Wentworth elected mayor again. Chicago ships 31,108,759 bushels of grain. On May 18, a "Great Wigwam" erected on Lake Street holds convention of newly-founded Republican Party that nominates Abraham Lincoln for President. On September 7, *Lady Elgin* sinks off Winnetka; 297 die.

1861 Julian S. Rumsey elected mayor. Civil War begins April 13. Three months later, 3,500 men in thirty-eight companies enlisted in city. In May, Dearborn Club founded. Wilbur Storey buys *Chicago Times*.

1862 Francis Sherman, war Democrat, elected mayor again; he serves until

1865 (two-year mayoral term begins in 1863).

1863 By winter, nine thousand hogs packed in three months— Chicago is "hog-butcher of the world," snatching title "Porkopolis" from Cincinnati. City's size is 24 square miles. First National Bank of Chicago opens July 1.

Memories of days such as this World Series game in 1935 have kept Chicago Cubs fans going for days, years, decades and generations.

Courtesy, the CTA

Cribs in Lake Michigan

At first sight, the water intake cribs in Lake Michigan, although rounded and immobile, look like ships a mile or two out in the lake. The cribs are protective walls for water-intake pipes covered by large screens cleaned continually by crews stationed on them. Nearly two hundred feet below the lake, sixteen-foot tunnels lead from the cribs back to Chicago's filtration plants. In the nineteenth century when the first tunnels were constructed, they had to be built progressively farther out from the shore to avoid pollution entering Lake Michigan from the Chicago River. This procedure was not completely successful. Finally, in 1900, the Chicago River was reversed, saving both Lake Michigan's purity and Chicago's water supply. In 1928, the newest crib—named after 1920s Mayor William E.

Dever—was towed out into the lake and sunk in its present position two miles off shore. The Dever Crib stands next to the no longer used Carter Harrison crib. Each week a boat goes out to the cribs, taking a four man relief crew and supplies.

Cubs

Since 1945 when the Chicago Cubs won their last pennant, adversity has stalked Wrigley Field (formerly Weeghman Field) at Clark and Addison streets. It is claimed this period of suffering has built character in long-suffering Cub fans. Known in the 1870s and 1880s as the Chicago White Stockings, under the management of baseball immortals A. G. Spalding and "Cap" Anson, Chicago's National League team garnered pennants in 1881, 1882, 1885 and 1886. At the turn of the century, the "White Stockings" name was taken over by Charles Comiskey's newly-founded American League franchise on the city's South Side. The origin of the name "Cubs," according to baseball historian Art Ahrens, "first appeared in the *Chicago Daily News* of March 27, 1902, when an unsigned sports column noted that 'Frank Selee will devote his strongest efforts on the team work of the new Cubs this year.' " Over the decades, many great and near-great players have worn the Cub uniform, but without doubt the very greatest was Ernie Banks. "Mr. Cub" joined the team in 1953. He played for nineteen seasons, hitting 512 homers and twice winning the National League's Most Valuable Player of the Year award. In the 1980s the Cubs became "America's" team—thanks to superstation WGN-TV, which broadcasts their games from the "friendly confines" of Wrigley Field nationwide. The Cubs were purchased in 1984 by the Tribune Company. But the North Side neighborhood, which on game days sells its frontyards for parking, rents its rooftops for game viewing and refuses to allow the Cubs to play night baseball, feels it owns the Cubs.

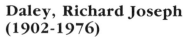

d
e
f
g

Daley, Richard Joseph
(1902-1976)

Master politician Richard J. Daley was born May 15, 1902, in the Irish bastion of Bridgeport. The last and most powerful "machine" politician to control a major American city, Daley was first elected mayor of Chicago in 1955. He served a record five and a quarter terms for twenty-one years. In his youth he had worked in the stockyards near Bridgeport. Although rather pudgy, Daley was always neatly tailored. A dedicated family man and devout Catholic, he attended daily Mass. His brick bungalow at 3536 South Lowe Avenue was a fortress protecting his wife, Eleanor "Sis," and four sons and three daughters. In the early 1920s, he honed his political skills as president for several years of the Hamburg Club, a close-knit neighborhood athletic organization. Daley earned a law degree at DePaul University, but his real education took place in the rough-and-tumble school of Chicago politics. In 1936 he was elected to the Illinois General Assembly as a write-in Republican filling the office of a candidate who had died. Daley switched immediately to the Democratic side of the aisle. He also served in the Illinois senate. After losing a campaign for sheriff, he ran for and was elected Cook County Clerk. Daley consolidated his fearsome political base by remaining chairman of the Cook County Democratic Party after being elected mayor. He fine-tuned the Democratic machine—he preferred the word "organization"—built in the 1930s and 1940s by boss Pat Nash and Mayor Edward Kelly. Patronage was the tool used to control workers until the Democratic machine was crippled by the Shakman Decree. During the riots following Dr. Martin Luther King's death in

1968, Daley issued an inflammatory "shoot to kill" order that drew wide-spread criticism. Daley reformed a corrupt police department, closed down the remnants of Chicago's vice districts and helped initiate a Loop building boom. On December 20, 1976, he suffered a heart attack and died in his doctor's office on North Michigan Avenue. A true product of the neighborhoods, Richard J. Daley rarely ventured into the suburbs, although he is now buried at Holy Sepulchre Cemetery in suburban Worth.

Dan Ryan Expressway

Finally completed in 1966, the Dan Ryan Expressway was named after a Cook County board chairman who had a hand in its building. Divided into express and local lanes, the fourteen-lane Dan Ryan cuts south from the Loop through the city. It can be a terrifying road to drive because of lane-switching drivers and high speeds. More vehicles pass over it daily than any other road in the world. A rapid transit line down the middle of the Dan Ryan was completed in the mid-1970s, providing service as far as 95th Street.

Darrow, Clarence Seward (1857-1938)

Clarence Darrow, a delightful cynic and agnostic, was the greatest criminal lawyer of this century. His most famous cases were the defense of Nathan F. Leopold, Jr. and Richard A. Loeb for their wanton murder of Bobby Franks (in

TIMELINE of CHICAGO HISTORY

1864 (Population: 169,353) Lyon and Healy found music store. Police commissioner rules two complaints from respectable house-holders necessary before brothels or gambling houses can be raided. Democratic National Convention meets in Chicago and selects George B. McClellan to run against Lincoln. "Sons of Liberty" charge an escape plot planned by prisoners at Camp Douglas on South Side. Conversion of City Cemetery to Lincoln Park begins.

1865 John B. Rice elected mayor. Union Stock Yards opens on Christmas Day.

Clarence Darrow, Chicago's great cynic and philosopher, was known as the country's top lawyer. His passion against injustice and brutality made him the country's most effective opponent of the death penalty.

Courtesy, the *Chicago Tribune*

1924) and the Dayton "Tennessee monkey" trial of teacher John Scopes when Darrow opposed the fundamentalist stand of William Jennings Bryan (in 1925). Some of Darrow's other famous trials were the Massie murder (Honolulu, 1932), the communists (Chicago, 1920), Sweet (Detroit, 1926), Kidd (Oshkosh, Wisconsin, 1898), the anthracite miners (Scranton and Philadelphia, 1903), Steve Adams and Big Bill Haywood (Idaho, 1907), and his own trial for alleged jury bribing (Los Angeles, 1912). Darrow fought for socialists, communists, the poor, blacks, people crushed by the "trusts" as well as railroad owners, William Randolph Hearst and other rich men. Darrow never asked if a client were guilty. The only client he lost to the gallows was a man whose appeal, rather than trial, he handled. Darrow abhorred capital punishment and, more than any other factor, his righteousness against this practice convinced judges and juries not to sentence his clients to death. Clarence Darrow has earned a significant place in American literature because of his skill with language in the courtroom. But Darrow also wrote novels, essays and dialogues. In one of the most revolutionary speeches ever delivered in Chicago history—his "Address to the Prisoners in the Cook County Jail" of 1902—Darrow said bitterly, "Most of our criminal code consists in offenses against property. It is of very little consequence whether one hundred people more or less go to jail who ought not to go—you must protect property, because in this world property is of more importance than anything else." Among the many delights of his autobiography, *The Story of My Life,* a caustic, unrepentant—if not always accurate—summing-up of his stormy life, he wrote: "I have followed my instincts and sought to rescue the suffering when I could. But I know that I have done it more or less involuntarily as a part of my being, without choice. If I had paused, I should probably still be wondering and doing nothing. I claim no credit, and I want no praise." Clarence Darrow died March 13, 1938, in Chicago. His ashes were scattered near his long-time Hyde Park home on the Japanese Island in the lagoon south of the Museum of Science and Industry.

Democratic Convention of 1968

Because of the opposition to the Vietnam War, President Lyndon Johnson announced in March 1968 he was not a candidate for reelection. The youth movement—a vocal flower child of rebellion—was growing in numbers, power and frequency of demonstrations. The Civil Rights movement provided a way to protest—civil disobedience—based on a willingness to go to jail and face police billy clubs. Led by Yippie's Abbie Hoffman and Jerry Rubin, anti-war spokespeople called all protesters from around the country to descend upon Chicago and make themselves heard. Rumors, to name but one, raged that the city's water supply would be tainted with psychedelic drugs. Mayor Daley, who treasured his role as kingmaker, had worked hard to win the Democratic convention for Chicago. He was determined his police—who had clashed with protestors before—would keep demonstrators in check. The route to the International Ampitheatre, where the convention was held, had been fortified with walls and barbed wire. Two nights before the convention convened, police with billy clubs brutally cleared Lincoln Park where the protestors had gathered. The same violent tactics on the next evening pushed demonstrators back into Grant Park in front of the Conrad Hilton hotel—an event labeled "a police riot" by a subsequent investigating commission. Daley's candidate, Hubert H. Humphrey, lost the election to Richard Nixon. After a circus-like trial for an alleged conspiracy to incite riots, the convictions of the Chicago Seven, charged with instigating the disturbances, were overturned.

Des Plaines River

The Des Plaines River runs from north to south, parallel to the western border of the city. In the early 1800s, it was used as a leg of the Chicago Portage. During the rainy season, it connected the Chicago River to the Illinois and Mississippi rivers. This was the route Indians and fur trappers took. Its banks were the site of seven or eight Indian villages. Today they are largely forest preserves. In September 1986, it overflowed its banks and caused millions of dollars in flood damage to homes situated in its 100-year flood plain.

Ditka, Mike (born 1939)

In his pre-game speech before the Chicago Bears beat the New England Patriots to win Super Bowl XX in 1986, coach Mike Ditka told his players, "Go out and play Bear football, smart and aggressive. If something bad happens, don't worry. Why? Because we're in this together. We are going to win it for each other." Ditka's frankness, demanding standards, and motivating bluntness helped result in the Bears' first Super Bowl championship. These leadership qualities stem from Ditka's childhood in steel-town Aliquippa, Pennsylvania. He grew up tough, played college football at Pitt and in 1961 joined the Bears.

Mike Ditka: Chicago Bears' head coach and sideline show.
Photo, Jonathan Daniel

Under George Halas, he played tight-end in the 1963 NFL championship. By the end of the 1960s, Ditka was playing for the Dallas Cowboys, scoring a touchdown in the Cowboys first Super Bowl in 1970. When Cowboy coach Tom Landry asked Ditka to switch to coaching, he jumped at the chance. Ditka coached for the Cowboys until Halas hired him to take over the trouble-plagued Bears in 1982. In the next four years of rebuilding the Bears, Ditka's temper, ire and impatience led him to be accused of immaturity. Even after winning the Super Bowl, he had his detractors. In his 1986 autobiography, Ditka wrote: "We are still going to play tough, aggressive defense. We will still be a team that challenges people. We will play more zone defense. We're also going to be radical where we play some people. People might raise their eyebrows, but that's life. If we decide to stand up William Perry and play him at linebacker, then we'll do it."

Douglas, Stephen Arnold
"The Little Giant" (1813-1861)
Stephen A. Douglas was an important force in the growth of Chicago. Landowner, real estate speculator and canal builder, Douglas defeated Abraham Lincoln for the office of Senator in 1858. But he lost the presidential election to Lincoln in 1860. A consummate politician, Douglas felt the slavery issue could be solved by a compromise. Ultimately he supported Lincoln's conviction that the Union needed to be defended. Douglas died of pneumonia in Chicago on June 3, 1861, in efforts to unite Illinois. "The Little Giant" is buried near land he owned beneath a monument at 35th Street, west of the Illinois Central tracks along the lake.

Drives Out of the City
Here are four interesting drives out from the Chicago area. Try one of these when you have a free afternoon:

■ Archer Avenue, southwest of the city, offers a winding drive through rugged, hilly and wild country. It seems more like southern Illinois or the Adirondacks in New York. One fascinating stop is the one-hundred-and-fifty-year-old St. James Sag Catholic Church whose cemetery first held the remains of the Irish canalers who had worked on the Illinois and Michigan Canal in the early 1840s.

■ Sheridan Road, north through Evanston, Wilmette, Kenilworth, Glencoe, Ravinia and Highland Park. This drive offers the sights of Lake Michigan, mansions, ravines, bluffs and lush landscapes.

■ Route 31 along the Fox river between Algonquin and Yorkville through quaint towns such as Oswego, Aurora, Geneva, St. Charles and Elgin. Sights here are the river, natural vistas, charming buildings and bridges. On the first Sunday of every month, the Kane County Fairgrounds flea market is open in St. Charles.

■ In Chicago, a favorite drive is always Lake Shore Drive north or south from the Loop. This is a scenic and relatively easy drive because of Lake Shore Drive's wide lanes, smooth banking and lack of truck traffic.

Du Sable, Jean Baptiste Pointe (1745-1818)

Awareness that the first permanent settler of Chicago, Jean Baptiste Pointe Du Sable, was a black man is not new. New is the respect now accorded his memory. In the 1880s a crude popular picture of Du Sable showed a black child with

TIMELINE of CHICAGO HISTORY

1866 Asiatic cholera strikes city. *Tribune* readers advised to bathe regularly, sleep between clean sheets and love their neighbors and God.

1867 Board of Health established March 9. Cornerstone of Water Tower laid March 25.

1868 Custom House records city imported $1,095,585 and exported $5,052,062

worth of goods. Field, Leiter and Co. opens store on October 12 at State and Washington streets, beginning shift of merchandisers from Lake Street to State Street.

large lips and a blank stare riding down the Chicago River on a log. Now Chicago has a museum dedicated to his memory. Du Sable settled at Chicago in 1779. The Indians were not happy to see white fur traders that they knew were forerunners of pioneers with guns that could take away Indian land. French on his father's side, Du Sable was dark-skinned from his mother, a native of Santo Domingo. His wife, Gohna, was daughter of a Potawatomi chief. This helped the Indians tolerate him. A bill of sale dated March 12, 1800, for Du Sable's rustic log cabin at the mouth of the river reveals he owned a "mansion," two barns, a horse-mill for flour grinding, bakehouse, poultry house, dairy, tools, fine furniture, art pieces, carts, plows and twenty-nine cows. It was a civilized encampment. Du Sable was an educated man who realized how valuable the Indians' land was. The newly founded United States and treaties it offered the Indians prefigured the future of Chicago. In the 1795 Treaty of Greenville, the Indians ceded six square miles at the mouth of the Chicago River to the government. Du Sable had moved away, however, three years before Fort Dearborn was built on the south bank of the Chicago River across from where his settlement had stood. Du Sable died in St. Charles, Missouri, on August 29, 1818. In 1968 his grave in the St. Charles Borremeo Cemetery was marked by the Illinois Sesquicentennial Commission.

Eastland

On July 24, 1915, the passenger vessel *Eastland* turned over in the Chicago River at the foot of Clark Street. Its crew, by emptying ballast tanks to allow more people on board, unbalanced the ship. When many passengers crowded one side to watch a passing ship, the *Eastland* capsized. Police and volunteers formed a human chain to rescue those on board, but 812—including twenty-two whole families—perished, most trapped below deck. Damage lawsuits dragged on for two decades until the Circuit Court of Appeals threw the last case out, contending blame could not be truly affixed.

Only now is the stark tragedy of the Chicago River's *Eastland* sinking beginning to fade from the city's memory. On July 24, 1915, the excursion vessel turned on its side, killing 812 people.

Courtesy, the *Chicago Tribune*

TIMELINE of CHICAGO HISTORY

1869 Roswell B. Mason elected mayor. Water Tower put into use. In April, System of boulevards created to surround the city limits. Railroads help finance project by paying $800,000 for right-of-way strip through what is now Grant Park. Refrigerated railroad cars expand potential of city's meat-packing industry.

1870 (Population: 298,977) Chicago White Stockings (predecessor not of White Sox, but Cubs) play first inter-city game on May 6, defeating New Orleans.

1871 George M. Pullman opens shop to manufacture "palace cars." Theodore Thomas leads symphonic orchestra. On Sunday night, October 8, fire devastates Chicago. It lasts until Tuesday, October 10. Joseph Medill elected mayor.

Edens Expressway

The Edens Expressway runs north from the Loop toward Milwaukee, Wisconsin. It branches off from the Kennedy five and half miles from downtown and ends ingloriously in Highland Park where—it is claimed—a driver who has been traveling from as far east as New York will encounter his first traffic light. It was a notorious spot for serious accidents until highway engineers put up five separate warning signs for motorists.

Eisenhower Expressway

Now named after President Dwight D. Eisenhower, this expressway is a high-volume corridor that funnels traffic toward and away from the Loop fairly efficiently in a straight east or west direction, except during the daily rush hour or when it is undergoing repairs—a not infrequent situation. At the city limit, the Eisenhower connects Oak Park quickly to the heart of the city, as well as linking up with the East-West and Tri-State tollways. While the expressway was proposed in the 1930s but not started until the 1950s, the Main Post Office was designed to allow the future expressway to pass through the building.

Essanay Studios

Located at 1345 West Argyle Street, the Essanay Studios, an old warehouse, was the home of a nascent movie industry between the turn-of-the-century and the end of World War I. The building stands today, holding its memories of a film colony that included such actors as Francis X. Bushman, Wallace Beery, Ben Turpin, Gloria Swanson, Colleen Moore, Charlie Chaplin and Tom Mix. Its name was drawn from the letters "S" and "A" which began the surnames of its founders, George Spoor and E. A. Ahmet.

Evanston

The suburb of Evanston lies immediately north of Chicago, ten miles from the Loop. It was born and exists intertwined with Northwestern University, a Big Ten school. The university gives Evanston intangible benefits such as musicians who were trained professionally at Northwestern and still live in the community. Evanston contains many beautiful mansions along its lakefront as well as an enviable mixture of upper-middle and middle-income housing. Its population—73,700 in 1980—is made up of whites, blacks, Mexicans, Haitians, and other ethnic groups generally found in lesser numbers in many suburbs. Evanston has one of the most respected and independent suburban newspapers in the U.S., the *Evanston Review.*

Everleigh Club

On February 1, 1900, Minna and Ada Everleigh (an alias that came from their grandmother's phrase "everly yours") opened the world's most opulent brothel at 2131–33 South Dearborn Street in Chicago's wide-open Levee district. In the words of reporter Jack Lait, "Minna and Ada Everleigh were to pleasure what Christ was to Christianity." The building was a three-story, fifty-room brownstone, which the Everleigh sisters spent $200,000 remodeling. Annual operating expenses were between $50,000 and $75,000, but profits have been estimated at $150,000 per year. The Everleigh Club had twenty gold-plated spittoons and six gilded pianos. The rooms, decorated in various motifs, were called Moorish, Gold, Silver, Copper, Red, Green, Oriental, Egyptian and Chinese. Two mahogany staircases were flanked by statues of Greek goddesses and potted

TIMELINE of CHICAGO HISTORY

1872 On December 24, temperature drops to 23 below. Record will last over one hundred years. *Tribune* editorial credits newly acquired territory of Alaska with sub-zero "gift."

1873 German population angered after Mayor Joseph Medill orders saloons closed on Sundays. Harvey D. Colvin elected mayor. Anshe Emet Synagogue founded. The $2 million Palmer House opens November 8 with barber shop floor studded in silver

dollars. Potter Palmer invites his competitors to attempt to set fireproofed rooms on fire. On December 24, ten thousand Chicagoans protest for food against cavalier policies of Relief and Aid Society.

The Everleigh Club at 2131 South Dearborn Street between 1900 and 1911 was possibly the most famous brothel in the world. It was known for its sumptuous furnishings, gentility of style and high prices ($50 a night). This photo of one of its parlors appeared in a 1911 brochure, prompting Mayor Carter Harrison II to close the club. The gold-plated spittoons reportedly cost $650 each.
KH collection

palms. Minna told her girls, "You have the whole night before you and one $50 client is more desirable than five $10 ones. Less wear and tear. You will thank me in later years." After he saw an advertising brochure with thirty photographs of it, Mayor Carter Harrison, Jr., closed the Everleigh Club on October 25, 1911. The Everleigh sisters took their wealth and retired to New York, spending the rest of their lives anonymously. Minna died at age 70 in 1948. Ada moved to Virginia where she died at age 94 in 1970. The building at 2131–33 Dearborn was torn down in 1933.

Farrell, James T. (1904-1979)

Born in Chicago on February 27, 1904, James T. Farrell died in New York on August 22, 1979. A pariah of the South Side Irish, he blossomed as a writer at the University of Chicago. Cleo Paturis, a New York editor and Farrell's companion at the time of his death, said, "You ought to read his work; he was a lonely man and a great writer, and if you're a Chicagoan, it's really central to the city." These comments sum Farrell up. *Young Lonigan* has the throbbing beat of Chicago's heart. It outshone his fifty-one subsequent books, but then Farrell took his ear away from Chicago's heart. A *New York Times* article stated the average sales of the nine novels Farrell published in the sixties and seventies were 8,000 copies. *The Nation* called the Lonigan trilogy "honest, unspectacular realism." The first edition of *Young Lonigan* was sold with a "scientific" introduction by Professor Frederic M. Thrasher, author of *The Gang*. The dust jacket states: "This novel is issued in a special edition, the sale of which is limited to physicians, surgeons, psychologists, psychiatrists, sociologists, social workers, teachers and other persons having a professional interest in the psychology of adolescence." Another excellent novel is *Gas House McGinty*. Farrell is buried in Calvary Cemetery, Evanston, Illinois. His major books are: *Young Lonigan: A Boyhood in Chicago Streets* (1932); *Gas-House McGinty* (1933); *The Young Manhood of Studs Lonigan* (1934); *Judgment Day* (1935); *A World I Never Made* (1936); *No Star is Lost* (1938); *Father and Son* (1940); *My Days of Anger* (1943).

Ferris Wheel

For the 1893 World's Columbian Exposition, George W. Ferris constructed the world's first Ferris Wheel in Jackson Park. Although not finished at the opening, it eventually became the greatest attraction and symbol of the fair. Each of its thirty-six cars held sixty people, for a total of 2,160 passengers. After the fair, it was taken down and moved to Broadway near Clark and Diversey. Later the wheel was rebuilt in St. Louis for the world's fair of 1904. Afterwards, its metal was used in the construction of several bridges.

Field, Marshall "The Merchant Prince" (1834-1906)

Marshall Field, future giant of retailing and philanthropy in Chicago, was twenty-two when he arrived in the city in 1856. The story of his rise has taken on mythic proportions, but its astonishing reality is indisputable. Field took a job as a clerk in the dry-goods firm of Cooley, Wadsworth & Company. According to legend, Field's frugality was such that he saved money by sleeping on a store counter. His knowledge and business acumen were rewarded when he became a partner in the firm in 1860. With Levi Z. Leiter, Field bought Potter Palmer's store in 1865. The world famous Marshall Field Store at Washington and State streets opened October 12, 1868. The growth of the business and Field's personal wealth made him the largest single taxpayer in America, although he refused to be assessed by the city on more than $2,500,000. Marshall Field died after contracting pneumonia while playing golf on January 1, 1906.

First Ward Ball

Around the turn of the century, the First Ward included the Loop and the red-light district known as the Levee to the south. It was the fiefdom of two staunch Democratic aldermen, "Bathhouse John" Coughlin and Michael "Hinky Dink" Kenna. They derived their political philosophy from their mentor Congressman Martin B. Madden who counseled them: "Stick to the small stuff." Coughlin once vociferously denounced a pamphlet written by a reformer: "It libeled me. It claims I was born in Waukegan. I was not. I was born in Chicago." On one of the biggest issues of their day—ending the reign of the great boodler (or briber) traction czar Charles T. Yerkes—Coughlin and Kenna surprised political watchers by voting with the reformers. Real reformers, however, they were not and nothing symbolized their power better than the annual, raucous First Ward Ball they alternately sponsored at the Coliseum during Christmas time. Tickets cost 50 cents. Every Levee denizen was expected to sell tickets, enriching the aldermen's coffers annually to the tune of $50,000. The balls were noisy, costumed occasions where liquor laws were suspended and the libertine spirit held sway. Zealous reformers such as Arthur Farwell and the Reverend E. A. Bell finally convinced Mayor Fred A. Busse to close the affair down. We are left with an immortal description of the First Ward Ball from the pen of Samuel Paynter Wilson: "This ball is usually held at the Coliseum. The renting of this hall being an everlasting disgrace to the directors of the Coliseum Company, who, having knowledge of the nature of this affair, rent it year in and year out, notwithstanding the storm of protest from the press and pulpit. As a mark of esteem, a box is reserved at the Coliseum for the owners of the houses of ill-fame so that they may attend with their string of white slaves, buy wine and liquor, and flaunt their shame before the curious multitude which throngs the building each year."

Forest Preserves

Cook County has a green border of forest preserves that many residents fully appreciate and regularly use. The Chicago Plan Commission and the Chicago Regional Plan Commission laid out the preserves at the beginning of this century. They have thrived and grown ever since. The forest preserves are composed of 66,746 acres. On this land are thirty-three fishing lakes and ponds, five nature centers, six charted bicycle trails, thirteen golf courses and driving ranges, six boat ramps, five toboggan slides, three swimming pools and 131 picnic areas. A free

TIMELINE of CHICAGO HISTORY

1874 On March 1, newspapers report saloonkeepers are secretly hiring feminine temperance groups to pray outside their taverns to get publicity. On July 15, Chicago hit by second major fire of the decade, destroying acres of buildings west of Michigan Avenue and south of Van Buren Street. Insurance companies for a while refuse to write policies in Chicago. Holy Name Cathedral replaces earlier Gothic church that burned down in 1871 Chicago Fire. On November 9 Joseph Medill acquires majority stock interest in *Chicago Tribune,* returning to editorial helm he had left nine years earlier.

"Bathhouse John" Coughlin and "Hinky Dink" Kenna, the
targets of many Chicago reformers, were the aldermen
of the turn-of-the-century First Ward, which included the
red light Levee district. They adhered to the philosophy,
"Don't steal anything big."

Courtesy, the *Chicago Tribune*

map of these natural assets is available from the Forest Preserve
District of Cook County, 536 North Harlem Avenue, River Forest,
Illinois 60305.

Fort Dearborn Massacre
(August 15, 1812)

In the flag of Chicago, one of the four stars
represents the Fort Dearborn Massacre (the other three stand for
the Chicago Fire, World's Columbian Exposition and A Century
of Progress fair). The Fort Dearborn Massacre, of these four, remained the most distorted, misunderstood and poorly researched
event in Chicago's history until Allen Eckert's 1983 book,
Gateway to Empire. Eckert collected over ten thousand refer-

ences to the massacre and revealed its context: the Indian tribes who attacked Fort Dearborn were allies of the British. During the War of 1812, outposts such as Fort Dearborn were of strategic importance to each side. The "massacre" must be understood as a military strike. Eckert does justice to all participants, describing their respective roles and later fates and corrects widely-circulated rumors, such as Black Partridge's alleged rescue of Margaret Helm from death by tomahawk. This fabricated incident was commemorated by a large statue that stood for years in the Chicago Historical Society lobby. Eckert's narrative provides an authoritative—if gory—account of the massacre. General Hull ordered the Fort Dearborn garrison to evacuate. Commandant Captain Nathan Heald ordered that all whiskey and gunpowder be destroyed, irritating the Indians. On August 15, the 148 soldiers, women and children marched and rode south out of Fort Dearborn, heading for Fort Wayne. Indians attacked when the procession reached the dunes at what is now approximately 1600 South Indiana Avenue. Eighty-six of the contingent were killed, sixty-two survived and twelve children were butchered. Some prisoners died and others were taken as slaves, sold to the British and later ransomed. Fort Dearborn was burned down. No American citizens returned to the region until the War of 1812 ended. The flood of sensational and popular accounts about the massacre, such as Margaret Helm's and Juliette Kinzie's, were first challenged and partially debunked at the end of the nineteenth century by Joseph Kirkland and J. Seymour Currey. It was almost another hundred years before the definitive work of scholar Allen Eckert dispelled the mountains of accumulated misinformation and showed what most probably occurred during the Fort Dearborn Massacre.

Fuller, Henry Blake (1857-1929)

Born in Chicago on January 9, 1857, Henry B. Fuller was a rarity: a native Chicago turn-of-the-century writer. In 1945 Vincent Starrett in his *Tribune* column wrote of Fuller: "A 'writer's writer,' his fine books are still unknown to the thundering herd and are likely to remain so; but critics give him a high rating as an artist, and collectors purchase his slim volumes with satisfaction. It is not a bad fate." Fuller was a painfully shy and lonely person who painted a picture of the canyon effect of skyscrapers in *The Cliff Dwellers*. Unbelievably he got his first kiss at age sixty-seven. Lorado Taft said Fuller "boasted to me a number of times he knew nothing of love whatsoever, that he had never been in love. That's the trouble with him." And perhaps with the popularity of his writing. Fuller died in Chicago on July 28, 1929. His major books are: *The Chevalier of Pensieri-Vani* (1890); *The Chatelaine of La Trinite* (1892); *The Cliff-Dwellers: A Novel* (1893); *With the Procession: A Novel* (1895); *Gardens of the World* (1929).

Gacy, John Wayne (born 1942)

On March 12, 1980, John Wayne Gacy was found guilty of more murders than anyone else in U.S. history. The northwest suburban contractor was convicted of the sex-related murders of thirty-three young men and boys between 1974 and December 11, 1978. Twenty-nine bodies were found buried in a crawl space beneath his house (since demolished) at 8213 Summerdale Avenue in unincorporated Norwood Park Township. In a difficult investigation pushed by the family of his final victim, the Des Plaines police solved the case in ten days, discovering the gruesome graveyard under the house. Having run out of room there, Gacy had begun throwing his victims' bodies into the Des Plaines River. A glad-hander who loved to have his picture taken with celebrities (such as Rosalynn Carter) and dress up as a clown, John Gacy—despite an insanity plea—was sentenced to death.

Galena and Chicago Union Railroad

Chartered and begun in 1836, the Galena and Chicago Union Railroad was not finished for twelve years. Originally proposed to run all the way to Galena, Illinois, in the northwestern corner of the state, the line never reached it. In 1848 a third-hand engine, the Pioneer, traversed the first ten miles of track. William B. Ogden, first mayor of Chicago, was president and prime mover of the railroad. To raise funds without becoming dependent on eastern capital, Ogden had ridden out on horseback to get farmers to subscribe to his railroad. Ogden relinquished control in a board dispute but later repurchased the railroad, folding it into the Chicago & North Western, a second railroad he founded.

Garden, Mary (1874-1967)

Opera star Mary Garden, a native of Scotland, was hired as a nanny by David Mayer, a partner in the Schlesinger and Mayer clothing store. Mrs. Mayer paid for Garden to take training as a singer in Paris. She returned to Chicago in triumph. Her performance of "Salome" stunned the city. Chicago Chief of Police Leroy T. Steward commented: "It was disgusting, Miss Garden wallowed around like a cat in a bed of catnip." She responded, "I always bow down to the ignorant and try to make them understand, but I ignore the illiterate." Garden later became director of the Chicago Opera Company.

Ghetto

Perhaps the best description of the word "ghetto" about the black community of Chicago appeared in the 1945 first edition of St. Clair Drake and Horace R. Cayton's *Black Metropolis:* " 'Ghetto' is a harsh term, carrying overtones of poverty and suffering, of exclusion and subordination. In the

TIMELINE of CHICAGO HISTORY

1875 Philip D. Armour and Gustavus F. Swift arrive in Chicago. Melville E. Stone founds *Chicago Daily News* on December 23, beginning era of penny newspaper. It will publish George Ade, Finley Peter Dunne and John T. McCutcheon. David Swing, Pastor of Fourth Presbyterian Church, resigns—having been convicted of heresy—and forms non-denominational congregation, which meets December 5 in Hooley's Theater.

1876 Monroe Heath elected mayor.

1877 Ferocious summer "Railroad Riots" rock Chicago streets. In December, Commercial Club opens.

The Pioneer, Chicago's first locomotive, was worn and dirty but still in service in the 1870s, when this photo was taken. It came to the city in 1848, a third-hand engine, to serve the Galena and Chicago Union Railroad. It was so small that in 1947 to get it out of the Museum of Science and Industry for the Railroad Fair they had only to open a door. It is now at the Chicago Historical Society.

Midwest Metropolis it is used by civic leaders when they want to shock complacency into action. Most of the ordinary people in the Black Belt refer to their community as 'the South Side,' but everybody is also familiar with another name for the area— Bronzeville. This name seems to have been used originally by an editor of the *Chicago Bee,* who, in 1930, sponsored a contest to elect a 'Mayor of Bronzeville.' A year or two later, when this newspaperman joined the *Defender* staff, he took his brainchild with him. The annual election of the 'Mayor of Bronzeville' grew into a community event with a significance far beyond that of a circulation stunt."

Giancana, Sam (1908-1975)

Sam "Momo" or "Mooney" Giancana, the son of an immigrant Sicilian fruit peddler in Chicago's Italian ghetto, rose to rule for nearly forty years what had been Capone's mob. A protege of Paul "The Waiter" Ricca and Tony "Big Tuna" Accardo, Giancana began as a wheelman. His ruthless streak and ambition soon removed all who stood in the way of his rise. By the late 1950s, Giancana wielded immense power in the underworld. He developed a taste for the high-life, befriending celebrities such as Frank Sinatra and Sammy Davis, Jr. Leaving his wife and three daughters in their expensively-furnished Oak Park home, he indulged in a flamboyant affair with singer Phyllis McGuire. Perhaps the most incredible episode in his career took place in the early 1960s when, in the aftermath of the Bay of Pigs fiasco, the CIA allegedly hired Giancana to murder Cuban dictator Fidel Castro. The target of unrelenting surveillance by FBI agents, Giancana sought an injunction to stop their harassment in 1963. He spent the rest of the decade living in Cuernavaca, Mexico, consolidating mob operations in Central and South America. In 1974 Giancana underwent gall-bladder surgery. He returned to Oak Park in failing health. On June 19, 1975, while cooking sausages in a basement kitchen in his home, "Momo" was shot eight times in the head by a still unknown assailant. In his biography of Giancana, *The Don,* William Brashler wrote, "His was a hit whose time had come. His depar-

---

TIMELINE of CHICAGO HISTORY

1878 Illinois Bell begins telephone service in city.

1879 Rebuilt, Academy of Design now called Art Institute. Its first collections are gifts from wealthy Chicagoans. Carter H. Harrison, Sr. elected mayor; he will serve four consecutive terms.

1880 (Population: 503,298)

1881 Marshall Field gains full control of Field and Leiter Department Store. Charles T. Yerkes arrives in Chicago.

1882 Bertha and Potter Palmer build a mansion at 1350 North Lake Shore Drive. Oscar Wilde visits Chicago and scandalizes its polite society.

Members of the Chicago City Ballet warming up at the town's favorite summer spot for culture, the Petrillo Band Shell in Grant Park.

Photo, Cathy Lange

ture in 1965 had been a blessing in disguise. If he'd known better he'd have let things lie. But that was something he had never done well, and wouldn't ever learn.''

Goose Island

When the earliest pioneers arrived in the area, Goose Island, a mile-long piece of land between two channels of the North Branch of the Chicago River, did not exist. This commercial area on the Near North Side extends between Chicago Avenue on the south and North Avenue on the north. It was created in 1850 when the Chicago Land Company, digging for clay, cut a channel that became the eastern edge of the island.

Originally it was called Ogden Island after William B. Ogden, Chicago's first mayor, who owned part of it. Goose Island was later settled by Irish-Americans who planted cabbage patches and raised geese.

Graceland Cemetery
At Irving Park Road and Clark Street, Graceland Cemetery offers a cornucopia of Chicago's history, legend, architecture and sculpture. If—rather, when—you visit Graceland, take along a good book on Chicago or pick up a free map at the main building. Look up the graves of famous Chicagoans. Here is what you might find. Four generations of the Marshall Field family—each unique in his own right—lie here. So does John Peter Altgeld, called by Vachel Lindsay, "The Eagle Forgotten." John Kinzie, survivor of the Fort Dearborn Massacre, and more than forty of his descendants are buried here. Daniel Burnham, co-author of the Plan of Chicago, and his wife are beneath the island in Lake Willomere. Bertha and Potter Palmer lie under a white, Greek-columned, Victorian exedra visible from the nearby Howard "L" line. One-time World Heavyweight Champion Jack Johnson is in an unmarked grave, even though performers in the play about "The Great White Hope" offered to purchase a stone marker. The monuments of Graceland as much as its illustrious roster are the source of its national fame. A stone baseball marks the grave of William A. Hulbert, founder of the National League. Architect Louis Sullivan has a simple geometric pattern on his tombstone. Lorado Taft executed a superb sculpture entitled *Eternal Silence,* an imposing, shrouded bronze figure over the burial place of the Graves family. The impregnable grave of George Pullman gives no impression that he was buried by his fearful family under tons of cement and railroad track to prevent any disgruntled Pullman employees from stealing his body.

Grant Park
The front yard of Chicago's Loop, Grant Park, was part of Lake Michigan until filled in with rubble from the Fire of 1871. The Chicago Cubs played here for a while, A. Mont-

gomery Ward protected it from being filled with too many museums or high-rise buildings and Pope John Paul II said mass here in 1979. It is also famous as the scene of a fascinating sports phenomena: sixteen-inch softball games. Grant Park contains a bandshell, the Art Institute, Goodman Theater and reconstructed facade from Louis Sullivan's Board of Trade building.

Gross, Samuel Eberly (1843-1913)

Samuel Gross, a Chicago real estate developer, was the author of *The Merchant Prince of Cornville,* a play that won international attention after he successfully established in court that Edmund Rostand plagarized it to write *Cyrano de Bergerac.* Gross amassed a fortune building twenty-one "suburban" towns (areas now within city limits) and 10,000 homes in Chicago. In middle life he became a "Chicagoan of leisure." One of his developments, Alta Vista Terrace, is a historic district and can be toured today. Gross dabbled at playwriting. On a trip to Paris in the summer of 1889, Gross left a copy of his play, *The Merchant Prince of Cornville,* at the Porte St. Martin Theater. Edmund Rostand subsequently produced *Cyrano de Bergerac.* In 1902 a U. S. Circuit Court found the coincidence unbelievable, stating in its decision "so many and such striking similarities and identities as clearly to demonstrate either a common origin or an appropriation of one play by the author of the other." In 1909, at age sixty-six, Gross moved to Battle Creek, Michigan. He then scandalized society by marrying an eighteen-year-old girl, Ruby Lois Haughey, a mere ten days after his wife obtained a divorce on grounds of desertion. Gross died in Battle Creek of kidney failure at age sixty-nine on October 25, 1913.

h
i
j
k

Halas, George Stanley
(1895-1981)

"Papa Bear" George Halas, for more than forty years the coach/patriarch of the Chicago Bears football dynasty, is credited with founding and developing the National Football League itself. Halas was preeminent, autocratic, loved and feared. He is the only man elected to the Football Hall of Fame in three categories—player, coach and owner. His coaching career began in 1919 when he became player/manager of a semi-pro football team sponsored by the Staley Manufacturing Company of Decatur, Illinois, to promote their cornstarch. In 1921 Halas moved his team to Chicago, striking a deal with William Veeck, Sr., then president of the Chicago Cubs, for the use of Wrigley Field. Among Halas' significant football innovations was refinement of the forward pass and T-formation. In 1922, after severing all ties with the Staley Company and taking over control of the franchise, Halas named his team the Chicago Bears, as he said, in "honor of the Chicago Cubs." By the 1930s, with the talents of such great players as Sid Luckman and Bronco Nagurski leading to the nickname "Monsters of the Midway," the Bears were the dominant force in professional football. Then the 1960s saw the emergence of all-time Bear great Gale Sayers, powerful defensive linebacker Dick Butkus, and future television sportscaster Johnny Morris. Halas' 1979 autobiography chronicles his outsize career with candor, frankness and simplicity.

Halper, Albert (1904-1985)

Albert Halper was born in Chicago on August 3, 1904. In 1932 when H. L. Mencken published Halper's story "My Brothers Who Are Honest Men" in the *American Mercury,* he was credited with discovering Halper. Actually Halper had been discovered by literary agent Max Lieber who watched popular story magazines for "new" writers in tune with the Depression era. Halper's Chicago novels—*The Chute, The Foundry, Sons of the Fathers,* and *The Little People*—are about average people caught in the Depression or the war. They are full of an O. Henry-like warmth and pathos. Paul Angle said *The Little People* was "very much like Dreiser's early writing, in which the intention was terrifically honest and the style terrifically awkward." In *This is Chicago,* Halper wrote Chicago "was always a good place for a writer to be born in, or to grow up in. And after a Chicago writer reaches adulthood it doesn't matter where he lives, in New York, Paris or Rome. The silver cord is never cut, he never really gets away." His most important books are: *Union Square* (1933); *On the Shore: A Young Writer Remembering Chicago* (1934); *The Foundry* (1934); *The Chute* (1937); *Sons of the Fathers* (1940); *The Little People* (1942); *This is Chicago: An Anthology* (1952); *The Chicago Crime Book* (1967); *Good-Bye, Union Square: A Writer's Memoir of the Thirties* (1970).

John Hancock Building

In the early 1970s, it was fashionable to refer to the Hancock Center by the nickname "Big John." The Standard Oil Building was then "Big Stan." However, after completion of the monumental Sears Tower, attention as well as popular affection shifted away from the 1,100 foot cross-your-heart steel structure between Chestnut Place and Delaware Street on the east side of North Michigan Avenue. Today the Hancock has its aficionados, not the least of which are those who live in its seven hundred apartments. The initial advertisement claimed these "begin where other high rise apartment buildings end and provide spectacular panoramic views of Chicago." Novelist Henry B. Fuller would call such people "cliff-dwellers," comparing them to Mesa Verde inhabitants and other Southwest tribes who a thousand years ago chose cliffs for their homes. The Hancock elevators travel 1,800 feet per minute, whisking visitors up to a must-see observatory on its 94th floor and expensive restaurant on the 95th. The top three floors of the one hundred story structure are filled with mechanical equipment. The Hancock is a Skidmore, Owings and Merrill design and was financed by the John Hancock Mutual Life Insurance Company. "Big John"—it deserves the affectionate name—was completed in 1968. Wall Climber "Spider" Dan Goodwin succeeded in scaling the Hancock, but in a case of classic mismanagement and near tragedy, the Chicago Fire Department sprayed Goodwin with fire hoses in a botched attempt to stop him.

Haymarket

On May 4, 1886, a Chicago that might have been, died. During a political rally, someone—the police never found out his identity—threw a bomb in Haymarket Square (now Randolph Street, east of the expressway). Seven policeman were killed, and other police fired into the crowd. An angered establishment used the incident as pretext to arrest, try, and sentence to death eight men who advocated the eight-hour day, socialism and anarchism. A number of Chicagoans—Jane Addams and Clarence Darrow among them—not only objected strenuously to the trial but also committed themselves more deeply to the cause of the poor and disenfranchised of the city as a result.

TIMELINE of CHICAGO HISTORY

1883 Seventy-five suburbs have population varying from 50 to 10,000. Each day 350 trains pass in and out of Chicago.

1884 On May 13, Cyrus McCormick dies. Fine Arts Building opens.

1885 Home Insurance Building begins, world's first skyscraper.

1886 On May 4, Haymarket tragedy. Seven policemen killed by a bomb thrown by unknown person. Trial follows. Rookery Building opens. Gurdon S. Hubbard dies.

1887 John A. Roche elected mayor. Four anarchist leaders who had been convicted of "conspiracy" in Haymarket aftermath—Spies, Parsons, Fisher and Engel—hang on November 11. James "Big Jim" Colosimo migrates to city from Italy. He will rise to control Levee District.

Henry B. Clarke House

At 1855 South Indiana Avenue, the Henry B. Clarke House is a testimony not only to how old this house is but how young the city is. It was built in 1837, the same year Chicago became a city. Its style is Greek Revival. Henry Clarke was a hardware merchant from Utica, New York, who arrived in Chicago in 1835. He built the house for himself, his wife and their three children a mile and a half south of the nearest other dwelling. At that time in the city of Chicago, anything south of Madison was considered in the country. In his *Reminiscences of Early Chicago,* E. O. Gale described this homesite: "Henry B. Clark(e), a typical pioneer, could not brook the narrow confines of a frontier village, but felt that the wide sweep of the lake and prairie in the remote southern part of the town would be more congenial to his taste. There, far removed from every evidence of civilization, save when the fall fires or the winter snows leveled the luxuriant rosinweed and exposed to his view the town, in the course of time the city found him. When vain North Siders would boast of William B. Ogden's grand white mansion, with equal pride the South Siders point to its beautiful counterpart on Wabash Avenue and 18th Street, the home of the former South Water Street hardware merchant." Clarke and his wife are buried in Graceland Cemetery. Because their house was considerably south, it escaped the path of the Chicago Fire in 1871. After the fire, its owner had the house moved twenty-eight blocks to 4526 South Wabash Avenue. There for twenty-five years it was used as a church office by St. Paul Church of God, whose congregation preserved it well. In 1977 the house was purchased by the city and moved a third time to a place near its original site. To make this final journey, the house was jacked up and pushed across the "L" tracks at Wabash and 44th Street.

Hirsch, Rabbi Emil Gustav (1852-1923)

From 1880 to 1923 Chicago developed its deep social conscience. Among its great advocates in the city were John P. Altgeld, Jane Addams, Clarence Darrow, Julia Lathrop, Ida B. Wells and Emil Gustav Hirsch. Rabbi Hirsch had perhaps the most municipal-oriented conscience of all. Hirsch was involved in many aspects of Chicago's life as a member of the City Club, president of the Chicago Library Board, member of Mayor Carter Harrison's 1911 Vice Commission, member of the Illinois State Board of Charities and Corrections, editor of *The Reform Advocate,* professor at the University of Chicago, and for forty-two years rabbi of the Chicago Sinai Congregation. Hirsch was a prominent activist who believed a better world was possible and that he had a moral duty to work toward its attainment. An immigrant, Hirsch spoke the languages of other immigrants. He understood human nature and attempted to mingle the philosophical traditions of Jews with Chicago. "May I ask you to remember," he once wrote, "that our religion, my religion, is really founded on the thought that the Kingdom is of this world, and if it is not now, it will be of this world. This world will be so constituted that ultimately it will be the kingdom of righteousness, founded on justice, and held together not by force, but by law." His grandson, Edward Levi, was president of the University of Chicago and attorney general of the United States.

Hubbard, Gurdon Saltonstall (1802-1886)

With the notable exception of Juliette Kinzie's *Wau-Bun,* a novelized history extolling her fur-trading father-in-law John Kinzie, literary critics often decry the dearth of Chicago literature prior to the World's Columbian Exposition.

TIMELINE of CHICAGO HISTORY

1888 "Long John" Wentworth dies.

1889 Major annexations of suburbs. Jane Addams and Ellen Gates Starr open Hull House. Auditorium Theater at Michigan Avenue and Congress Street dedicated.

1890 (Population 1,099,850) Census finds Chicago second largest U.S. city.

1891 Hempstead Washburne elected mayor. Theodore Thomas organizes Chicago Symphony Orchestra (CSO).

Monadnock Building opens.

1892 Newberry Library and Art Institute open. On June 6, first elevated rapid transit line begins service between Congress and 39th streets.

Too frequently ignored is the powerful and moving autobiography written by another early fur-trader, legislator and Chicago business tycoon Gurdon Saltonstall Hubbard. At age sixteen, he left his home, paddling against the strong current of the St. Lawrence River as an apprentice fur-trader into the little-explored Great Lakes region. Hubbard went to work for the American Fur Company at its headquarters on what is now Mackinac Island. The voyageur's diet "consisted of one pint of lyed or hulled and dried corn, with two to four ounces of tallow, to each man." On Saturdays, they were alloted flour to make Sunday pancakes. New recruits were mockingly called "mange du lard" or "pork eaters" because they kept the taste for it. Hubbard soon earned the respect of the Indians who dubbed him "Pa-pa-ma-ta-be" or "the Swift Walker" because of his ability to outwalk the ablest of them. He first visited Chicago on September 30, 1818, and then used the Chicago Portage. He later wrote a graphic description of its difficulties. In the early 1830s Hubbard served in the Illinois Assembly and was instrumental in determining that the Chicago River, not the Calumet, should be part of the Illinois and Michigan Canal. Settling in Chicago, Hubbard opened the city's largest warehouse, became for a time its biggest meat-packer, and was also a shipping magnate. A. T. Andreas said of Hubbard: "Only a single man became identified with the modern commerce of the city, who had been connected with the rude Indian traffic." Lloyd Wendt in 1986 wrote an excellent biography, *Swift Walker,* of Hubbard.

Hull House

At 800 South Halsted Street, Hull House had been a residence, hospital, saloon, tenement and desk factory before Jane Addams and Ellen Gates Starr took it over in 1889. It became known internationally as the first settlement house in the United States. Under the direction of Addams and Starr, Hull House housed an art gallery, music school where Benny Goodman got his start, coffee house, gymnasium, the Jane Club, boy's club, day nursery, apartments, craft studio, classes for immigrants, dining hall and large residence. In *Twenty Years at Hull House,* Jane Addams described Hull House as "an attempt to relieve, at the same time, the over-accumulation at one level of society and the destitution at the other.'' Among the people associated with it were Florence Kelley, Julia Lathrop, Grace and Edith Abbott, Sophonsiba Breckenridge and Mary McDowell. Closed in 1963, the restored Hull House building was opened in 1967 as a museum.

Indian Boundary Line

The thirteen colonies' 1783 claim to the Northwest Territory (Ohio, Michigan, Indiana, Illinois and Wisconsin) arose from George Rogers Clark's successful and daring raids into the area during the Revolutionary War. The territory was passed to the new United States by the Treaty of Paris with England. In 1791, the United States sent an expedition under General St. Clair to wrest control of this territory from the Indians. He was defeated in battle. Two years later, General "Mad Anthony" Wayne led a larger, better-prepared and more-organized army. The defeated Indians were forced to sign the 1795 Treaty of Fallen Timbers. One provision called for a fort at the mouth of the Chicago River. A subsequent treaty in 1816 drew lines ten miles each side of the Chicago River and running parallel to it, creating the eventual opening up of the Illinois and Michigan canal. The northern line starts at the lake and cuts southwest through Rogers Park. The southern line starts at the mouth of

*T*IMELINE *of CHICAGO HISTORY*

1893 Carter Harrison Sr. reelected mayor. World's Columbian Exposition opens May 1. Governor John P. Altgeld pardons three surviving Haymarket prisoners—Fielden, Neebe and Schwab—on grounds their trial was illegal. Marshall Field donates $1,000,000 for a museum of natural history in former Palace of Fine Arts from World's Columbian Exposition. Mayor Harrison is assassinated October 31 by Eugene Prendergast. John P. Hopkins elected mayor.

1894 On February 24 British editor W. T. Stead publishes *If Christ Came to Chicago,* outlining vice and corruption of city. Pullman strike broken by U.S. troops.

Hull House as seen on a 1912 photo postcard. When it was opened in 1889 by Jane Addams and Ellen Gates Starr, the structure at 800 South Halsted Street was the first neighborhood settlement house in the United States.
Courtesy, G. Schmalgemeier

the Calumet and runs south southwest toward Blue Island. The cession focused sharply on the future of Chicago as the gateway to the Mississippi Valley and the West.

Indians

When the first settlers moved into the area, the native Indians who lived in and around Chicago were the Potawatomies, Ottawas and Kickapoos. The Illinois Indians had been driven from the area because of their alleged involvement in the betrayal of Pontiac, the great Ottawa chief, who forged a confederation to fight the white men. Tecumseh, a Shawnee chief at the time of Fort Dearborn, had worked to build a larger but looser confederation. In the War of 1812 he aligned his forces with the British. One tragic battle was the Fort Dearborn Massacre on August 15, 1812. Two decades later, in 1833, the Indians were forced to sign the Treaty of Chicago which removed them farther west in return for goods, money and promises. Greedy traders had wrested much of the Indians' new-found wealth from them before the ink of their X's had dried on the agreement.

Iroquois Theater Fire (1903)

On Randolph Street where the Oriental Theater now stands, the Iroquois Theater was the site of one of the greatest tragedies of Chicago's past. During a Christmas show on December 30, 1903, the Iroquois was swept by fire. A drape, stirred by a breeze, touched an arc lamp and caught fire. The asbestos curtain was lowered but jammed half way down. The dead numbered 603. Of these, 212 were children. "Mr. Blue Beard" was playing. Actor Eddie Foy, at risk to his own life, tried to calm the stampeding audience. Many died piled up in front of the exit door that was locked despite a city ordinance requiring accessible emergency exits. Five city and theater officials were indicted but never convicted.

Jackson, Jesse (born 1941)

A South Side civil rights leader and 1984 Presidential candidate, Jesse Jackson pulled together a multi-racial and ethnic "Rainbow Coalition." Blacks, the poor, women, Latinos, whites and Asians united behind his candidacy, based on his message of concern for the needy. An early protege of Dr. Martin Luther King, Jr., Jackson founded PUSH (People United to Save Humanity) after King's death. He is undoubtedly one of the most eloquent speakers in the city's history. Critics charge his pro-Arab position and failure to denounce Black Muslim Louis Farrakan make Jackson an anti-semite. Generally, his opposition prefers to attack Jackson for his style rather than his views and positions. His effectiveness as a politician was demonstrated in the voter registration campaigns he organized that helped elect Harold Washington mayor of Chicago.

Joe Podsajdwokiem

This Polish phrase translates literally "Joe under the sidewalk." It was used for generations in Polish neighborhoods. Since Chicago had been built on a swamp, the water table was too high to permit basements or sewer pipes. This problem was solved by raising the grade, building the streets up from six to eight feet. Lawns of houses built before this grade-raising seem sunken. The area under the raised sidewalks was used in the early 1900s for coal storage and as the family outhouse. Polish Chicagoans answering the call of nature would say they were going to see Joe "under the sidewalk." Older Poles in Chicago recall the phrase with a smile.

Joliet Limestone

The color of hundred-year-old Chicago stone two and three flats is not the brownstone of New York, but a nondescript grey. Most of this stone is Joliet limestone, the material used to build the Water Tower. The town of Joliet had a small mountain of limestone until it was quarried and then shipped by rail and canal to Chicago to construct residences and commercial buildings here. Chicago later stopped moving mountains and dug quarries in the southwest suburban area for the face it showed to the world. The town of Joliet, while named for Louis Jolliet, was originally Juliet and chose to use one less "l" in its name than the explorer did.

Jolliet, Louis (1645-1700) *and*
Marquette, Father Jacques (1637-1675)

The first Europeans known for certain to have traversed the site of Chicago and to have used the Chicago Portage were Louis Jolliet and Father Jacques Marquette in 1673. They set out to explore the Mississippi from a fort at Michilimackinac near the meeting point of Lake Huron and Lake Michigan. After portaging across Wisconsin, they headed southward. Following advice from Indians in the area, they returned to Lake Michigan via the Illinois, Des Plaines and Chicago Rivers. Marquette returned the following autumn and spent the winter of 1674 on

"Kup," Irv Kupcinet, (left) ex-football star, and as a *Sun-Times* columnist, a Chicago institution. He's always happy to greet a fan.

Photo, Mike Zajakowski

the south branch of the Chicago River (near present day Damen Avenue). Suffering continuously from diarrhea, Father Marquette nevertheless said Mass every day. He died May 18, 1675, near the present day Ludington, Michigan. In 1677 Christian Iroquois and Algonquin Indians took his remains to St. Ignace, Michigan, for reburial.

The Jungle (1906)

In an advance blurb for Upton Sinclair's *The Jungle,* Jack London wrote: "Here it is at last! The *Uncle Tom's Cabin* of wage slavery! Comrade Sinclair's book is alive and warm! It is brutal with life. It is written of sweat and blood, and groans and tears. It depicts, not what man ought to be, but what man is compelled to be in this, our world, in the Twentieth Century." *The Jungle* was first serialized in *Appeal to Reason,* a socialist weekly. Sinclair, a writer of socialist propaganda, sought to improve the lot of common workers. *The Jungle* graphically describes the harrowing life of an immigrant family headed by Jurgis Rudkus, one of the most unforgettable characters of literature. Their exploitation by stockyard owners, the sales of slum dwellings by unfair land contracts, the crying need for unionization of the yards, the digging of tunnels under the Loop and Chicago itself make up parts of *The Jungle*'s indelible ingredients. The greatest public outcry grew from the novel's savage description of unsanitary packing conditions in the yards. President Theodore Roosevelt was particularly revolted by what he read. As a direct result, laws creating the Food and Drug Administration and mandating federal inspection of all meat products were enacted. Published by Sinclair's own Jungle Publishing Company (this "Sustainer's Edition" is today a collectible) and then released by Doubleday, Page and Company, *The Jungle* has been translated into twenty-seven languages and gone through almost a thousand editions. It stands as the classic story of the brutal abuse of Eastern European immigrants in the big city.

John F. Kennedy Expressway

The Kennedy Expressway runs northwest from its juncture with the Eisenhower and Dan Ryan expressways at a point a half mile west and south of the Loop. When completed in the early 1960s, it was first known as the Northwest Expressway. It was renamed the John F. Kennedy Expressway on November 23, 1963. It splits away from the Edens and continues west and north to O'Hare International Airport where it also connects with the Northwest and Tri-State tollways.

Kerr, Charles Hope (1860-1944)

Charles H. Kerr, publisher of the *International Socialist Review,* was one of those most deeply affected by the injustice of the deaths of the Haymarket "martyrs." His publishing company—Charles H. Kerr Company—was founded the same year as the Haymarket Affair, 1886, and it has been one of the most effective and continuing voices in the struggle against social injustice. The firm published reform pamphlets, populist tracts, utopian novels. In 1894 it published the Rev. William H. Carwardine's expose *The Pullman Strike,* and between 1906 and 1909 the three-volume English language standard edition of Karl Marx's *Das Kapital.* The Haymarket victims were hanged for what they said, wrote and published. Charles H. Kerr Company has for over a century published the very kind of statements for which they died.

Kinzie, John Harris (1803-1865)

The son of famous fur trader John Kinzie, John Harris Kinzie was brought to Chicago at age one in 1804. Fort Dearborn was just being completed. Kinzie was nine when the Fort Dearborn Massacre occurred. His family escaped death when friendly Indians rescued them by paddling out into the lake. After an apprenticeship with the American Fur Company in Mackinac, Kinzie became an expert trader and then Indian agent. He married Juliette A. Magill in 1830. She is considered Chicago's first author. Her *Wau–Bun: The Early Day in the Northwest,* published in 1856, chronicles the life of the Kinzie clan. Although scholars have cast doubts on its accuracy, the book remains an indispensable source of information about Chicago's earliest settlers. In 1834 John H. Kinzie returned to Chicago, the year after it had been incorporated. After selling parts of his father's land,

*T*IMELINE *of CHICAGO HISTORY*

1895 George B. Swift elected mayor. Julius Rosenwald has become vice president of Sears, Roebuck and Company. Civic Federation prosecutes ballot manipulators, gaining twenty-one convictions. First Ward Ball raises $25,000 for

"Bathhouse" John Coughlin and Michael "Hinky Dink" Kenna. Kenna opens Workingmen's Exchange at 307 Clark Street.

1896 Annie Field donates two bronze lions weighing three

tons apiece to Art Institute.

1897 (Population: 1,490,937) Carter H. Harrison, Jr. elected mayor in April. George Pullman dies. Chicago Public Library Building (now Cultural Center) opens.

Louis Jolliet and Father Jacques Marquette, two French explorers, were in 1673 the first Europeans to record visiting the site of Chicago. The detail in this picture is from a bronze relief on the Marquette Building.
KH collection

Kinzie built a considerable fortune. His attempt to enter politics, however, proved unsuccessful as in 1837 he lost the election for mayor to William B. Ogden. Kinzie was a tireless builder and prominent citizen until his death on June 21, 1865, while on leave from the Union Army on his way to the seaside for a rest. According to *Chicago and Its Makers:* "A blind beggar asked for alms, and Mr. Kinzie died of heart failure while in the act of taking a coin from his pocket to relieve the blind man."

Krause Music Store

Louis Sullivan wrote in his book *Kindergarten Chats:* "I would place a modest wreath upon the monument of him who stood alone, an august figure in his art, and now, across the bridge invisible, made vital by these stones, breathes forth

88

a strain of noble poetry.'' The Krause Music Store at 4611 North Lincoln Avenue is such a poem by Louis Sullivan. It was his last design, completed in 1922, three years before his death. The small store that since 1929 has housed a funeral home is on a street known for its ethnic flavor, specifically its German grocery stores, traditions and architecture. A commercial structure on Lincoln Avenue must have a Bavarian Alps facade to be considered beautiful. In such surroundings, Sullivan's work does not blossom—it explodes. The store, in his best style, is functionally simple yet rich in ornamentation. The building was commissioned by William P. Krause, the music store owner, who selected architect William Presto, a neighbor, to design a store front with a second floor apartment for the Krause family. Presto turned to his former employer, Sullivan, for the design of the facade.

Kupcinet, Irv (born 1912)

Kup is a native West Sider, Harrison High School student and then University of North Dakota graduate. He played football alongside future president Gerald Ford on the 1934 College All–Star Team. When his professional football career with the Philadephia Eagles ended with a shoulder injury, Kup took up a pen. For over fifty years, Kupcinet has written for Chicago, first on the *Chicago Times* and then its successor the *Chicago Sun-Times.* ''Kup's Column'' began January 18, 1943. Known for its breezy, gossipy style, his column shares the same friendly tone he used for years when, with Jack Brickhouse, he announced Bears games over *WGN* radio and also on his own long-running television discussion program ''Kup's Show.'' Like Ford, Kup may trip or fumble, but is given the benefit of a doubt because he is not vicious or close-minded . His favorite effort is an annual Purple Heart Cruise on Lake Michigan, begun in 1945, for disabled veterans.

l
m
n
o

La Salle, Robert Cavelier Sieur De (1643-1687)

In 1679 Frenchman Robert De La Salle set out to explore the Mississippi and other rivers in what is now the Midwest, claimed then by France. In 1680 he laid out Crevecoeur at the present site of Peoria; the Indians called it "Fort Checagou." A year later La Salle built an impromptu fort near the present site of Chicago and in a letter referred to the location for the first recorded time as "Checagou." La Salle attempted to establish the first shipping on the Great Lakes, but his vessel *The Griffin* was lost, apparently during a storm in Lake Michigan. La Salle was assassinated March 19, 1687, by his own men while exploring the Mississippi.

Lady Elgin

Lake Michigan is not an ocean. Compared to one, the lake remains relatively calm. In fact, on Great Lakes ore-carrying vessels the engine rooms are located in the stern, a placement that could break an ocean-going ship in half. Even so, Lake Michigan can be violent and demanding. The worst officially recorded disaster on Lake Michigan occurred on September 8, 1860. (Although the Eastland sinking resulted in a greater loss of life, it happened on the Chicago River.) The *Lady Elgin* had left to return a contingent of supporters of Stephen Douglas to Milwaukee. He was running for President against Abraham Lincoln and they had attended a Chicago rally. The *Augusta,* an unlit lumber schooner, struck the *Lady Elgin* in the lake off the suburb of Winnetka. The extent of damage was not immediately apparent and the *Augusta* continued toward Chicago. The boilers of the *Lady Elgin* soon became swamped and the ship began to sink. The lake was choppy. Many of its passengers tried to swim for shore but high waves and the undertow made the last hundred feet difficult. Northwestern student Edward Spenser risked his life swimming out to rescue sixteen people. Altogether three hundred lost their lives. Because maritime laws at the time were lax, a board of inquiry absolved *Augusta* skipper Captain D. M. Malott of blame. Malott and a later crew subsequently drowned in a separate ship disaster.

Lager Beer Riot of 1855

"The Germans Prepared for War" proclaimed a newspaper headline. The year was 1855 and the Germans were residents of Chicago. These immigrants from Bavaria, Prussia and Saxony made up a fifth of Chicago's population. The mayor was Dr. Levi Boone, nephew of wilderness explorer Daniel Boone. He had been elected by the Know Nothings, a nativist American political party suspicious of all foreigners and Roman Catholics. It was staunchly for temperance. This coalition flared briefly in popularity. Newspaper editorials were particularly vitriolic in attacking German and Irish Catholics. These bigots worried about the drinking habits of immigrant ethnic groups. Mayor Boone, playing to the Know Nothings, proposed the city council pass an ordinance closing taverns on Sundays and raising the annual cost of liquor licenses from $50 to $300. The Germans often spent Sundays, their one day off work, at *bierstuben*

TIMELINE of CHICAGO HISTORY

1898 New library at Michigan and Randolph opens on January 1.

1899 Joseph Medill dies.

1900 (Population: 1,698,575) Everleigh Club, Chicago's most elegant brothel, opens in Levee District.

1901 Philip Armour dies. Marshall Field and Co. grosses $50 million.

1902 Potter Palmer dies in May. On September 13, Cub immortals Tinker, Evans and Chance first play together.

1903 A fire at Iroquois Theater on Randolph Street kills 603 people. Famed advertising man Albert Lasker made partner at Lord and Thomas agency.

---

such as Mueller's and Ostendorf's on Randolph Street as well as ones in their North Side neighborhood. A series of confrontations and incidents took place and the situation came to a boil on April 21. After a number of saloonkeepers were taken in for selling beer on Sunday, protestors and police clashed near the Cook County Court House. Dispersed at first, the crowd regrouped later in the day on their own turf north of the river and marched on the Court House at Randolph and Clark streets. The Clark Street drawbridge was quickly raised to impede their approach but a traffic back-up made lowering it necessary. The mob rushed across. Shots were fired. One policeman had his arm mangled. His fleeing assailant was shot in the back. Rumors flew of other deaths though names were never given. The Know Nothing party soon lost its political base. Boone was a one-term, one-year mayor. Chicagoans joined the new Republican party and were allowed to have their beer for another sixty-five years until Prohibition. Levi Boone, it was said, was known on occasion to enjoy a cold beer.

Lake Michigan

The greatest asset of Chicago, besides its people, is Lake Michigan. It supplies the city with a shipping port, water supply, fishing place, sailing area, swimming pool, and constantly changing source of dramatic natural beauty. A thousand years ago Chicago lay under the lake that emptied westward at Summit, toward the Mississippi River. At its greatest width, Lake Michigan is 118 miles across. A few tips about the lake:

■ It can be dangerous. Many drown in it every year, some who are swept into the water while walking along the rocks.

■ It is available. People fish, catch smelt, swim free (especially in August), sail and just watch the passing show.

■ After rainfall, the lake can be deceptively polluted because the North Shore Channel gates are sometimes opened and their polluted contents poured into Lake Michigan.

Leopold, Nathan F. (1906-1971) and Loeb, Richard A. (1907-1936)

Eighteen-year-old Nathan Leopold and seventeen-year-old Richard Loeb were the sons of newly wealthy parents in Chicago. Both were indulged and bright young men, looking for a way to end their boredom. They wanted to do something challenging that would prove to the world how intelligent and clever they were. They had graduated from the University of Chicago at an age when most boys were just getting out of high school. On May 21, 1924, Leopold and Loeb for the thrill of it murdered fourteen-year-old Bobby Franks. Afterwards, to make Franks' disappearance look like a kidnapping, they sent a fake ransom note to his parents. They were eventually recalled by a forest ranger who identified Leopold as a frequent visitor to the wooded area where Franks' body had been discovered. Leopold's eyeglasses, found near the body, were traced to him, as was a Royal typewriter they used to write the ransom letter. The killers were pinpointed and then arrested. They gave complete confessions. Clarence Darrow, staunchly opposed to capital punishment, defended Leopold and Loeb. Darrow pleaded eloquently that the judge look to the future rather than the past and not sentence them to death. The judge heeded Darrow's plea, sentencing them to life plus ninety-nine years. In 1936 Loeb was murdered in jail during a sexual attack. After serving thirty-three years in prison, Leopold was paroled. He moved to Puerto Rico where he worked in a tiny Church of the Brethern hospital, doing social and medical research. Leopold said, "All I want is to find some quiet place where I can sink

TIMELINE of CHICAGO HISTORY

1904 Orchestra Hall opens on Michigan Avenue. CSO founder and conductor Theodore Thomas dies one month later.

1905 Reform mayor Edward F. Dunne elected.

1906 City Hall begun. Upton Sinclair's searing expose of stockyards, *The Jungle,* published. Marshall Field dies after catching pneumonia while playing winter golf in Chicago. Both Cubs and White Sox win national pennants. South Shore Country Club incorporated.

1907 Fred A. Busse elected mayor (four-year mayoral term takes effect). DePaul University founded.

1908 Cubs win pennant.

1909 Commercial Club publishes Daniel Burnham and Edward Bennett's *Plan of Chicago.*

This rare drawing of the red light Levee district appeared in *Harper's Weekly* in 1899. In an accompanying article, the author quoted Mayor Carter Harrison II as denying that Chicago was a wide-open town.

from sight and live quietly, and serve others to atone for my crime." Their gruesome crime inspired many books; perhaps the most well known is Meyer Levin's novel *Compulsion,* which was later made into a movie.

Leutgert, Adolph

In 1897 Chicago sausage maker Adolph Leutgert was convicted of murdering his wife. Leutgert's story that the woman was visiting relatives appeared unlikely after her wedding ring was discovered in a sausage vat. Leutgert was put on trial and Chicagoans for a while ate less sausage.

The Levee

In 1890's Chicago, the "old" Levee was a wide-open red light district along Clark Street between Polk Street and Roosevelt Road. It was lined with gaming houses, shot-and-a-beer taverns and, above all, brothels. The Levee competed for customers with other Chicago vice districts such as Little Cheyenne and the Bad Lands. In *Lords of the Levee,* Herman Kogan and Lloyd Wendt described what happened next: "When the old Levee on the southern edge of the Loop was outgrown, a newer and more elaborate and infinitely viler section sprang up in the choice area around Clark Street, Wabash Avenue, Eighteenth and 22nd (now Cermak Road) streets, its vicious tendrils still extending into other parts of the town. Here was the new Levee, the notorious Levee, the internationally famous home of sin and evil. Here were the brothels and peep shows and dime burlesque houses, the cheap saloons and smelly cribs." This Levee was home to the aristocratic Everleigh Club brothel, Big Jim Colosimo's brothels, and Al Capone's Four Deuces at 2222 South Wabash Avenue. Other brothels here were Bed Bug Row, the House of All Nations, the Why Not?, the Bucket of Blood and the Library. Among madams who ran these brothels were Carrie Watson, Lizzie Allen, Vic Shaw, Zoe Millard, French Emma Duval and Aimee Leslie. Infamous Levee pimps and white-slavers who plied their evil trade included Harry Guzik, Roy Jones, Ed and Louis Weiss and "King of the Brothels" Ike Bloom. Many Chicago gangsters who came to power in the 1920s got their start here, while new-to-the-city young women were trapped into the Levee's degrading life of white slavery. By the first decade of this century, efforts to end the Levee's commercialized prostitution increased. In 1909 reformer Gypsy Smith led a march on the Levee. The Vice Commission of 1911, a coalition of civic leaders, started the final drive to close it down. By the end of the 1920s, the Levee red-light district was no more.

Levin, Meyer (1905-1981)

Author Meyer Levin was born October 8, 1905, on South Sangamon Street in the Maxwell Street market area. His first published article was about the son of a Maxwell Street peddler. From 1922 until 1928, Levin was a reporter for the

Chicago Daily News, a literary hotbed that produced many great writers. Levin also worked for *The Chicago Evening American.* He wrote three Chicago novels: *The Old Bunch, Citizens,* and *Compulsion.* He felt his first two books, *Reporter* and *Frankie and Johnnie: A Love Story,* were his attempts to pass as a WASP writer. His later works are profoundly Jewish. He tried to stage *The Diary of Anne Frank* and wrote a book about this, *The Fanatic.* It is the story of Broadway's distortion of the manuscript left by a survivor from the death camps. In 1937 Levin covered the Spanish Civil War. Ira Berkow's *Maxwell Street* provides an interesting perspective on Levin. Meyer Levin's major books are: *Reporter* (1929); *Frankie and Johnnie* (1930); *Yehuda* (1931); *The New Bride* (1933); *The Old Bunch* (1937); *Citizens* (1940); *My Father's House* (1947); *In Search: An Autobiography* (1950); *Compulsion* (1956); *The Fanatic* (1964); and *The Architect* (1981).

Abraham Lincoln Statue
(The Standing Lincoln—1887)

By whatever route one takes to the appreciation and enjoyment of sculpture, the superb 11½-foot statue of Abraham Lincoln, popularly known as *The Standing Lincoln,* in Lincoln Park behind the Chicago Historical Society, stuns visitors with its sublime beauty. The sculptor, Augustus Saint-Gaudens (1848-1907), was invited to enter a competition to create a statue, but he refused. The contest was abandoned and he was chosen anyway. Saint-Gaudens had been deeply moved by Lincoln whom he had seen as a boy and later viewed in death. To create this statue, Saint-Gaudens used a life mask of Lincoln that Leonard Volk, a Chicago sculptor, had made before Lincoln went to Washington. The President-elect had not yet grown his beard. The incredible likeness to life of the statue is not due to a mere accumulation of exact details, but to a deep, powerful vision arising from the soul of the artist. Thirty years later, Saint-

This illustration of four prominent Chicago statues was part of a book published in 1900 titled, *Chicago of Today: The Metropolis of the West.*

KH collection

96

Ottawa Indian Monument

La Salle Statue

Lincoln

Schiller Monument

Gaudens created another sculpture of Lincoln, *The Seated Lincoln.* This statue is in Grant Park north of Congress Parkway. In their book, *Chicago's Public Sculpture,* Ira Bach and Mary Lackritz Gray say, "Critics consider it the less successful of the two works, but the artist preferred this figure." It was not erected until nineteen years after Saint-Gaudens died.

Lincoln Park

Lincoln Park was originally Chicago's city cemetery, but today it is a lively place—one of the great, public-oriented parks of the world. In the 1860s, the graves were removed. Lincoln Park gained a zoo in the 1870s. It has been noted over the years for a variety of much-loved animals, including the ape Bushman, now stuffed and on display in the Field Museum. There is also a farm. Visiting Lincoln Park Zoo on Sunday is a favorite activity of Chicagoans. Lincoln Park is noted for its statues such as *The Standing Lincoln, Shakespeare, John Peter Altgeld* and—in the zoo—*Winken Blinken* and *Nod.* Paddle boats can be rented in the lagoon. Other activities in Lincoln Park include baseball, football, tennis, golf, fishing, sculling, bicycle riding, jogging and picnicking. Lincoln Park's ultimate asset is its neighbor, Lake Michigan.

Lingle, Alfred "Jake" (1892-1930)

One of the most notorious "hits" ordered by Al Capone was the killing on June 9, 1930, of *Chicago Tribune* crime and underworld reporter Jake Lingle. Lingle was shot in the pedestrian right-of-way to the tunnel of the Illinois Central Railroad while on his way to catch a train to Washington Park race track. A public uproar ensued and the authorities became determined to find Lingle's murderer. The story that unfolded, however, cast its victim in a different light than had at first been presented. Jake Lingle was portrayed as a greedy, behind-the-scenes power broker who traded his prestige and influence with Police Commissioner William F. Russell and personal relationship with Capone for cash and favors. Even the *Tribune,* which had defended his reputation, admitted Lingle was crooked.

The Art Institute and the friendly lions of Michigan Avenue
have been there almost 100 years.

Photo, Michael Paul Caplan

Lions (Art Institute)

The much-beloved sculptures of two lions
standing proudly on the steps of the Michigan Avenue main entrance to the Art Institute were cast for the World's Columbian
Exposition of 1893. They were exhibited separately during the
fair. As the result of a donation by Henry Field's wife Annie, they
were brought together and installed in front of the newly-built
Art Institute. Their creator was Edward Kemeys (1843-1907),
a self-taught sculptor who was the most famous of the nineteenth-century American school of animal sculptors. He achieved
realism by studying lions in the wild. The mouth of the south
lion is tightly closed and the north one is eagerly open. Kemeys
was a democratic sculptor who said, "I never doubted the judgment of the people." He shunned sculpture that needed "a college professor to explain it." He was serious in the exercise of
his art and would be proud of the lasting appeal his lions have

99

had in Chicago. With Water Tower and the Daley Center Picasso, the Art Institute lions are popular symbols of the city. Kemeys certainly would not have found sacrilegious the wear on the lion's tails from countless hands rubbing them or the large Bear football helmets that the lions wore in 1986 before the Super Bowl.

The Loop

Technically "The Loop" is the traditional commercial heart of Chicago bounded on four sides by the raised "L" tracks on Lake Street, Wabash Avenue, Van Buren Street and Wells Street. Use of the name "The Loop" predates the "L" which was built in the 1890s. Originally, "The Loop" denominated the area bordered by Lake, Wells, State and Madison streets that was "looped" by streetcar tracks. The name is loosely used to designate downtown Chicago.

McCormick, Edith Rockefeller (1872-1932)

Mrs. Harold Edith Rockefeller McCormick never exchanged words with her chauffeur. He was given detailed instructions about her destination and time of return to ensure she never had to speak to him. Even her children required appointments to see her. This true grande dame of Chicago society, the daughter of John D. Rockefeller, married Harold, son of reaper king Cyrus McCormick. She believed erroneously that she descended from a French nobleman, La Rochefoucauld. In fact the Rockefellers were of German origin. She also believed she was the reincarnation of King Tut's child bride. Who could prove her wrong? Such grandiose ideas, aided immeasurably by the wealth of her father and husband, accompanied her taste for expensive things. The McCormicks owned two of the most extravagant Chicago area mansions: 1000 Lake Shore Drive (since torn down) and the Villa Turicum in Lake Forest (also no longer standing). She owned a rug valued at $185,000 given by the Shah of Iran to Peter the Great, Czar of Russia. Four of her chairs had belonged to Napoleon. One of her many necklaces contained stones from the Russian crown jewels. Edith had four children, but after the death of one from scarlet fever she slowly grew away from them. Menus in her mansion, at her insistence, were written in French. Edith moved for eight years to Switzerland, undergoing the controversial new therapy of psychoanalysis by Carl Jung. She donated large sums to advance Jung's work. In his own way, Harold McCormick was rather odd. According to one account, "he was nothing if not fun-loving. He was also very much of a dandy, fond of jeweled cufflinks and stickpins and rings, bright striped shirts with contrasting collars, embroidered waistcoats and grey mohair spats." His frequent extra-marital dalliances he blamed on Edith's sojourn for analysis, although he had indulged in affairs before she left for Europe. The McCormicks lavishly patronized Chicago opera. After a many-course meal ending just in time to reach the performance before it started, Edith would arrive at the opera in a plum-colored Rolls Royce. She wore an ermine cape, its 275 skins falling around her like a tent, and a gold bracelet on her bare ankle. Crowds would turn out just to witness her arrival at the opera. Edith lost a fortune building a city she dubbed "Edithton," south of Kenosha on the shore of Lake Michigan. When the Crash of 1929 struck, she lost heavily. She moved into the Drake Hotel, where she lived on $1,000 a day until her death at age sixty.

TIMELINE of CHICAGO HISTORY

1910 (Population: 2,185,283) William Randolph Hearst's *Chicago American* battles *Tribune* in circulation war.

1911 Carter Harrison, Jr. elected mayor again. Chicago Vice Commission reports. Everleigh Club closes. Attacks by reformers continue on Levee District. City Hall building completed.

1912 Harriet Monroe starts *Poetry: A Magazine of Verse.* Dr. Preston Bradley founds People's Church. Medinah Temple built.

1913 On November 13, city council passes ordinance unifying separately owned streetcar and bus lines. Five-cent fare established.

1914 Margaret Anderson begins publication of *Little Review,* one of the country's most respected literary magazines. On April 23, Weeghman Park (now Wrigley Field) opens. In November, Union Stock Yards temporarily closes due to outbreak of hoof-and-mouth disease. Colonel Robert R. McCormick takes control of *Tribune.*

Magnificent Mile

Michigan Avenue, from the Chicago River to Oak Street beach, was formerly Pine Street and known for its boarding houses. When the Michigan Avenue bridge was completed in 1920, replacing the time-worn-and-honored Rush Street bridge, Pine Street became North Michigan Avenue. A public relations firm called it "The Million Dollar Mile." In 1947 real estate magnate Arthur Rubloff announced an ambitious plan to develop North Michigan Avenue into "The Magnificent Mile." It has its charm. So did the parallel Clark Street from Grand to Chicago Avenue. In the 1950s and 1960s when it was full of strip shows and skid row bars, this portion of Clark Street was known as "The World's Worst Half Mile." On North Michigan Avenue, property values have soared and every block on it today is worth more millions.

Mamet, David (born 1947)

A number of now successful actors began their careers on Second City's stage. "The lion of Chicago theater," as *Tribune* critic Richard Christiansen called David Mamet, started his career as a busboy there. Perhaps the reason for Mamet's success is that he does not believe in pretending—but in real emotion. Mamet insists actors express anger, sadness or happiness about something real in their lives. Mamet's rise has been intertwined with Chicago's professional theaters. Fritzie Sahlins, former wife of Second City producer Bernard Sahlins, produced and directed Mamet's early play, *The Duck Variations.* Mamet brought together a group of actors who established the St. Nicholas Theater. He also worked with Stuart Gordon and the Organic Theater on the original production of *Sexual Perversity in Chicago.* This played at the Organic, which was then at 4520 North Beacon Street. Mamet's highly acclaimed *American Buffalo* was directed by Gregory Mosher at the Goodman Theater, beginning a long and fruitful collaboration between playwright and director. Mamet has written about Chicago's history. His *The Water Engine* is set during the 1933 A Century of Progress Exhibition and his Pulitzer Prize winning *Glengarry Glen Ross* depicts conniving Chicago real estate salesmen. Mamet has written motion picture screenplays for *The Postman Always Rings Twice* and *The Verdict*. And he has recreated Chicago in the 1930s for the motion picture version of *The Untouchables*. Mamet will stand on any platform that will give him a more interesting view of life. He researches his subjects deeply. David Mamet treats his words like his actors' emotions: they have to be real.

Marquette, Jacques (1637-1675)
See *Jolliet, Louis*.

Maxwell Street
Centered around Halsted Street (800 west) and Maxwell Street (1300 south), the open air Maxwell Street market is more than a hundred years old. It extended farther east before construction of the Dan Ryan Expressway pushed it westward. Anchored by a Polish sausage stand on Halsted Street open twenty-four hours a day, Maxwell Street comes alive on Sunday mornings beginning at 4 a.m. when bargain-hunting shoppers descend on the temporary stalls of outdoor vendors. Many consider it a marketplace of junk, but others are exhilarated by its bargains, second and third-hand goods and special treasures. Prices are, as a rule, negotiable and often so low a buyer can get cheated but not lose much money. If you need a rusty pair

---

TIMELINE of CHICAGO HISTORY

1915 William Hale Thompson elected mayor; he serves until 1923, will be reelected in 1927. On July 24 Eastland capsizes, killing 835 people. *Birth of a Nation,* considered first full-length major motion picture, shown in city. This exhibition touches off boycott because many consider its depiction of blacks' role in U.S. history flagrantly biased.

1916 Republican National Convention nominates Charles Evans Hughes and Charles Fairbanks. Carl Sandburg's *Chicago Poems* published. George William Mundelein named third archbishop of Chicago. Navy Pier opens.

The Merchandise Mart, pictured here in the early 1930s, was the world's largest building. It would later be purchased for back taxes by Joseph Kennedy, father of the Kennedy clan. The view is from Clark Street and Wacker Drive.

Courtesy, the CTA

of pliers, an old bathtub fixture or items from last year's biggest fad, Maxwell Street is the place to go. Socks without heels, watches, electrical items that may or may not work and are possibly stolen make the emphatic motto for Maxwell Street shoppers, "caveat emptor."

Merchandise Mart

Until completion of the twice-as-large Pentagon in Washington, D.C., the twenty-five story Merchandise Mart with ninety-seven acres of floor space was the world's largest building. It was begun in 1928 and finished in 1931. Until the Sears Tower was completed, it still held the title of world's largest commercial building. Constructed at an original cost of $32 million, it housed wholesale operations of Marshall Field and Company. These closed during the Depression. During the 1930s in one of the shrewdest deals of his legendary career, tycoon Joseph P. Kennedy (1888-1969) purchased the Merchandise Mart by paying only its past-due real estate taxes. Sargent Shriver, John F. Kennedy's brother-in-law, once headed it. The Mart remains a jewel in the crown of the vast Kennedy family portfolio. Most of its tenants are wholesale furniture distributors and jobbers who showcase new design trends in furniture for retail stores and interior decorators. The Merchandise Mart stands on the north side of the Chicago River at Wells Street where the original Chicago and North Western Railroad Station stood. In the 1830s, Miller's Tavern, an establishment so busy it scarcely had room for chairs, was here.

Merchandise Mart Hall of Fame

Along the edge of the Chicago River—in front of the Merchandise Mart—stand a series of oversize bronze busts on marble columns honoring eight of the greatest merchants in American history. They are: Marshall Field (1834-1906), the early owner of Marshall Field & Company; George Huntington Hartford (1833-1917), founder of the Great Atlantic and Pacific Tea Company; John R. Wanamaker (1838-1922), founder of John Wanamaker, Inc.; Frank Winfield Woolworth (1852-1919), founder of the F. W. Woolworth Company; Edward A. Filene (1860-1937), president of William Filene and Sons; Julius Rosenwald (1862-1932), president and chairman of the board of Sears, Roebuck & Company; General Robert E. Wood (1879-1970), president and chairman of the board of Sears, Roebuck & Company; and Aaron Montgomery Ward (1843-1913), founder of Montgomery Ward and Company.

Meyer, Karl (born 1937)

War tax protestor and conscience of Chicago, Karl Meyer refuses to sanction violence or killing, either personally or by the U.S. government. To protest capital punishment, he once pushed a cart with a mock electric chair in it over the roads to Springfield. Protesting nuclear weapons in 1960, Meyer walked across the United States, Europe and the Soviet Union, passing out leaflets critical of the policies of both super-powers. During the early 1960s, he went on the Walk to Moscow, but he angered other protestors in his group when he said he had not spoken to enough Russians to find out their opinions about peace. He has been jailed many times for his protests, including one against C.T.A. fare increases. Meyer's most persistent cause has been the fight against using federal taxes for killing. He has preached and practiced a way to refuse paying income taxes. On his W-4 form, Meyer lists as many extra dependents as are needed to reduce the balance due to zero. In 1971 he served nine months in Sandstone Federal Penitentiary for this offense. When he was released, he was as adamant as ever about not paying taxes. In a 1984 *Chicago Reader* article, Meyer said, "I hope I wouldn't go too many years without experiencing jail from time to time. It's an indication you're making at least a small impact." Meyer's "crimes" have landed him in Cook County Jail. He has been called "the complete idealist." What most people consider impractical and against every day common sense, Karl Meyer commits himself to do in the name of love for others.

Mickey Finn

Chicago has contributed its share of words and phrases to the American language including "clout," "the Loop," "The Magnificent Mile," "sundae" (the suburb Evanston claims this often challenged credit), "copper" (for policemen who wore copper badges during Mayor Haynes' 1850 administration), and "paddy wagon" (after policemen who before picking up skid row drunks would say "Paddy, get the wagon"). Chicago's most well-known linguistic contribution, however, derives from a belligerent, pugnacious and bullet-headed man even the lowliest hoodlums looked down on: Mickey Finn. He claimed at various times to be from Ireland and Peoria. His professions ranged from jack-rolling to bartending. His reputation derives from a crafty combination of these two skills. In the late 1890s, Finn opened the Lone Star Saloon and Palm Garden near Harrison Street on a part of State Street then known as "Whiskey Row." A sign advertised "Try a Mickey Finn Special." This concoction was probably hydrate of chloride. It would knock out a customer for up to twelve hours, long enough for the unfortunate to be robbed of all valuables, including clothing. After several accomplices testified against him, the city got tough with Finn and revoked his license. Mickey Finn sold his potent formula to other dive-keepers and disappeared from Chicago.

Midway Airport

Midway Airport on Chicago's Southwest Side at 5500 to 6300 South Cicero Avenue was once the busiest airport not only in the city but also in the world. The title "busiest airport" was taken by large-jet-capable O'Hare International Airport in the late 1950s. Midway was dedicated in 1927 as the Chicago Municipal Airport. It took over airmail service from Maywood Airport, where Charles Lindbergh had delivered mail. It occupies a square mile of land whose use or sale, in the original sectioning of this area, was designated to benefit public schools. As a result, the land is rented from the Chicago Board of Education. The airport was renamed in honor of the United States World War II naval victory at Midway Island.

TIMELINE of CHICAGO HISTORY

1917 On March 24, city gets its first motorcoaches. United States enters war in Europe; registration for draft begins on June 5. Irwin St. John Tucker, Chicago Episcopal priest, writes an anti-draft pamphlet for which he will be sentenced to twenty years in prison. U.S. Supreme Court will reverse conviction for pronounced prejudice in Tucker's case by Federal Judge Kenesaw Mountain Landis. On December 22, Mother Cabrini dies. She will be first U.S. citizen canonized a saint.

1918 Chicago encourages war effort by instituting "heatless Mondays" to conserve fuel. On September 10, airmail initiated to New York. On October 17, 381 people die in one day from influenza epidemic. Bertha Palmer dies. Goodman School of Drama opens.

At the time of this 1946 photo, Midway Airport, then known as Chicago Municipal Airport, used a billboard to proclaim itself the "Aviation Center of the World." Midway remained the "world's busiest airport" for another dozen years until O'Hare International Airport took over the title.

Courtesy, the CTA

Mies van der Rohe, Ludwig (1886-1969)

Master architect and visionary Ludwig Mies van der Rohe shaped the direction of twentieth century architecture so completely that only now, almost two decades after his death, have counter-reactions to his brand of austere modernism begun to gain force. He fled Nazi Germany where he had been the leader of the famous Bauhaus School of Architecture. In a 1964 statement summing up his principles, he said, "It was my growing conviction that there could be no architecture of our time without the prior acceptance of the new scientific and technical developments. I believe that architecture has little or nothing to do with the invention of interesting forms or with personal inclinations. True architecture is always objective and is the expression of the inner structure of our time, from which it stems." This stern view is also encapsulated in his widely quoted dictum, "less is more." Critics contend his buildings are cold, almost inhuman creations. A visit to his designs for the Illinois Institute of Technology (IIT) from 31st to 35th Streets on South State Street—with its austere, squared buildings—will do little to alter such an opinion. Mies came to Chicago in 1938 to teach at the Armour Institute (later renamed IIT). He left his imprint on the cityscape in a series of high-rises, perhaps the most frequently seen of which are the Lake Shore Drive Apartments built between 1948 and 1951.

Mr. Dooley

Martin J. Dooley, a fictional turn-of-the-century Chicago saloonkeeper and political pundit, was created by newspaper columnist Finley Peter Dunne. Mr. Dooley has been called the Doonesbury of his day. His name, it was said, was better known than the vice president's—except for the year Theodore Roosevelt held the office. Mr. Dooley's pragmatic philosophy is summed up in his dictum: "Trust iv'rybody, but cut the cards." Mr. Dooley's acerbic comments on current events—from the condition of the stockyards to American imperialism in the Philippines—won admiration and respect for this character and his witty creator.

Monadnock Building

The sixteen-story Monadnock Building at 53 West Jackson Boulevard could serve as the entire curriculum for a course on architecture. Occupying a square block, it is actually made up of four integrated buildings. The northern half—originally known as the Monadnock and Kearsarge Building—was designed by Burnham & Root (mainly John W. Root). Boston developer Peter Brooks and his Chicago agent Owen Aldis called for the structure to be located on the south end of downtown (before the "L" was built encircling the Loop). It was adjacent to the city's red light district. Brooks asked for "an avoidance of ornamentation" and "the effect of solidarity and strength." Root, who loved ornamentation, nevertheless met the challenge. It was completed in 1891. It is the tallest and heaviest wall-bearing building in Chicago and, most likely, the world. Louis Sullivan said of it, "the Monadnock went ahead; an amazing cliff of brickwork, rising sheer and stark, with a subtlety of line and surface, a direct singleness of purpose that gave one the thrill of romance. It was the first and last word of its kind." He also called it "the high tide of masonry construction as applied to commercial structures." It was one of the first attempts at a portal windbracing system. The weight-bearing walls at their base are six-feet thick. The building has set two feet since it was finished. The two buildings on the south half of the block were originally known as the Katahdin and Wachusett buildings (for mountains in New Hampshire). They were developed by Peter Brooks' brother, Shepherd Brooks. They continue the bay lines of the northern structures. They were designed after Root's untimely death by Holabird & Roche and completed in 1893. In 1940 when the subway was put through, new hardpan caissons were used to support the eastern wall.

Monroe, Harriet (1860-1936) *and* "Poetry: A Magazine of Verse"

Harriet Monroe, author of the "Columbian Ode" for the World's Columbian Exposition of 1893, led the way from such classic poetry forms to the experimental verse of the modern era. Monroe was the niece of John Wellborn Root (she wrote a biography of him in 1896), the architect who helped break the mold of imitative architecture. She founded *Poetry: A Magazine of Verse* in 1912. The first issue was dated September 23, 1912. At the start, she paid 50 cents a line. Monroe published new poets such as W. B. Yeats, D. H. Lawrence, Vachel Lindsay, Carl Sandburg, Sara Teasdale, Edna Vincent Millay, H. D. (Hilda Doolittle), Rabindranath Tagore and Wallace Stevens. Her roving European editor, Ezra Pound, discovered poems by an American working in a London bank—T. S. Eliot. The poets Monroe nurtured led a revolution in poetry that created innovative forms and dealt with controversial subjects. Vachel Lindsay, an itinerant poet who had traded his poems for food, was one of her discoveries. *Poetry* published Lindsay's great "General William Booth Enters Heaven." Carl Sandburg's "Chicago," and T. S. Eliot's seminal "The Love Song of J. Alfred Prufrock" also first appeared in her magazine. For decades, poets have received constructive criticism and comments rather than simple rejections from the magazine that carries on Monroe's original two-fold intention to encourage poets and publish their work. Harriet Monroe died on September 26, 1936, in Arequipa, Peru, on her return journey from an international writers' congress in Buenos Aires. She is buried there.

Motley, Willard (1912-1965)

Born in Chicago, as a child Willard Motley lived on West 59th Street in a "respectable" part of Englewood. A black, he attended Englewood High School and earned the nickname "The Little Ironman" while playing football. In a 1960 *Tribune* interview, he said, "I moved to the slums of Chicago after being bored in the middle class neighborhood in which I was reared; there I discovered myself and the sort of thing I wanted to put on paper." Nelson Algren claimed "among others" Motley imitated the style of Farrell, Dreiser, and Sandburg. Both Motley and Algren wrote about drug addiction in similar Chicago settings. Motley wrote about Italians from a white point of view. He studied and painted the Chicago scene with meticulous notes

*T*IMELINE *of* CHICAGO HISTORY

1919 On June 9, *Chicago Tribune* scoops world by publishing secret draft of Versailles Treaty leaked by a Chinese delegate angered at the autocratic behavior of the major powers.

On July 27, a group of whites drown a young black man when he enters a segregated South Side beach. A race riot breaks out, inflaming city; fifteen whites and twenty-three blacks die. Al

Capone arrives in city from New York. In the "Black Sox" Scandal, White Sox players throw the World Series. Chewing-gum magnate William Wrigley buys Cubs.

(six years of them for his first novel). He wrote endlessly, the first draft of one of his novels ran to 500,000 words. He wrote about characters the reader could care about; for example, Nick Romano in *Knock on Any Door* as an altar boy is painfully powerful. He believed Chicago had the potential to become a means of human salvation. His first novel was a major best-seller. Two of his novels were made into movies. Motley moved to Cuernavaca, Mexico thirteen years before he died on March 4, 1965. His major books are *Knock on Any Door* (1947); *We Fished All Night* (1951); *Let No Man Write My Epitaph* (1958); *Let Noon Be Fair* (1966).

Navy Pier

Jutting out more than half a mile at the end of Grand Avenue into Lake Michigan, Navy Pier offers a healthy stroll to its end—3,040 feet. It was one of five piers serving a thriving maritime Chicago. Its official name was Municipal Pier No. 2. At the 1916 opening, a streetcar line ran out almost to the tip. Loss of the streetcar ride was only one of many tribulations the pier has survived. The first 2,340 feet were designed as double-decked ship freight and passenger terminals. Passenger runs that crossed the lake dwindled and Chicago failed to emerge as the international shipping port that optimistic planners predicted. The docks stood empty. The 660 square foot recreation area at the far end once featured a cafeteria, amusement rides, concert hall, emergency hospital and rest rooms. Its Roof Garden Restaurant—a naturally air-conditioned spot—seemed destined for a prosperous future until federal agents raided it during the early days of Prohibition to stop illegal liquor sales. During World War II, it served as a training school for the navy and marines. In 1946, the pier became a campus for the University of Illinois, Chicago Undergraduate Division. The school remained here until 1965 when it moved to the newly-built campus at Harrison and Halsted streets and was renamed the University of Illinois at Chicago Circle. By the 1980s, Navy Pier, after a remodeling and facelift, became the site of a vast annual international art exhibit, Indian powwows and a wide variety of ethnic festivals. Now, if only they would reinstitute the streetcar!

"Terrible" Tommy O'Connor—some said he was innocent—
was to be hanged Dec. 19, 1921, for the murder of Maxwell Street detective Paddy O'Neil. He escaped four days
before the scheduled hanging. They kept the gallows for
him for half a century but he never showed up to use them.

Courtesy, the *Chicago Tribune*

Oak Park

The suburb of Oak Park is located nine miles
straight west of the Loop. Oak Park's prosperity dates from the
1840s when Chicago's first railroad—the Galena and Chicago
Union—reached it. Wide avenues lined with ample trees preserve
Oak Park's beauty. It is rich in both architectural and literary
traditions. In Oak Park, L. Frank Baum worked on his *Wizard
of Oz* stories and Edgar Rice Burroughs wrote his *Tarzan* tales.
It was the childhood home of Ernest Hemingway, who unfortunately was not Oak Park's greatest booster. "It is a town of
wide lawns and narrow minds," Hemingway said bitterly. The
impressive and innovative homes Frank Lloyd Wright designed
here belie Hemingway's criticism. Oak Park has twenty-one

schools and colleges, three public libraries, sixteen parks and seven recreation centers. In 1980 its population was 54,887, a drop from the 1970 population of 62,511.

O'Connor, "Terrible" Tommy

"Terrible" Tommy, should he show up one of these days, would be nearly a hundred years old. He is invited to show up for a hanging that he failed to attend—his own. On December 19, 1921, O'Connor escaped from the old county jail at 54 West Hubbard Street, now the site of condominiums. Resourcefully, he got out of jail through a shaft and over the wall four days before his scheduled execution. He had been sentenced to death for the murder of Maxwell Street detective Paddy O'Neil. Despite reported sightings of O'Connor over the years, no one could ever confirm seeing him. The gallows remained stored in the basement of the county jail for the next fifty years in case authorities got the chance to fulfill his sentence: "to be hanged until death."

Ogden, William Butler (1805-1877)

However wild and woolly one might want to paint early Chicago, the sophisticated, literate, gentlemanly entrepreneur William B. Ogden should be remembered. Ogden was also elected Chicago's first mayor. Of his contributions, A. T. Andreas wrote: "To the citizens of Chicago and to the people of the Northwest: would you behold William Butler Ogden's monument, look around you!" In 1835 the thirty-year-old Ogden arrived in Chicago as an emissary of his brother-in-law, a speculator in Chicago real estate. Ogden quickly made a minor fortune for his relation by selling a small part of his holdings. Ogden also invested on his own. In 1837 he ran for mayor against John H. Kinzie and defeated him. Chicago suffered a terrible financial panic during Ogden's term in office. A nationwide de-

William B. Ogden, elected Chicago's first mayor in 1837, also gave the city its first railroad, the Galena and Chicago Union, in 1848. He lost personally and financially in the Chicago and Peshtigo fires, both of which occurred on the same day, Oct. 8, 1871.
KH collection

W. B. Ogden.

pression and questionable currency caused the panic that hit Chicago's land boom particularly hard. Almost alone, Ogden stood against repudiation of the city's debt and won. In the next decade, Ogden rode out on horseback to raise money from area farmers to finance the city's first rail line, the Galena and Chicago Union Railroad. He became first president of the railroad but resigned after some board members impugned his motives. Ogden then founded the Chicago and North Western Railroad, which eventually purchased the Galena and Chicago Union line. Ogden became president of the Union Pacific Railroad and was present in 1869 when the Union Pacific and Central Pacific joined rails at Promontory Point, Utah. Ogden owned considerable property both in Chicago and Peshtigo, Wisconsin. The two cities were both destroyed by fires the same day, October 8, 1871. Ogden lost two fortunes and a number of friends in the fires. Ogden retired to his New York home on the Harlem River where he died on August 3, 1877.

O'Hare, Edward Henry "Butch" (1914-1942)

A young World War II Congressional Medal of Honor winner, Lt. "Butch" O'Hare was shot down over the Pacific. He has the world's busiest airport named after him. O'Hare graduated from the U.S. Naval Academy at Annapolis despite the fact his father, Edward J. "Artful Eddie" O'Hare, ran Al Capone's Hawthorne dog track in Cicero. The elder O'Hare told the federal court Capone had the names of the jurors in his income tax evasion trial and was attempting to bribe them. Jurors were switched at the last moment and Capone convicted. Years later Eddie O'Hare was gunned down the week Capone was released from prison. The plaque at the airport commemorating Butch O'Hare's brave deeds reads: "For conspicuous gallantry and intrepidity in aerial combat at grave risk of his life above and beyond the call of duty, as section leader and pilot of squadron three, when on February 20, 1942, having lost the assistance of his teammates, he interposed his plane between his ship and the adjoining enemy formation of nine attacking twin engine heavy bombers, without hesitation, alone and unaided, he repeatedly attacked this enemy

The Our Lady of Angels fire on Dec. 1, 1958, claimed the lives of 92 children and 3 nuns. It gave the city one of the saddest days in its history.

Courtesy, the *Chicago Tribune*

formation at close range in the face of their intense combined machine gun fire, and despite this concentrated opposition, he, by his gallant and courageous action, his extremely skillful workmanship, making the most of every shot of his limited ammunition, shot down five bombers and severely damaged a sixth before they reached the bomb release point. As a result of his gallant action, one of the most daring in the history of combat aviation, he undoubtedly saved his carrier from serious damage.''

Oriental Institute

The Oriental Institute at 1155 East 58th Street can be considered misnamed. More properly, it should be called the "Middle East Museum." Located on the campus of the University of Chicago, it catapulted to fame through the scholarship and archaeological work of Dr. James Henry Breasted. The Institute is a treasure house of artifacts and relics from the civilizations of Babylonia, Assyria, Egypt, Palestine, Sumer, Akkad, Nubia and Asia Minor. Its collections include pieces from the Dead Sea Scrolls, a model of the Tower of Babel, mummies, the Great Stone Bull, which once guarded the palace entrance of Sargon II, greatest of all Assyrian kings. The Oriental Institute has aided the researches of many scholars in putting together an extraordinary record of the time when Western Civilization was evolving from agrarian societies to technologically developed ones. The best example of this is the 4,000 year old chariot in the Oriental Institute that represents the oldest recorded use of the wheel. The museum is open from 10:00 a.m. to 4:00 p.m. Tuesday through Saturday; 12:00 p.m. to 4:00 p.m. Sunday; and closed Monday.

Our Lady of the Angels Fire

On December 1, 1958, a devastating and tragic fire swept Our Lady of the Angels parochial school at 3814 West Iowa Street. The fire started in a rubbish basket in the basement and raged through the classrooms, killing children at their desks. Others died while leaping from second floor windows. It claimed the lives of ninety-two pupils and three nuns. As a result, all Chicago area schools were ordered to install sprinkler systems. The archdiocese settled all claims for $3.2 million.

p
q
r

Palmer Mansion

It was not Camelot, although some people imagined it was. The Palmer Mansion stood for seventy years at 1350 North Lake Shore Drive. It was the home of Bertha and Potter Palmer. He founded the department store that is now Marshall Field & Company and also built a succession of Palmer House Hotels, but he made his main fortune in real estate. In the 1880s and 1890s, Bertha Palmer was the undisputed queen of Chicago society. She was also president of the Lady Board of Managers at the World's Columbian Exposition. Her reign in Chicago was highlighted by her sister's marriage to the son of President Ulysses S. Grant. The Palmers built their castle on an almost-abandoned stretch of north Lake Shore Drive in 1882. On its walls hung a prominent art collection—especially of Impressionists. The Palmer mansion's outer doors had no doorknobs or keyholes. They had to be opened from the inside. It was replaced by a twenty-two story apartment building, but Chicagoans were able to tour the Palmer mansion for a fifty cent admission just before it was torn down in the 1950s.

Patronage/Shakman Decree

"They charge us with patronage," Mayor Daley complained in March, 1972. "There's nothing wrong with patronage. What kind of man is there who would not give a friend a job? I have done it many times and I will do it again and I have no apologies to make." Despite Daley's definition, patronage has come to imply the trading of public-sector jobs for unremunerated service usually in the form of electioneering or precinct work in support of a political sponsor. One of the most hallowed traditions for getting a city job in Chicago was a letter of introduction from an alderman, ward committeeman or Democratic official. Those hired in this way worked for the Democratic party and were expected to sell tickets for party fund-raisers. This long-entrenched and quasi-feudal system persisted until the early seventies. Attorney Michael Shakman, on behalf of the Independent Voters of Illinois, filed a lawsuit contending political labor in return for government employment was a violation of a person's civil rights. Federal Judge Abraham Lincoln Marovitz—he had sworn in Daley as mayor—initially threw the case out. An appeals court remanded it back to the U. S. District Court for a decision. Judge Nicholas J. Bua negotiated a consent decree on May 5, 1972, which subsequently became known as the Shakman Decree. This order prohibits forced political contributions by public employees, bans them from political activity during working hours and bars their being disciplined or discharged for political reasons. In a famous Shakman Decree case, Jane Byrne's administration was forced to grant a six per cent cost-of-living allowance to Deputy Chicago Public Library Commissioner G. Patrick Green. He claimed his raise was refused because he was a cousin of Byrne's arch-rival, State's Attorney Richard M. Daley.

Perry, William "Refrigerator" (born 1962)

"The Fridge," a three-hundred-plus-pound defensive lineman, blocker and sometime offensive ball carrier for the Chicago Bears, in his rookie year (1985) helped the Bears win their first NFL (and Super Bowl) championship in twenty-three years. Perry's nickname came from his fondness for raiding his family's refrigerator in high school. He has been compared to both a monster and pixie. Capturing the imagination of virtually everyone—football fans and non-fans alike—Perry has reaped the rewards of celebrity stardom, acting in many television commercials and giving product endorsements. Probably his most memorable play was one for which he was penalized after attempting to carry his teammate Walter Payton, who was toting the ball, across the goal line.

The Potter Palmer mansion at 1350 North Lake Shore, built in 1882, represented the first turn of the soil that transformed the sandy, swampy lake shore into the Gold Coast. Reluctantly at first, members of Chicago's upper social strata moved there from Prairie Avenue and Washington Boulevard.

Courtesy, the *Chicago Tribune*

Phillips, Wally

In every city one radio commentator/disc jockey usually captures the imagination and ratings of the listening audience. Wally Phillips of WGN, for twenty years on mornings and now with lunch-time interviews, has earned the love and respect of Chicago. He has an upbeat, "I love Chicago because it cares" and "let's get something happening" style. Phillips has found this attitude works here. The poor benefit as he annually collects over a million dollars for them through his Neediest Children's Christmas Fund effort.

The Plan of Chicago (1909)

Also known as The Burnham Plan. Daniel Burnham and Edward Bennett were commissioned by the Commercial Club to make a plan for the city. Published by the club in 1909, this plan was adopted the next year by Chicago. Major portions were implemented over the next two decades. Though broad and imaginative, the plan was also flawed. It gave the city North Michigan Avenue, but proposed filling Grant Park with museums. Its greatest limitation was it was not a plan for Chicago, but a plan for the downtown area. It ignored the neighborhoods and outlying areas, probably because the use of eminent domain was more limited at that time than it would later be. This was an omission for which the city is still paying. Its greatest strength was focusing on the river and lake.

Prairies

The ecology of Chicago's past—the tall grass prairie—is a dominant and extraordinary one which still thrives in secluded portions of this area. In undisturbed stretches along railroad right-of-ways, in set-aside areas and even in some back yards, prairie grasses five and six feet high proclaim what once was and may again some day be. Once upon a time in northern Illinois, tall grass prairies swayed in the wind like vast seas, magical in color and lushness. In the month of May, prairies burst into rich hues that surprise onlookers: dark blue, shades of yellow, bright purple, and green. Insects buzz, grasshoppers click, and birds sing while the winds cause a symphony of undulating movement across the prairie surface. A beautiful tapestry is created, woven of colors from plants with roots hundreds of years old. Encroaching environments, primarily those made by humans, theaten the ecology of the prairie. Often fire, either set by people or caused by nature, cleanses the prairie, burning tree roots and non-tall grass prairie weeds, and beginning the ecological cycle again. Patches of true prairie are occasionally spotted along road embankments. Some of the better expanses of virgin prairie in their full glory can be observed at the north end of Illinois State Beach Park in Winthrop Harbor or at the Goose Lake Prairie State Park southwest of Joliet.

Prairie Avenue

In the 1880s and 1890s, Prairie Avenue—just southeast of the Loop—was the unchallenged street of social prestige in Chicago. But it was more than just the street where the fashionable of Chicago lived. Some of the great names of the Chicago School of Architecture received early and significant commissions and created homes here. The scions of nineteenth century Chicago and most of their dwellings are gone today, but the influence the architecture wrought persists. Among the residents of Prairie Avenue were Marshall Field, George Pullman, and Gustavus Swift. Lake Michigan and the Illinois Central Railroad tracks lay to the east, and the infamous Levee to the west. Prairie Avenue blossomed originally with the help of the Fire of 1871. The earliest Prairie Avenue settlers were the envy of relatives hit by the holocaust. By the 1890s more than one hundred men and women (most of the women were widows of wealthy men) were millionaires in the burgeoning metropolis. West Washington Boulevard and North Lake Shore Drive competed as fashionable locations, but pre-World War I Prairie Avenue was the city's Nob Hill. When Bertha and Potter Palmer built their castle on the north side lakefront, the northward exodus officially began. Many Prairie Avenue residents retaliated, refusing to ''receive'' the apostates as callers. By the 1920s and 1930s many Prairie Avenue mansions had been abandoned and were torn down. In the 1970s, the area was made a historic district and a portion of Prairie Avenue restored. The thirty-five

TIMELINE of CHICAGO HISTORY

1920 (Population: 2,701,705) 18th amendment (Prohibition) takes effect on January 17, Al Capone's 21st birthday. On May 14, bi-level Michigan Avenue bridge opens. On May 11, Colosimo shot in lobby of his restaurant, allegedly by Capone. In a smoke-filled room during the Republican National Convention, dark horse candidate Warren Harding of Ohio is selected to be nominated for president. Drake Hotel opens.

1921 On November 11 first Chicago radio station—KYW—begins to broadcast. It will relocate to Philadelphia in 1934. George Halas moves Chicago Bears to Wrigley Field.

room Glessner Mansion at 1800 South Prairie Avenue is open to the public today. It was designed in 1886 by Henry Hobbs Richardson for John J. Glessner, a director of International Harvester. The Glessner House influenced Louis Sullivan and Frank Lloyd Wright and now is the home of the Chicago Architectural Foundation.

Printing House Row Historic District

The geographical reference points for the Printing House Row district south of the Loop were strikingly different when they were built than they are today. The commercial area was developed during the early 1890s. The Van Buren "L" had not then been built. Its construction extended the southern edge of the Loop from the previous boundary of Madison Street. The Eisenhower Expressway, Congress "L" and Union Station did not exist. The area where the core of Chicago's large printing business was located was bordered to the north by shanties, to the east by the red-light Levee District, to the west by the river and to the south by Dearborn Railroad Station. On this unprepossessing site, businessmen and architects joined forces, constructing the magnificent buildings that now, almost a hundred years later, are being re-habbed to create a highly successful residential and commercial community noted for its design, large lofts and advantageous location. Among the buildings that have been remodeled:

THE PONTIAC BUILDING at 542 S. Dearborn Street. Designed by Holabird & Roche and completed in 1891, it was one of the first skyscrapers with a steel frame construction. The Pontiac is now primarily office and retail space.

THE TERMINAL BUILDING at 537 S. Dearborn Street. This fifteen story building was designed in 1892 by John Van Osdel, Chicago's first professional architect. After seeing many of his buildings destroyed in the Fire of 1871, he started from scratch. The exterior was preserved in 1985-86, but the interior, after being gutted, was remodeled with fifty-two one and two bedroom apartments.

THE TRANSPORTATION BUILDING at 600 S. Dearborn Street. The first major renovation in the area, this 1911 structure was re-habbed in 1978 creating 294 apartments on its twenty-two floors.

Other important renovations in the Printing House Row District include: the NEW FRANKLIN BUILDING at 720 S. Dearborn Street, the OLD FRANKLIN BUILDING at 525 S. Dearborn, the DONAHUE at 711-727 S. Dearborn and the ROWE at 714-716 S. Dearborn. The DUPLICATOR and the MORTON buildings at 530 and 538 S. Dearborn have been renovated and combined to create the Morton Hotel. Immediately south of this district is the historic Dearborn Street Station, a Romanesque structure long treasured by the city. A $6.8 million renovation of this station and its annex created a mix of retail and commercial space.

Prohibition

Chicago, almost from its beginning, struggled with the issue of alcohol use and abuse. In the 1840s, certain hotels proudly proclaimed themselves "temperance houses." The Beer Riots of 1854 brought turbulence and division to the young city. In the 1870s, pray-ins took place in front of saloons. The law allowed precincts to vote themselves dry. The issue became crucial in the late 1880s when dry suburbs and unincorporated areas feared they would lose this status if they were annexed to the city. Chicago and eventually Evanston became the home of the Woman's Christian Temperance Union. In 1920, after the Volstead Act (18th Amendment) established national prohibition,

TIMELINE of CHICAGO HISTORY

1922 Radio stations WMAQ (then WGU) and WGN on air. Construction of Soldier Field begins.

1923 Chicago banker and civic leader Rufus Dawes proposes a world's fair for 1933 to celebrate city's centennial. On

November 6, William Dever, a reform candidate, elected mayor, replacing scandal-ridden administration of Big Bill Thompson.

1924 Thirty thousand factories in city produce $7 billion

worth of goods. On May 21, Nathan Leopold and Richard Loeb murder 14 year-old Bobby Franks. Eloquence of attorney Clarence Darrow saves them from a death penalty. On October 9, Soldier Field officially opens.

Chicago turned to beer-runners. Little Italy wine-makers, bathtub gin concocters and illegal importers helped to make its name as the town that even revivalist and former Chicago Cub outfielder Billy Sunday could not shut down. In 1931, the election of Anton Cermak as mayor revealed the voters' attitude toward Prohibition. Cermak had risen to power as the representative of the city's saloons. On December 5, 1933, the "noble experiment" ended, thirteen years, ten months and eighteen days after it had begun.

Prudential Building

The completion of the Prudential Building at 130 E. Randolph Street in 1955 broke the logjam and began an explosion of high-rise construction in and near the Loop. Not a single commercial skyscraper had been built in the twenty-two years before it was finished. Doubters felt the Prudential Building might not become fully occupied. Since then more than a hundred skyscrapers, with many times the Prudential Building's floor space, have joined Chicago's skyline.

Pullman, George Mortimer
(1831-1897)

When he came to Chicago in 1855, George Pullman literally helped lift the city out of the mud. The streets needed to be raised eight to ten feet for installation of a sewer system. Building entrances then had to be made level with the new grade. In his early days in Albion, New York, Pullman had moved houses that were too near the Erie Canal. His first business venture here was raising the Tremont Hotel in 1858. In his book, *Pullman,* Stanley Bruder describes this operation: "Heavy timbers were propped along the cellar's walls and ceiling, and a thousand men and five thousand jackscrews were placed in position to raise the four-story brick hotel. On Pullman's command the men turned the jackscrews a set number of notches. At intervals the process was repeated, and quickly the structure rose. People and furniture remained in the hotel undisturbed." The principal reasons for his fame are a railroad sleeper car he perfected, the Pullman Palace Car; the town he built and lost; and a bitter strike he technically won. In 1864 he built his first sleeping coach, the "Pioneer." It was selected to carry Abraham Lincoln's body from Chicago to Springfield. Pullman's Palace Car Company was chartered on February 22, 1867. By the 1870s, railroad track gauge had become standardized throughout most of the United States. Pullman's sleepers could be transferred among different railroad lines and the market for them grew nation-wide. To house his expanding plant operations, Pullman in 1880 chose a site near Lake Calumet at 105th Street and Cottage Grove Avenue. This was far from downtown Chicago, so Pullman decided to build a town where his employees could live. However, the fanatic attention to detail that aided him in perfecting the sleeper misfired when applied to planning of his company town. Workers did not want their lives as regimented as Pullman envisioned. In 1894 when business slowed down, Pullman cut jobs, wages and working-hours. He did not lower rents or gas and water charges. His workers wanted to bring in arbitrators and tried to negotiate with him. But Pullman adamantly refused to yield and a bitter strike ensued. With the help of U.S. Army troops sent by President Grover Cleveland technically to protect the mails, Pullman was able to break the strike. He died a broken-spirited man at age sixty-six on October 19, 1897. His body was buried in Graceland Cemetery beneath tons of steel and cement to prevent anyone from desecrating it.

*T*IMELINE *of* CHICAGO HISTORY

1925 On July 6, thirty-three story Tribune Tower opens. Its gothic design, based on Malines Cathedral in Belgium and Butter Tower in Rouen, wins a $100,000 design competition for John Mead Howells and Raymond M. Hood. On August 19, Victor Lawson, publisher of *Chicago Daily News* for almost fifty years, dies. Hack Wilson joins the Cubs, slamming 190 homers in six years.

1926 Assistant state's attorney William McSwiggin slain April 27. City's ire aroused by question, "Who killed McSwiggin?" In June, Roman Catholic International Eucharistic Congress held at Mundelein and Soldier Field. Mercantile Exchange opens trading in pork bellies.

Resurrection Mary, the ghost of the Southwest Side, is created in this award-winning photo by *Chicago Tribune* photographer Karen Engstrom, with the help of her daughter. . . .

Courtesy, the *Chicago Tribune*

Read, Opie (1852-1939)

Nicknamed "The Arkansas Traveler," Opie Read was born in Nashville, Tennessee, on December 22, 1852. Read came to Chicago in 1887. He wrote twenty novels in his first twenty years in the city, including four in one year—1900. His "Chicago period" novels extended the reputation he had earned as editor of the humorous *Arkansas Traveler,* begun in Little Rock, Arkansas, in 1882. To the delight of northern readers, Read interpreted the South and delineated southern characters. His last book was *The Autobiography of the Devil—Satan's Side of It* (1938). He served as president of the city's press club and found a publisher for newspaperman L. Frank Baum, author of *The Wizard of Oz.* Read spent fifty-two years in Chicago and died here on November 2, 1939. His major books are: *A Ken-*

tucky Colonel (1891); *Odd Folks* (1897); *Judge Elbridge* (1899); *In the Alamo* (1900); *The American Cavalier* (1904); *"Turk"* (1904); *Old Jim Jucklin: The Opinions of an Open-Air Philosopher* (1905); and *I Remember* (1930).

Resurrection Mary

Tradition says Resurrection Mary, the young female ghost of Chicago's Southwest Side, appears on Archer Avenue in or around Resurrection Cemetery. Her often told story begins with two young men who encounter an attractive girl at a dance. She asks them to dance with her and is a superb, light-footed dancer, but seems rather distant. The boys offer to give the young girl a ride home. Asking to be let out at Resurrection Cemetery, she promptly disappears. They have learned, however, her name and an address in the Back of the Yards neighborhood. The next day when they visit the home, an older woman answers the door. The men ask about the girl and the woman replies that she had a daughter named Mary who has been dead for ten years. She shows them a picture; it is the girl they met the night before. Other tales are told of Mary hitchhiking along Archer Avenue, getting out at the cemetery and disappearing. Supposedly, Mary left her hand print on the cemetery's iron gate. These tales have surfaced in other versions elsewhere. But in Chicago her name is always Mary. Resurrection Cemetery is her home and on the Southwest Side of Chicago they know she exists.

Rice, John Blake (1809-1874)

On July 30, 1850, during a performance of the opera *La Sonnambula,* a fire broke out at Rice's Theater which was run by actor John Blake Rice. Hastening to the footlights, according to A. T. Andreas, Rice reassured the audience, "Sit down. Sit down. Do you think I would permit a fire in my theater?" Heeding his words, the crowd sat calmly until the prompter bellowed, "Mr. Rice, the theater *is* on fire!" The alarm sounded and the audience fled from the theater, averting disaster. People remembered Rice's authoritative behavior afterward when he solicited donations to rebuild his establishment, the first permanent theater in Chicago. The voters apparently remembered this incident when they elected Rice mayor fifteen years later. Or maybe the citizenry refused to face the possibility Chicago could have a fire. The Chicago Fire of 1871 was still six years in the future. Rice avoided political involvement with the Chicago Fire because a reform ticket by Roswell B. Mason had been elected that year. Ironically, Rice, an avid book collector, had sold his extensive collection before the fire destroyed his home. Rice was elected to Congress in 1872, surprising many who felt an actor could never be elected to such a high office in America.

River Locks

The Chicago River flows out of Lake Michigan or, as Chicagoans like to say, "backwards." Attempts to reverse the river had been made prior to the Fire of 1871. The feat was finally engineered in 1900. Chicago annually faced the problem of river effluvia polluting its essential water source, Lake Michigan. River sewage reached the water intake cribs no matter how far out into the lake they were placed, causing cholera and the need to boil all water on certain days. The discovery that moving water oxidized led to a feasible plan for reversing the river. The Ship and Sanitary Canal was dug, with locks at the mouth of the Chicago River. St. Louis was unhappy about the pollution but Chicago had the locks opened and the lake flowed into the river before a lawsuit could be filed. The city also had a canal that could handle large ships.

Riverview

Frank Sinatra's elegiac "There Once Was A Ballpark Here" could also express the nostalgia Chicagoans feel about Riverview Amusement Park, which stood at Belmont Street and Western Avenue. A Chicago landmark from 1904 until its closing in 1967, Riverview billed itself as the "World's Largest Amusement Park." It had two and a half miles of midway, a towering parachute ride, and seven roller coasters. "The Bobs" at sixty-five m.p.h. was considered by its fans the fastest and roughest ride in the world. Its most serious competition was the Cyclone Coaster at Coney Island. Chuck Wlodarczyk in *Riverview:*

Gone But Not Forgotten claims a 150-pound man weighed fifteen pounds at the top and 400 pounds going down "The Bobs" hill. Riverview differed from today's more elaborate theme parks because the admission prices were quite low. Two-cent and five-cent nights were common. "The Bobs" cost 25 to 50 cents a ride and 20 to 35 cents for an immediate second ride. People with very little money were encouraged to visit Riverview, walk its Midway, see the free samples from its side show exhibits and watch others spend literally pennies in the Penny Arcade. Wlodarczyk's epitaph for Riverview concludes: "Much speculation has been said about why the park closed. Some feel that racial fears closed the park, some say the stockholders were offered a good deal and didn't want to pass it up. Whatever the reasons, Riverview was sold to the dismay and sadness of millions. The park was sold for approximately six and a half million dollars on October 3, 1967, and never reopened. Interestingly enough today that six and a half million could not even rebuild 'The Bobs.' "

Rookery Building

The Rookery, an eleven-story building on the southeast corner of Adams and La Salle streets, is a memorial to a classic era of Chicago architecture—the mid-1880s—and a memento of the city's two truly great Chicago architects, John Wellborn Root and Frank Lloyd Wright. Young architects wish-

TIMELINE of CHICAGO HISTORY

1927 Average weekly wage in Chicago, according to Association of Commerce, is $15.43. Incredibly, discredited former mayor William Hale Thompson reelected. Capone's men reputedly work with his precinct captains. Mary Bartelme, first woman judge in Chicago, assigned to Juvenile Court. Municipal Airport (later renamed Midway) opens to air traffic in December.

1928 On August 16, work begins on world's largest commercial building, the twenty-five story Merchandise Mart. Urbine J. "Sport" Herrman, Chicago library board member and close friend of Mayor Thompson, initiates a campaign to cleanse library of "tainted" books—those considered pro-British. Ben Hecht and Charles MacArthur write *The Front Page.*

ing to study one historical Chicago building might well pick the Rookery. Its name derives from the post-Chicago Fire building boom of the early 1870s. In 1872 the building on this site, which was part water-tank, was a temporary city hall and Chicago's first public library. Legend has it pigeons roosted in the eaves, leading to its nickname "The Rookery." When the new structure was erected between 1884 and 1886, the informal old name was officially chosen over a long list of proposed Indian names. Its style combines traditional construction with the then-new skyscraper method. The Rookery has thick, load-bearing walls on its street sides and open, skeleton-supported walls in the inner courtyard. Root, like Louis Sullivan, loved to weave in foliage ornamentation. The Rookery features such designs. Root wondered if the design would stand the test of time. Architectural historian Carl Condit observes: "It has [survived] through his sure sense of organization and his subordination of detail to mass and structure." It also survived pigeons who use its ornamentation for a rookery. The lobby was remodeled in 1905 by Frank Lloyd Wright. He introduced white marble and flowing simplicity into an area marked with lacy, iron arabesque and Victorian metalwork. Historian Donald Hoffman summed up Root's great creation: "Through the constant interplay of dualities—solid and void, structure and space, stasis and kinesis, opacity and transparency, darkness and light—Root achieved a dynamic balance, a vital resolution."

Rosenwald, Julius (1862-1932)

In 1893 Julius Rosenwald, a manufacturer of men's clothing, invested $35,000 in the fledgling Sears, Roebuck and Company. The firm, directed by the imaginative Richard Sears, had reached out to the burgeoning American middle class. Rosenwald became president of Sears in 1910 and chairman in 1925. He masterminded the evolution of Sears from solely a mail order house into a retailer with hundreds of stores across the country. Rosenwald was also a consummate philanthropist, giv-

The parachute ride at Riverview was a landmark for the city as well as the park. As scary as it was, the ride was never involved in a major or fatal accident. Some Chicagoans still boast they rode it—others, that they didn't.
Courtesy, Chuck Wlodarczyk.

132

ing away $36 million because be believed in "giving while I am still alive." He helped build twenty-five YMCAs and YWCAs in urban areas containing large black populations. In the South, the Julius Rosenwald Foundation contributed to the construction of nearly five thousand schools for blacks. A rumor spread there that Alvah S. Roebuck, the other person after whom Sears, Roebuck is named, was a black. Roebuck had long before left the company, to lose a fortune speculating in Florida real estate. Roebuck was hired by Sears' public relations department to make appearances in the South. Rosenwald also donated $7.5 million to help rehabilitate the old Palace of Fine Arts from the World's Columbian Exposition, turning it into the Museum of Science and Industry, which for a brief time was known as the Rosenwald Museum.

Royko, Mike

Historically, there have been two kinds of Chicago writers: Those who stayed and those who left. Among those who could not be lured away: Franc Wilkie, Eugene Field, Gwendolyn Brooks, Saul Bellow and columnist Mike Royko. Royko moved, but it was only across Michigan Avenue from the Rupert Murdoch-purchased *Sun-Times* to his sometimes target, the *Chicago Tribune.* He quickly established he could, on occasion, put his finger in the eye of both papers. Royko is as much a Chicago phenomenon as a lackluster Cubs team, an exciting performance by the Chicago Symphony or a brilliant Louis Sullivan piece of architecture. His roots go deep into the immigrant neighborhoods. He has held onto the earthy, sometimes acidic and grubby flavor of genuine Chicago. It has helped win him a nationally-syndicated column, carloads and not infrequently barloads of friends, choirs of enemies, a Pulitzer Prize and several near misses for other awards. Mike Royko can be playful as he is in his Slats Grobnik neighborhood stories or in his annual Ribfest to find the best non-professional ribmaker in Chicago. He can be powerful as in his political exposes. He can also stew a rancorous soup, especially in responding to letters of people who want to one-up, curse or pray for him to obtain enlightened guidance. Through it all, he can write with the best and make a reader give out a laugh as loud as the one that used to surround the Fun House at Riverview.

St. Valentine's Day Massacre

This ignoble event occurred February 14, 1929, in the S-M-C Cartage Company garage at 2122 North Clark Street. The killers dressed as Chicago policeman. Virginia Kay, the late *Daily News* columnist, once called it "the spot of spots where seven of Bugs Moran's henchmen were wiped out along with a curious ophthalmologist. Frank Gusenberg, one of the dying victims, was asked who shot him. 'Nobody shot me,' the noble man snarled." Bugs Moran, who narrowly missed participating in the historic event, later commented, "Only Capone kills like that." Capone was conveniently on vacation in Florida that day. John Kobler in *Capone* quotes gangster Al Karpis on the members of the execution squad: Fred Burke, Claude Maddox, George Ziegler, Gus Winkler and "Crane Neck" Nugent—a group regularly employed by the Capone syndicate for executions.

Sandburg, Carl (1878-1967)

This writer was "indubitably an American in every pulse-beat," to borrow H. L. Mencken's phrase. Carl Sandburg found success as a journalist, poet, historian, children's author, folksinger and autobiographer. He won three Pulitzer Prizes: two for poetry and one for history. Even more perhaps than Walt Whitman, Sandburg popularized free verse. His poems about Chicago—and he wrote many—linked his name with the power and vigor of the city. He penned the immortal description of the city as "Hog Butcher for the World/Tool Maker, Stacker of Wheat/Player with Railroads and the Nation's Freight Handler,/Stormy, Husky, Brawling, City of the Big Shoulders." During his Chicago years as a newspaperman for the *Daily News,* Sandburg covered the race riots of 1919 and produced a still popular book about the tragedy. Sandburg crossed two vital strains of literary creativity: a sensitivity to what he saw and heard and a willingness to fiddle with the language. Sandburg played with language and grammar, acknowledging near the end of his life that he liked "adjectives not as much as nouns and verbs." Sandburg was born of Swedish immigrant parents on January 6, 1878, in Galesburg, Illinois. When he was a young man, the Sandburg family changed the spelling of their name from "Sandberg." He attended West Point in Douglas MacArthur's class, but dropped out after two weeks because his test scores in math and grammar were not high enough. Sandburg married the sister of photographer Edward Steichen, Lilian, in 1908. From 1912 to 1928, they lived first in Chicago and then in Elmhurst. Sandburg served as assistant to the socialist mayor of Milwaukee. He preferred the first name "Charles" but his wife convinced him to change it to "Carl." Sandburg died on July 22, 1967, in his Flat Rock, North Carolina home.

Sears Tower

The Sears Tower in the early 1970s brought to Chicago the right to boast of having the world's tallest building. Sears, Roebuck and Company, for years housed on the far West Side, announced plans to construct the Sears Tower on the block bounded by Franklin Street, Wacker Drive, Adams Street and Jackson Boulevard. The black steel and glass structure built as Sears' corporate headquarters staggers upward to stand as the tallest building in the world. Completed in 1974, the Sears Tower has 110 stories and is 1,468 feet high. Its architect was Bruce Graham. The construction is similar in principle to bridges and other structures that high school physics students sometimes make to measure stress. The Sears Tower is constructed of nine elongated tubes, each seventy-five feet square. Banded together to form a mega-tube, they provide lateral strength to withstand the winds which whip up from Illinois' prairies and buffet the tower. Its observatory offers a breathtaking view of the city and on clear days visibility can reach as far as four states. Hours are 9 a.m. to midnight.

Second City

Journalist A. J. Liebling in a series of *New Yorker* articles later published as a book pasted the derisive label "Second City" on Chicago. It has had a lasting effect on the city. In 1959, a young University of Chicago graduate, Paul Sills, chose this name for an improvisational group he founded adjacent to the urban-renewal-removed Art Colony in Hyde Park. Second City, the comedy ensemble, has invigorated American humor and served as a training ground for up-coming comedic talent for three decades. Among its many illustrious alumni are Shelly Berman, Joan Rivers, Barbara Harris, Howard Alb, Bernard Sahlins, John Belushi, Harold Ramis, Elaine May and Mike Nichols. The improv comedians from the Wells Street theater have attained national fame on "Saturday Night Live" and in movies.

Skyscraper

The most significant architectural development of the late nineteenth century was the invention in Chicago of the skyscraper. The Home Insurance Company, which stood at La Salle and Adams streets, has been determined to be the world's first real skyscraper (1885). The term "skyscraper" technically refers not to a building's height but to whether its weight is carried by masonry walls or by a steel skeleton. To be a true skyscraper, a building's weight must be borne by a skeletal steel structure rather than the masonry walls. It was not ascertained

*T*IMELINE *of* CHICAGO HISTORY

1929 On February 14, seven men slain by Capone's gunmen in a North Side garage—the St. Valentine's Day Massacre. On November 4, Chicago Civic Opera House opens with a performance of "Aida." On September 3, Samuel E. Thompson founds *Daily Times,* first afternoon tabloid.

1930 (Population: 3,376,438) Adler Planetarium, gift of Chicago merchant and philanthropist Max Adler, dedicated May 10. On June 9, *Chicago Tribune* police reporter Jake Lingle gunned down in Illinois Central passageway at Randolph Street east of Michigan Avenue. Later Lingle's close ties to Capone revealed.

for certain that the steel skeleton of the Home Insurance Building rather than the walls bore the weight of the building until it was torn down in 1931 to make way for construction of the Field Building.

Skyway

The seven-and-a-half mile Chicago Skyway links the Dan Ryan Expressway to the Indiana Toll Road. At its opening in 1958, a city public works director said overconfidently: "It is the bridge over the congested streets of the city's industrial district, over railroad switch tracks and over the Calumet River. It can't fail." Economically it has failed. Interest payments on bonds that financed construction and a sinking fund to pay off principal necessitate 40,000 vehicles a day use it. On an average day, approximately only 30,000 pass over it. The giant bridge over the Calumet River offers a spectacular view of Lake Michigan and of the southwest side of Chicago. The Skyway does save time for most travelers going east or west. But traffic tends to use the slightly longer route via the Dan Ryan, Calumet and Kingery expressways, saving drivers a dollar Skyway toll and Indiana Toll Road tariffs. The Skyway is a classic study in lost potential. It needs someone to sell the public on it. Perhaps Chicago could use the wily New Yorker who sold the Brooklyn Bridge.

Soldier Field

The landmark stadium, located near Burnham Harbor and surrounded by north and south-bound lanes of Lake Shore Drive, opened as Grant Park Stadium on October 9, 1924. It was dedicated as Soldier Field on November 11, 1925, by Governor Frank O. Lowden, who said, "Let it be a memorial to all the fallen heroes of all the wars ever fought." On September 23, 1927, World Heavyweight Champion Gene Tunney defeated Jack Dempsey at Soldier Field despite the legendary "long count." The largest crowd to attend an event here gathered on September 8, 1954, when over 250,000 showed up for the Marian Year Tribute. Soldier Field, built of concrete, is faced with cast stone of granite texture. Its design recalls ancient Greek and

Roman stadia. Classic Doric colannades soar one hundred feet above the arena. Overall dimensions are 678 by 1,184 feet. A tier of bleachers, installed in 1970, divides the stadium. Seating capacity of the south field is 60,875. The Chicago Bears—amid rumors they would move to the suburbs—played their 1985 home games at Soldier Field on the way to their first championship in twenty-three years.

Solti, Sir Georg (born 1912)

Born in Budapest, Hungary, Sir Georg Solti studied and worked in the opera houses of Austria. Fortunately he was in Lucerne, Switzerland, on March 11, 1938—the day Hitler's troops marched into Austria. He survived World War II living in Switzerland, where first prize in the 1942 Geneva International Piano Competition kept bread on his table. Taking on ever greater musical tasks, Solti outdid himself as music director in Bavaria, Generalmusikdirektor in Frankfurt and finally, by 1961, as director of the Royal Opera at Covent Garden in London. For his work in England, he was rewarded with knighthood in 1972. Solti was named in 1969 principal conductor of the Chicago Symphony, an orchestra on the verge of exploding as a world-class musical entity. Under his discipline, talent and drive, the CSO reached a pinnacle of international acclaim, retaining its special quality. The clear and distinct "Solti sound" keeps even non-music-loving patrons awake and has re-

TIMELINE of CHICAGO HISTORY

1931 On April 7, Anton Cermak elected mayor, defeating Thompson 671,189 to 476,922. Oak Forest poorhouse turns away 19,000 poor people. Capone found guilty of income tax evasion and sentenced to eleven years in federal penitentiary. Charles L. Comiskey and William Wrigley die. P.K. Wrigley inherits Cubs.

1932 Franklin Delano Roosevelt nominated at Democratic National Convention in the Chicago Stadium. Devastated by the Depression, Chicago has 750,000 unemployed. Public school teachers and civil servants work without pay.

vitalized the musicians' morale. Solti and his CSO have taken New York, Europe and the Far East by "bravo," stupifying audiences who thought Chicago's hallmark sound was the "rat-a-tat-tat" of a machine gun.

South Shore Line

In the late 1920s, the Chicago South Shore and South Bend Railroad (popularly known as the South Shore) advertised itself as the "First and Fastest" among the hundreds of American electric railways. It is both the fastest and the last interurban. In 1908 when its predecessor company—the Chicago, Lake Shore & South Bend Railway—opened, the line was part of a plan to unite all major American cities by electric interurban. Linking cities along the southern shore of Lake Michigan, this line was to be a key part of the span between Chicago and New York. It ran on the newest power source: alternating current. By 1925 it had suffered major losses and faced bankruptcy. Chicago utility czar Samuel Insull took over and sank millions of dollars into the interurban. He had the rails torn up, replacing the 70 and 80 pound rails with 100 pound ones. Insull changed the interurban's electric power source to direct current. This allowed the trains to run into Chicago using the Illinois Central tracks. Insull also bought new cars and engines. In 1929 the South Shore won the Charles A. Coffin medal "for distinguished contributions to the development of electric transportation for the convenience of the public and the benefit of the industry." It also won the Electric Traction Interurban Speed Trophy for the fastest regular schedules between terminals. It staggered through the Depression when Insull lost control but rebounded during World War II. With their long-outdated equipment, most interurbans did not survive the rise of the automobile as the means of transportation Americans preferred. In the 1950s the South Shore traded some of its land to the Indiana Tollway, which agreed to help finance improvements and restore its bridges and tracks. The South Shore today retains the most important title of its history: "survivor."

stuv

South Water Street Market

The earliest stores of Chicago were the back ends of wagons that belonged to the farmers and produce merchants who brought food to the burgeoning village. For almost a hundred years, their traditional place of business lay along the south bank of the Chicago River on what was known as South Water Street. Sellers grew into wholesalers. The market soon supplied not only Chicago but the Midwest and much of the Eastern seaboard. Shipments of produce from California and the Southwest came to Chicago in refrigerated cars. From here the fresh produce was distributed throughout the Midwest as well as the East. The Burnham Plan called for replacing the South Water Street Market with Wacker Drive. In 1926 the market moved to 14th and Morgan streets. The development of refrigerated trucks after World War II ended the need to break up shipments of lettuce, fruits and vegetables at Chicago. The market began to lose its national character. It still prospers, however. Check it out early some morning. It now serves the Midwest. Most produce houses say they are doing even better than twenty or thirty years ago when they served the Eastern seaboard as well as Chicago. A revolution in American eating habits that focused on fresh vegetables and fruit caused a dramatic comeback for the South Water Street Market.

TIMELINE of CHICAGO HISTORY

1933 Chicago celebrates one hundred years since it was incorporated as a town. Anton Cermak dies March 6 from a bullet intended for President Roosevelt fired February 15 by Guiseppe Zangara in Miami, Florida. Frank Coor and then Edward J. Kelly appointed interim mayors. A Century of Progress officially opens on May 27. Fair closes November 12 but reopens next year.

1934 On May 19, Union Stock Yards hit by $8 million fire. On July 22, FBI agents ambush and kill John Dillinger, most wanted criminal, in an alley south of Biograph Theater in 2400 block of Lincoln Avenue. July 24 is hottest day in Chicago history—104.8 degrees.

1935 Jane Addams dies. On April 1, Edward J. Kelly elected mayor. Leo Burnett opens advertising agency on August 5.

Spaghetti Bowl

The interchange of the Dan Ryan, Eisenhower and John F. Kennedy expressways, completed in 1961, seems to be in a continual state of repair. Generally, it is considered well-engineered, but tends to become a bottleneck heading south toward the Dan Ryan where eastbound traffic from the Eisenhower joins it. The "spaghetti bowl" is a familiar reference point for radio traffic reports during rush-hour because of the looped exits from one expressway to another.

State of Illinois Center

Few buildings have become legends as quickly as the State of Illinois Center at Randolph and Clark streets, which was dedicated May, 1985. It represents a daring break with traditional concepts of public architecture—too daring, many have since concluded. Governor James Thompson chose the architect and was as euphoric as an Egyptian king about his pyramid. Wunderkind Helmut Jahn, of C. F. Murphy/Jahn, was chief architect and Lester B. Knight & Associates was responsible for the engineering and mechanical systems. The Illinois Capital Development Board, supposed to oversee state-financed construction, uncritically endorsed the project. The most visually stunning—if environmentally stifling—feature of the center is a seventeen-story glass-enclosed atrium. On summer days, the temperature inside can soar into the high nineties. State employees resorted to setting up umbrellas next to their desks for relief from the heat. It has been beset with continual air-conditioning problems in the summer and heating failures in the winter. In contrast with other structures where lower fuel prices have brought declining utility bills, its power costs ran as high as sixty-nine percent above projections. The comfort index inside the center can be horrendous. However, these extra fuel costs, estimated to run as high as $500,000 annually, pale in comparison with the gigantic cost-overruns incurred during construction. A *Tribune* critic commented, "The project seemed a way to leap over the next few decades and land Illinois directly in the Twenty-First Century. It may take until the next century just to figure out how to make the thing work."

State Street

First known in the mid-1800s as State Road because it was part of the main road south through Illinois, State Street was nowhere near a "great street" until the late 1860s when Potter Palmer decided to invest in it. The fashionable shopping street then was Lake Street. There was no "L" in those days. And as drivers of stylish carriages quickly learned, in spring there did not seem to be any bottom to the mud on unpaved Lake Street. Field & Leiter (now Marshall Field & Co.) on Lake Street was originally owned by Potter Palmer. It was the first major firm to move to State Street. Palmer built a glorious new Palmer House hotel on State Street, only to watch it burn down days later in the Fire of 1871. State runs south through old neighborhoods and north through the Rush Street night club area and Gold Coast. Today State Street in the Loop is a broad mall closed to traffic, except C.T.A. buses. Its continual throng of pedestrians is punctuated by street musicians, food kiosks and sidewalk preachers.

Statues in Chicago

It is certainly no exaggeration to say Chicago has one of the finest collections of public sculptures by great artists in the United States. Here is a brief list of them.

UNTITLED PICASSO (1967) (known in Chicago as the Picasso), by Pablo Picasso. Daley Plaza, between Washington Boulevard and Dearborn Street. Vilified, praised, misunderstood and finally

TIMELINE of CHICAGO HISTORY

1936 "Duchess of Bubbly Creek" and settlement house founder Mary E. McDowell dies October 14. Lorado Taft, sculptor of the *Fountain of Time* statue in Washington ⁻...k, dies on October 30.

1937 On February 7, first giant panda in U.S., Su-Lin, arrives at Brookfield Zoo. On Memorial Day strikers and families organize demonstration at Republic Steel plant. Someone allegedly throws a rock and 10 people are shot and

killed by police. On October 5, President Roosevelt dedicates Outer Drive bridge over river, opening infamous S-curve with two 90 degree angle turns, and delivers famous "Quarantine" speech, setting policy toward Nazi Germany.

accepted grudgingly by Chicagoans, Picasso's 50-foot high cubist-inspired head of a woman has become, along with the Water Tower and the Art Institute lions, an immediately recognizable icon of Chicago. Models and pictures of the Picasso lack the impact of actually visiting it. The size engulfs the viewer. It is bigger than we are and this dimension is important for its impact.

MIRO'S CHICAGO (1981) by Joan Miro. 69 West Washington. Sitting across the street from the Daley Center Picasso, *Miro's Chicago* is a mixture of surreal imagination, whimsy and queenly stateliness. It mingles elements of what has been called, for better or worse, "found art."

BEING BORN (1982) by Virginio Ferrari. Corner of Washington and State streets. A large semi-circular stainless steel piece standing on a marble reflecting pool that could represent a slice of either a ball-bearing (it was donated by the Tool and Die Institute) or an eyeball.

HEALD SQUARE MONUMENT (1941) by Lorado Taft and Leonard Crunelle. At Wabash Avenue in the middle of the East Wacker Drive. George Washington, Robert Morris and Haym Salomon—three Revolutionary War heroes—stand in this square named for Nathan Heald, the commander of Fort Dearborn at the time of the massacre.

MONUMENT A LA BETE DEBOUT (1985) by Jean Dubuffet. State of Illinois Center. This thirty-foot black and white painted fiberglass creation by the self-proclaimed "wild man" of French art lies somewhere between a kindergartener's doodles and the powerful-yet-playful vision of an artist. To appreciate it perhaps requires both perspectives. No one feels neutral about Dubuffet!

THE FOUR SEASONS (1974) by Marc Chagall. First National Plaza at Dearborn and Monroe streets. Chicago's early brickmaking industry is commemorated by bits of common brick mixed with stone and glass shards of every color and provenance in Chagall's 3,000-square foot fantasia of year-round life in the city. Explosions of color, wheeling figures, and parts of the city's skyline are parts of this vibrant work.

FLAMINGO (1974) by Alexander Calder. Federal Plaza at

Picasso statue in the Daley Plaza, doing an imitation of Bears' quarterback Jim McMahon.

Photo, Kim Tonry

Dearborn and Monroe streets. Graceful, strange, and delicate. Calder said of this sculpture, it is "sort of pink and has a long neck, so I called it *Flamingo.*" This 53-foot-tall "stabile" is as much the work of an engineer as a sculptor. It effectively breaks up the straight grids of the buildings surrounding it and attempts to draw visitors toward, into and around it. Another Calder, his second important Chicago commission, *Universe,* sits in the Sears Tower Lobby.

BATCOLUMN (1977) by Claes Oldenburg. To see it is to believe it and it can be seen in the plaza of the Social Security Building at 600 West Madison Street. Considering the horrendously long period since either the White Sox or Cubs won a pennant, much less a World Series, Oldenburg (a former Chicagoan) picked an ironic symbol—a baseball bat 100 feet tall—with which people can humbly, rather than proudly, identify.

ULYSSES S. GRANT MEMORIAL (1891) by Louis Rebisso. Grant, astride his horse, overlooks Cannon Drive at the south end of the zoo. He is in Lincoln Park, just as Lincoln *(The Seated Lincoln)* is in Grant Park. This proud, military statue was installed on October 7, 1891.

HANS CHRISTIAN ANDERSEN (1896) by John Gelert. This classic statue is east of Stockton Drive next to the zoo. Danish sculptor Gelert left Chicago with this monument to a story-teller and swan (a former ugly duckling).

EUGENE FIELD MEMORIAL (1922) by Edward McCartan. Chicago's children donated their pennies to purchase this statue-group of two sleeping children watched over by an angel in Lincoln Park Zoo. Eugene Field, *Chicago Daily News* columnist from 1883 to 1895, was also the author of such loved children's poems as "Little Boy Blue" and "Wynken Blynken and Nod." He was also a glib-tongued social critic.

WILLIAM SHAKESPEARE (1894) by William Ordway Partridge. West of Stockton Drive at 2300 north, this statue of the Bard of Avon has a comfortable lap that countless children climb onto every year. This friendly statue provides them with a good first impression of Will Shakespeare.

JOHN PETER ALTGELD (1915) by Gutzon Borglum, who also sculpted Mt. Rushmore. Located in Lincoln Park, south of Diversey, Governor Altgeld—who suffered severely because of his concern for the poor, immigrants and prisoners—is fittingly portrayed protecting the huddled figures of a man, woman and child.

ALEXANDER HAMILTON (1952) by John Angel. At the junction of Cannon and Stockton Drives in Lincoln Park, founding-father Hamilton—like Lincoln— is commemorated by statues in both Grant and Lincoln Park, thanks here to one million of Kate Sturges Buckingham's dollars.

JOHANN WOLFGANG VON GOETHE (1913) by Herman Hahn. Poet and writer Goethe, at Diversey Parkway and North Sheridan Road, has survived two wars with Germany and Chicagoan's painfully inaccurate mispronunciation of his name (the umlaut is not recognized). Despite these setbacks, this statue of Goethe as a godlike youth with an eagle perched on his knee is not unadmired by Chicagoans.

GENERAL PHILIP HENRY SHERIDAN (1923) by Gutzon Borglum. At Sheridan Road and Belmont Avenue, the statue of Sheridan beckons troops to battle. The horse General Sheridan rides is named Winchester. He called it that after the place he left to lead a charge and rout a Confederate attack. The efforts of horse and rider were immortalized in Thomas Buchanan Read's poem, "Sheridan's Ride." Winchester's raised leg symbolizes his rider was wounded in battle (the legs of Grant's horse are on the ground, meaning he was not wounded). Sheridan, after whom Fort Sheridan and Sheridan Road are named, took command of maintaining law and order in the days following the Chicago Fire of 1871.

*T*IMELINE *of* CHICAGO HISTORY

1938 Clarence Darrow dies. Cardinal Mundelein attacks Hitler. Nazis try to go through the Vatican to get a retraction. Mies van der Rohe arrives at Armour Institute (now Illinois Institute of Technology).

1939 U.S. Supreme Court rules illegal a sit-down strike at Fansteel Metallurgical Corporation in North Chicago. On July 14, Saul Alinsky and Joe Meegan organize Back of the Yards Neighborhood Council.

1940 (Population: 3,396,808. Metropolitan population is 4,499,126) Republican presidential candidate Wendell Wilkie splattered with egg when he arrives at La Salle Street Station. Chicago apologizes but city's image hurt.

A SIGNAL OF PEACE (1894) by Cyrus Dallin. East of Lake Shore Drive, south of the Gun Club, at Diversey Parkway, this statue portrays a Sioux chief riding a pony and giving the Indian peace signal. He holds his spear above his head. Judge Lambert Tree donated the statue, which was first exhibited at the World's Columbian Exposition of 1893.

THE ALARM (1884) by John J. Boyle. A different Indian statue stands east of Lake Shore Drive, north of the Gun Club. Lumber millionaire Martin Ryerson, who began his career trading furs with the Ottawa Indians (one of the tribes pushed out of the area by the 1833 Treaty of Chicago), donated this statue. It is the oldest on park land and commemorates Ryerson's Indian friends.

Elsewhere in the city:

VICTORY, or THE BLACK DOUGHBOY (1927) by Leonard Crunelle. This World War I monument stands on East 35th Street and Dr. Martin Luther King Drive. The statue atop the column was added in 1936 to honor the dead of the black regiment (370th, 93rd Division) in World War I. It also is a reminder of the segregation that then existed in the armed forces.

THE REPUBLIC (1918) by David Chester French. Jackson Park at Richard and Hayes Drive (6300 south). The original statue of *The Republic* was part of the Court of Honor at the World's Columbian Exposition. It was 65-feet tall, whereas this statue is only 24-feet tall. The "Golden Lady" faces the opposite way, lending a confused credence to an old Chicago tale that she occasionally is turned on her pedestal. The first statue was destroyed after the fair and this copy was created from a 12-foot model.

THOMAS GARRIGUE MASARYK MEMORIAL (1955) by Albin Polasek. Midway Plaisance at 1400 east. Masaryk, a one-time visiting professor of Slavonic studies at the University of Chicago, was president of Czechoslovakia from 1918 to 1935. The barrel-chested statue of a knight honoring him is St. Wenceslaus, who helped free Bohemia hundreds of years ago.

FOUNTAIN OF TIME (1922) by Lorado Taft. Washington Park, West End of Midway Plaisance. Taft's masterpiece, a circle of men, women and children crowding around the inscrutable figure of Time, took fourteen years to complete. It is made of steel-reinforced, hollow-cast concrete that unfortunately due to Chicago's harsh weather is slowly being eroded.

Stevenson Expressway

The Stevenson—the newest, simplest and safest expressway in Chicago—runs southwest from the Loop to the suburbs and continues downstate as I-55 through Joliet to Springfield and St. Louis. It follows the route of the Illinois and Michigan Canal formed in the 1830s and 1840s. The expressway was named after Adlai Stevenson, former governor of Illinois, two-time Democratic presidential candidate and United Nations Ambassador under John F. Kennedy.

Street Numbers

We can thank the city fathers in 1908 for the easy and consistent numbering system for street addresses in Chicago. It is a blessing and boon. Major streets running east and west or north and south are laid out half a mile or 400 numbers apart. The dividing lines are State and Madison streets. Belmont Avenue, for example—eight major streets or four miles north of Madison—is 3200 north. Western Avenue—six major streets or three miles west—is 2400 west. If you cannot read a house or building number, look at the lightpoles. They show the first two numbers on every block. Fifty-six will be stamped, for example, on poles in the 5600 block. Diagonal streets are a little more complicated, but comparison with grid streets will usually help. The front of the Chicago Yellow Pages lists how far north, south, east or west every Chicago street is. In Chicago the traditional

TIMELINE of CHICAGO HISTORY

1941 New daily newspaper founded by Marshall Field III, *Chicago Sun,* debuts; its first Sunday edition on December 7 is same day Japanese bomb Pearl Harbor.

1942 On December 2, in the squash courts (the west stands of Stagg Field) at the University of Chicago, scientists led by Enrico Fermi achieve world's first self-sustaining nuclear reaction.

1943 Chicago gets its first public subway. A five-mile stretch is dedicated on October 17. Edward Kelly reelected mayor for third term. Lord and Thomas becomes Foote, Cone and Belding advertising agency.

distinction between a street (running north and south) and an avenue (running east and west) is not consistently observed. If you want to translate a pre-1909 street number into a current one, you can get help through the Chicago Public Library (269-2830).

Streeter, Captain George Wellington (1837-1921)

Captain Streeter was a character, phenomenon and unique presence in Chicago history. His title, he said, was a remnant of his Civil War service. Afterward, he had a brief career as a showman, traveling the Midwest with a menagerie of animals and carnival acts. This "George S. Wellington Show" folded in its second year. Arriving in Chicago in the mid-1880s, he tried show business again, buying a half-interest in the shabby Apollo Theater. When this venture proved fruitless, Streeter bought a semi-seaworthy hulk in which he installed a used boiler. Christened the *Reutan,* this rickety vessel made one journey to Milwaukee on July 10, 1886, although its passengers all took the train back to Chicago. On its return, the *Reutan* shipwrecked on a neglected area of shore north of the Chicago River's mouth. As sand piled up, the mosquito-riddled area became a marshy, cat-walked landfill where Streeter lived in his boat. The Chicago police rarely ventured here to stop illegal sales of booze and gambling. Soon other squatters built shacks, joining Streeter and Maria, his wife, to create a crude settlement. Streeter claimed that since his land had not appeared on earlier maps, it was consequently part of neither Chicago nor Illinois. He proclaimed it "The District of Lake Michigan" and sold lots cheaply to all comers. During the era when reporters would visit Captain Streeter, Lloyd Lewis and Henry Justin Smith, authors of *Chicago: The History of Its Reputation,* described one meeting with him: "He clung on through hard times and good, growing constantly in pride, aware that the newspapers had made him a public figure; always glad to be interviewed, but holding a long Springfield rifle, with a bayonet, on his arm as a threat to constables." Rich powerbrokers owned mansions on nearby Lake Shore Drive. Among them were Potter Palmer and N. K. Fairbank, who insisted Streeter must go. His shabby encampment spoiled their view of the lake. Numerous assaults were made by the authorities. One in May of 1900 involved five hundred police. Eventually Streeter lost his land. He died January 24, 1921, of pneumonia at age eighty-four. Of Chicago, Streeter said: "This is a frontier town, and it's got to go through its redblooded youth. A Church and a W.C.T.U. never growed a big town yet."

Subways

Subways had been proposed for Chicago during the nineteenth century, but excavation work did not officially begin until December 17, 1938. Despite the interference of World War II, the State Street route was completed five years later on October 17, 1943. The Dearborn Street Subway, begun in early 1939, was finished in 1951. The Congress (now Eisenhower) Expressway route was completed in 1958. This was the first significant project in the United States to provide rapid rail transit in a grade-separated right-of-way constructed in the middle of a multi-lane expressway. All Chicago subway routes emerge and eventually go above ground. The Logan Square "L" was extended to Jefferson Park on February 1, 1970. Three additional stops were added in February 1983. On September 3, 1984, the line reached O'Hare International Airport. On the way is a Southwest Side route to Midway Airport.

TIMELINE of CHICAGO HISTORY

1944 When Montgomery Ward and Co.'s board chairman Sewell Avery balks at wartime government regulations, he is unceremoniously carried by two soldiers from his office. At Democratic National Convention held at Chicago Stadium, Franklin Roosevelt nominated for an unprecedented fourth term; he chooses Senator Harry S. Truman of Missouri as running mate.

1945 End of World War II initiates phenomenal growth of suburbs. Cubs win National League pennant but lose World Series to Detroit Tigers.

1946 A fire at La Salle Hotel on June 5 leaves 61 people dead.

Sullivan, Louis (1856-1924)

Louis Sullivan was deeply involved in the relationship between culture and democracy, especially in architecture. Lewis Mumford called him "the Whitman of American architecture" after the poet who believed that culture did not come from the upper classes, but from the people. Having studied architecture at the Massachusetts Institute of Technology and the Ecole des Beaux-Arts in Paris, Sullivan came to Chicago in 1875. In 1883 he became a partner of Dankmar Adler, a relationship that lasted for twelve years. During this time, Sullivan and Adler, who was a superb engineer, created a style of architecture that broke radically with earlier models. Nowhere was their innovative work more dramatically displayed than at the World's Columbian Exposition of 1893. Other architects had imitated classic Greek and Roman architecture, but Sullivan and Adler offered a glimpse of the future with their Transportation Building, in which function rather than tradition dictated form. His Schlesinger & Meyer retail store (now Carson Pirie Scott & Co.), built between 1899 and 1904, demonstrated that such a structure can and should be a showcase from the outside in. Frank Lloyd Wright called Sullivan's Getty tomb at Graceland "a symphony in stone." Sullivan's philosophical writings on architecture, *Kindergarten Chats* and *The Autobiography of an Idea,* although written in a flowery *fin-de-siecle* style, have guided younger architects in creating a revolution in architecture. During the last two decades of his life, Sullivan's authentic style went unappreciated. He received fewer commissions and died April 16, 1924, near penniless. He was shown a copy of the just published *The Autobiography of an Idea* on his deathbed.

Terkel, Louis "Studs" (born 1912)

A tough and tender chunk of Chicago, Studs Terkel was born May 16, 1912, in New York. In the 1930s, he was a University of Chicago Law School graduate and struggling WPA writer aligned with causes of working people and the unemployed. Terkel has become a true legend. His television program "Studs' Place" is recognized as a classic of the Chicago School of Television. His radio interview show on WFMT is con-

The Congress Expressway (now the Eisenhower) was at last being dug in the early 1950s. This photo looks toward downtown.

Courtesy, the CTA

sidered among the most literate and intelligent radio in the country. And his bestselling series of oral histories chronicling Chicago in the Depression, Jazz era greats, the work place, and World War II have helped make him a national celebrity. His strong values and commitments—he was blackballed during the McCarthyism of the 1950s—have not stopped him from ascending to the special place that Chicagoans reserve for individuals who represent the best in their city.

Thompson, William Hale (1867-1944)

Legendary for his tolerance of corruption, "Big Bill" Thompson served a total of three terms as mayor of Chicago: from 1915 to 1923 and 1927 to 1931. Lloyd Wendt and Herman Kogan in their rollicking biography of him quoted two conflicting views of Big Bill: "He has given the city an international reputation for moronic buffoonery, barbaric crime, triumphant hoodlumism, unchecked graft and a dejected citizenship," or he was "a master politician, a firm patriot, a defender of American ideals, a friend to the oppressed, a humanitarian who yearned only to do miracles for the city he ruled." At death, Thompson left $1,488,250 in cash and gold certificates in $50, $100, $500 and $1,000 denominations, lending credence to the widely held belief his Capone era administration was cash-oriented. "Big Bill the Builder," as he had wanted to be known, had built a personal fortune.

Tommy Gun

The Thompson submachine gun, popularly called the Tommy Gun, was developed to be a "trench broom" by Brigadier Gen. John T. Thompson, director of arsenals in World War I. It was not perfected until 1920. Since the gun did not violate concealed weapon regulations in the early 1920s, it was sold openly in hardware and sporting goods stores. Advertisements for the Tommy Gun claimed it was excellent for "protecting large estates and ranches." In 1923 the price was $175, and it came with a twenty-cartridge magazine. A fifty-cartridge magazine cost an additional $21. In the hands of an unskilled person, fifty shots by the gun might not be sufficient to hit a target. The Saltis-McErlane gang was first to use the Tommy Gun. The gun was hard to handle and posed a greater threat to bystanders than to gangsters. Al Capone quickly recognized the Tommy Gun's potential. He used it to murder Jim Doherty, Tom "Red" Duffy and Assistant State's Attorney William McSwiggen. Later work Capone left to Vincent De Mora, alias "Machine Gun" McGurn, or the gang who handled the St. Valentine's Day Massacre. Upset about how his pet idea was being used, General Thompson traveled to Chicago to see if he could aid law enforcement efforts. He couldn't.

Tunnels Under the Loop

Forty feet below street level, the Loop and surrounding blocks are laced with tunnels that once carried supplies and coal to buildings. Electric locomotives pulled 3,304 cars through fifty-nine miles of tunnels. The tunnels measure six by seven feet. Most still exist. Construction, begun in 1899, was completed in 1909. Jurgis Rudkus, the major character in *The Jungle,* is described as a digger of these tunnels. The last tunnel was dug in 1954 for the Prudential Building but was never used. By 1959 the general shift away from the use of coal for heating caused the demise of the tunnel system. A few tunnels are still partially used to carry heating pipes and other conduits. The *Tribune* used one of these tunnels to deliver large rolls of paper from a dock on the river to a subbasement of Tribune Tower until its printing operations were moved in the early 1980s to the Freedom Center plant at Chicago and Halsted.

Tunnels Under the Chicago River

In the 1860s, Chicago was controlled by bridge-tenders who created traffic jams on city streets by raising bridges over the river. The bridge-tenders were issued guns, presumably to protect themselves from irate travelers who were delayed. Part of the problem was solved on January 1, 1869, when a tunnel beneath Washington Street was completed, and then on July 4, 1871, when a La Salle Street tunnel was opened. Three months

TIMELINE of CHICAGO HISTORY

1947 On January 25, Al Capone dies after a brain hemorrhage. Buses, streetcars, subways and elevated lines brought under municipal ownership of Chicago Transit Authority. Reform candidate Martin H. Kennelly elected mayor. Real estate developer Arthur Rubloff unveils his plan to turn Michigan Avenue into the "Magnificent Mile." Field buys *Daily Times* and merges it with *Chicago Sun.*

1948 Chicago spawns new industry of manufacturing television sets. City commemorates one hundredth anniversary of its first railroad with Railway Exposition and Fair along lake.

1949 Old Chicago Stock Exchange merges with ones from St. Louis, Cleveland and Minneapolis-St. Paul to form Midwest Stock Exchange. Greyhound bus terminal opens at Clark and Randolph streets.

later, this tunnel saved many lives during the Chicago Fire. Both tunnels are now blocked off, although the La Salle Street tunnel remained open until 1939 and the Washington Street tunnel until 1953.

Union Stock Yards

For more than one hundred years, the Union Stock Yards left an indelible mark on life in Chicago. By 1900 the yards and their one hundred neighboring meat-packing firms employed 30,000 workers. In that year, Chicago slaughtered 300,000 hogs, 75,000 cattle, 50,000 sheep and 5,000 horses. The Union Stock Yards opened on December 25, 1865. This Southwest Side industry affected more than Chicago's economy. Prior to 1900 when the Chicago River was reversed, Bubbly Creek, a small tributary of the South Branch of the river and sewer of the stockyards, carried water and the overflow waste through the city out into Lake Michigan. This polluted the lake and gave Chicago its distinctive, pungent odor. Reversing the river helped to solve this problem, although Chicagoans old enough to remember attest that the smell of the stockyards lingered in the air of the city until the yards closed in 1971. The 475-acre site of the Union Stock Yards at Exchange Avenue and Halsted Street is today an industrial park. Only the imposing Stock Yards Gate stands as a historical landmark. The stockyards, background for Upton Sinclair's 1906 novel *The Jungle,* had a lasting impact on Chicago's development. The jobs here drew Irish, German, Polish, Hungarian, Czech, Yugoslavian, Lithuanian and black workers to Chicago. The yards—at least until they were unionized—continually needed new sources of cheap labor. Other important industries for Chicago were spawned from the use of stockyard by-products: leather goods (especially shoes), canned meats, soap (made from animal fat), medical compounds and sausages. Meatpacker Philip Armour was noted for his ingenuity in the use of by-products. His chief competitor, Gustavus Swift, uttered the immortal words about the stockyards: "In Chicago, meatpackers use everything from the pig except the squeal." The yards' importance ultimately gave way to more diversified yards across the country, closer to the farms and ranges where animals were bred. The number of competing yards elsewhere jumped from sixty-four in 1929 to 2,300 by 1959.

University of Chicago

In *Chicago: An Extraordinary Guide,* Jory Graham wrote: "The University of Chicago was founded by the most prodigious young academic overachiever of the nineteenth century and one of the era's most prodigious multi-millionaires. William Rainey Harper (1856-1906) was a high school graduate at age nine, a college graduate at age thirteen, a college teacher at sixteen, a Ph.D. and the principal of a Tennessee College at nineteen. Before he was thirty he had become the country's leading instructor of Hebrew and had made the study of Hebrew a national challenge." Harper subsequently headed the Chautauqua movement. A committed Baptist, Harper was a good salesman of his idea for a university. He founded the University of Chicago in 1891 as a showpiece between 55th and 61st streets and the Illinois Central tracks and Cottage Grove Avenue. It was opened in time for the 1893 World's Columbian Exposition, a fact that helped recruit professors and students. Harper got multi-millionaire oil magnate John D. Rockefeller to donate the start-up funds. He would ultimately donate $35 million to the school. The Rockefeller Foundation subsequently contributed another $45 million. Harper wished to keep higher education unpretentious. The only people called "doctors" at the University of

*T*IMELINE *of* CHICAGO HISTORY

1950 (Population: 3,621,000. Metropolitan population: 5,600,000) On May 25, 34 people killed and 50 injured when a streetcar crashes into a gasoline truck at 63rd and State streets.

1951 Chicago's second subway, Milwaukee Avenue-Dearborn Street line, opens. Martin Kennelly re-elected mayor.

1952 Major steel strike lays off 80,000. Republican National Convention at International Amphitheatre nominates Dwight D. Eisenhower and Richard Nixon. Democrats meet in the city too, nominating Illinois Governor Adlai E. Stevenson and John J. Sparkman.

Eddie Vrdolyak, chairman of the Cook County Democratic
Committee, but mayoral candidate of the Solidarity Party.
Photo, Kim Tonry

Chicago are medical ones. The University of Chicago, the jewel
of Hyde Park, ranks among the preeminent educational institutions in the United States, and at the top of midwestern schools.
On its faculty are dozens of Nobel Prize winners. The University of Chicago Press, its publishing concern, is the largest scholarly
press in the country. Also renowned are its Oriental Institute,
libraries, nuclear and medical facilities and undergraduate college. Among its innovative and illustrious presidents have been
Robert Maynard Hutchins and Hannah Grey.

Veeck, Bill (1914-1986)

What P. T. Barnum wished to be—the consum-
mate hustler—Bill Veeck accomplished. He also happened to be
an extraordinary *mensch*. His father had been the Cubs general

manager during his childhood. From him Veeck learned how to sell peanuts, draw crowds and horse-trade players. In World War II, Veeck was wounded and lost his left leg. Afterward, he put together a group of investors to purchase the St. Louis Browns, a team with the worst record and lowest attendance in baseball. He increased attendance and tweaked the noses of other owners who blocked his dream of moving the team to Los Angeles. Later Veeck bought the equally hapless Cleveland Indians. Under his direction, they won a record number of games and set attendance records. Veeck brought Satchel Paige into the big leagues. Paige, whose skin color had kept him out for decades, could play baseball at almost fifty as well as players half his age. In 1959 Veeck's Chicago White Sox garnered their first pennant since the Black Sox scandal of 1919. Veeck shared ownership with a group of others under a tax scheme of his devising. The little things, from not wearing a tie to sitting in the bleachers, made Bill Veeck a shining example of a man of the people.

Vrdolyak, Edward (born 1937)

Formerly alderman of Chicago's east side 10th ward, Edward Vrdolyak, served as chairman of the Cook County Democratic Committee and kingpin of a powerful city council bloc opposed to Mayor Harold Washington. No one ever disputed this University of Chicago Law School graduate's abilities at political infighting and resiliency. He survived accusations of conniving, of political pay-offs, of ambulance chasing in the 1972 Illinois Central Gulf Railroad crash, of being part of an "evil cabal," of being "Fast Eddie," of offering to help the Republicans and of leading a "coffee revolt" against Mayor Daley. Like an able street fighter, Alderman Vrdolyak remained quick on his feet and tough-skinned. His opponents usually shook their heads and backed off. Only Mayor Washington resolutely fought him. The gargantuan clashes of these two politicians and the civic turmoil they caused led pundits to dub their battling "Council Wars." He did not run for another term as alderman but tried for mayor on the Solidarity Party ticket and lost April 7, 1987, to Harold Washington.

w
x
y
z

Wacker Drive

Running along the south bank of the Chicago River, Wacker Drive turns south at the point where the river forks. It was named for Charles H. Wacker, president of the Chicago Planning Commission, which promoted its development. When Wacker Drive replaced the city's South Water Street fruit and vegetable market in the 1920s, one commentator called the two-level drive, "flatly, a new concept." It remains so and has, at one point east of Michigan Avenue, a third level. Wacker is a fast shortcut from Michigan Avenue to the west side of the Loop with its train stations, expressways and commercial developments. Wacker Drive moves quickly and is the route of preference for buses, newspaper trucks and savvy Chicagoans who know where a driver can and cannot exit it.

Washington, Harold (1922-1987)

Harold Washington was born on April 15, 1922. In 1939, at age seventeen, he won a city championship in the 120-meter high hurdles. Forty-four years later, in 1983, Washington ran a longer race and overcame higher hurdles—some of his own making—to be elected the first black mayor of Chicago. However, the battle was far from over as Washington clashed repeatedly with a city council majority bloc of white aldermen led by Edward Vrdolyak and Edward Burke. Aided by Washington's disorganization, this bloc held the upper hand until—half way through Washington's term—two factors turned the odds in his favor. A botched attempt to exploit a secretly tape-recorded private conversation of Washington back-fired. Instead of portraying his worst side, the taping incident made Washington look good. Then in 1986, after special elections in reapportioned city wards, the political make-up of the city council shifted in his favor. Washington won the crucial support of the new Hispanic aldermen elected to the council. Many Chicagoans thought Mayor Washington unusually eloquent and, more than some of his opponents would admit, a credible reformer. He was re-elected to a second term as mayor April 7, 1987. He died in office of a heart attack on November 25, 1987.

Water Tower

The gothic encasement at Michigan and Chicago avenues, Water Tower was built between 1867 and 1869 to cover the standpipe of the city's waterworks across the street. A. T. Andreas wrote, "Much credit was justly accorded to W. W. Boyington, the architect of the building, for the professional skilled taste and judgment displayed and work entrusted to him." At the time it was a block away from the lake. The beaches have gradually been filled in and now Water Tower is a half mile from the lake. It survived the Fire of 1871, standing proudly amid the ruins. The pump was removed in 1904. Water Tower is a memorial to the fire and one of the most recognizable symbols of Chicago. In the early 1980s, Water Tower was turned into a tourist information center.

TIMELINE of CHICAGO HISTORY

1953 Freitz Reiner appointed conductor of CSO. Hugh Hefner publishes first issue of new magazine he calls *Playboy*.

1954 Ray Kroc purchases rights to new way of cooking hamburgers and french fries, opening first McDonald's "speedee service system" hamburger stand in northwest suburban Des Plaines.

1955 Key year in city's growth. Completion of Prudential Building, first major new office building constructed downtown since 1930s, initiates wave of commercial construction. *Chicago Tribune* publisher Colonel Robert R. McCormick dies April 1. Richard J. Daley elected mayor April 5. O'Hare International Airport opens to commercial flights in October. In November, first spadeful of dirt turned on expansion of Calumet-Sag Channel.

1956 Congress (now Eisenhower) Expressway completed. Lyric Opera of Chicago evolves from Lyric Theater of 1954.

Weil, Joseph "Yellow Kid" (1876-1976)

Joseph "Yellow Kid" Weil, an extraordinary conniver and swindler, rose to fame and fleeting wealth in Chicago during the heady era when "The Sting," as practiced in the movie with Robert Redford and Paul Newman, was often worked in the city. "You can fleece a lamb many times," Weil claimed, "but you can take his hide only once." His nickname "Yellow Kid" derived from an early comic-strip character. Weil began his career selling Meriwether Elixir, a supposed cure for tapeworms. His scams were always on a gargantuan scale. He cheated wealthy people who were greedy for more. "The police and daily press have estimated," Weil wrote in his autobiography, "that I acquired a total of about $18 million in my various swindles. They may be right. I never kept books." He accounted for the loss of his fortune through fast living and poor investments. Whatever Weil made was spent quickly. Yellow Kid's autobiography is more fascinating than most history. Weil lived a long life, spent a minimum amount of time in jail, and had achieved the status of a genuine folk hero when he died at the age of 100. Near the end, Yellow Kid reflected on the vicissitudes of his work: "There are no good confidence men any more because they do not have the necessary knowledge of foreign affairs, domestic problems and human nature."

The Chicago White Sox

If the Cubs have been "America's team," the White Sox have been not only blue collar, but provincial South Side. This team can claim more stockyard workers rooted for it than any other team in history (for more than three generations the team was located either just southeast or, after 1915, just northeast of the Union Stock Yards). In 1919 the White Sox were in the World Series, having won it two years earlier. The Sox were composed of some of the great players of the era, such

Harold Washington: Chicago's first black mayor, who commanded attention with his fine bearing.
Photo, Michael Paul Caplan

162

as Shoeless Joe Jackson and Ed "Knuckles" Cicotte, both of whom were implicated in the throwing of the 1919 World Series to the Cincinnati Reds and banned for life from baseball. Until 1959, it appeared the ban included the South Side team ever again winning a pennant. Other American League teams could record the feats of Babe Ruth, Ty Cobb and Ted Williams. White Sox fans had Ted Lyons (21 seasons without playing for a pennant winner) and Luke Appling. He hit .388 in 1936 to bring the team into the first division for the first time since the Black Sox scandal, but he became better known as a hitter of foul balls than a superstar. Frank Lane, who was hired in 1948 as general manager of a team that had just lost 102 games, started building toward a pennant winner (11 years later). He operated under the theory that if you had nothing and you traded, you might get something better. It worked, and he assembled a marvelously loved team with such players as: Nellie (tobacco-chewing) Fox, Luis Aparicio (who led the league in stolen bases eight straight years), Jungle Jim Rivera, Billy Pierce, Minnie Minoso and, for 1959, Ted Kluszewski. The Stock Yards were winding down and many Chicagoans had moved to the suburbs, but the faith of the years bore fruit in 1959 when they won the American League pennant. The team won its division title in 1983, but baseball had been taken out of the hands of those without personal fortunes, such as the Comiskeys and the working man's friend, Bill Veeck. It had become one of the hobbies of millionaires Jerry Reinsdorf and Eddie Einhorn. The Sox no longer were a cause, no longer part of the South Side's class struggle. The team, to the owners, no longer seemed on a foot-entangled mission to undo the Black Sox Scandal. The two owners tried to mold the White Sox team to the style of what had become a high-priced Yuppie sport. The owners then argued that because the park was a has-been their team was out of place on the South Side. They were, without knowing why, right. The state and city came to their rescue with a deal that will keep it there.

Wentworth, "Long John" (1815-1888)

Chicago and North Western Railroad passengers riding north through the city see in the northeast corner of Rosehill Cemetery a tall obelisk. "Long John" Wentworth erected this monument wishing it to stand as the loftiest tombstone in the West. He paid almost $50,000 for it. Wentworth also commissioned, at the cost of $30,000, a two-volume genealogy of his family tree. Wentworth had three separate careers—journalist, politician, and real estate developer—in the course of his outsize life. He arrived in Chicago in 1836, purchasing the city's first newspaper the *Chicago Democrat* on November 23. He published the *Democrat* for twenty-five years, mainly as a vehicle to promote his own political ambitions. Elected to Congress at age twenty-eight, Wentworth served there with Abraham Lincoln. In the campaign for senator that made Lincoln nationally known, both Stephen Douglas and Lincoln worried that Wentworth might enter the race. "Long John," who weighed three hundred pounds and stood six-and-a-half feet tall, was elected mayor of Chicago in 1857 and again in 1860. Wentworth fought with nearly every-

TIMELINE of CHICAGO HISTORY

1957 Edwin Berry, executive director of Chicago Urban League, charges Chicago is most segregated city in nation. Nineteen story Inland Steel Building built. Designed by Bruce Graham, it is the first high-rise to use external steel for support.

1958 A self-styled hustler and inimitable showman, Bill Veeck, buys White Sox. Albert Cardinal Meyer named archbishop of Chicago.

1959 On January 4, *Chicago Sun-Times* publisher Marshall Field IV purchases *Chicago Daily News* for $24 million.

Completion of St. Lawrence Seaway fulfills Chicago's dream of a direct outlet to Atlantic Ocean for vessels up to 710 feet long. Queen Elizabeth visits Chicago. White Sox for first time since 1919 Black Sox scandal win American League pennant.

body. Once, as the result of a battle with the city council, he fired the entire police force. He died at age seventy-three on October 16, 1888. His *Tribune* obituary said: "To the last, he was the same self-reliant, self-assertive, colossal embodiment of defiant, intellectual egotism, unrelieved by sweetness and light." His extensive land holdings in Summit and on the Southwest Side made him a very wealthy man at death—despite the lavish sums he spent to perpetuate his name!

Wigwam

In 1860 a building popularly called the "Wigwam" was erected on the southeast corner of Market (now Wacker Drive) and Lake Street to house the Republican National Convention. This was the first national political event held in Chicago. Temporary structures in this era were commonly called wigwams. Built at a cost of $5,000, this wigwam was the scene of well-orchestrated gallery packing and raucous demonstrations in favor of the Illinois favorite, dark horse candidate Abraham Lincoln. On May 18, after the third ballot, Lincoln had 231½ of the required 233 votes. After the Ohio delegation swung several votes in his favor, Lincoln won the nomination of the Republican party for president.

Wilkie, Franc B.

Wilkie was born in Saratoga County, New York, on July 2, 1830. He came to Chicago after working as a journalist in Davenport, Iowa. Using the pen name "Poliuto," Wilkie was among the most enterprising journalists and best humorists of Chicago's early literary history. During the Civil War, he walked across the battle lines and for a short period covered the war from the Rebel side. In the 1860s and 1870s, Wilkie wrote editorials for Wilbur B. Storey's extraordinary newspaper, the *Times.* He was president of the Chicago Press Club in 1879 and translated "racy" tales and sketches from French into English. A. T. Andreas in his *History of Chicago* wrote, "Mr. Wilkie's style is strongly marked with cynical humor, and he can rail in good set terms at all the world. He entered fully into all the

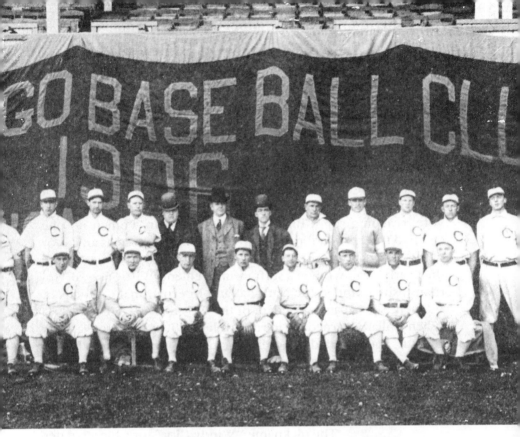

The 1906 Chicago White Sox, although known as "The Hitless Wonders," were good enough to defeat the Chicago Cubs in the World Series. The two teams have played only rarely in it since then and never against each other.

KH collection

audacities of the *Times* and was no more discriminating than his chief as to where his blows fell, so that they only fell hard. He excels as a reporter or descriptive writer, is always picturesque and readable." Wilkie's major books are: *Davenport: Past and Present* (1858); *Walks About Chicago: and Army and Miscellaneous Sketches* (1869); and *Sketches and Notices of the Chicago Bar* (1871).

Willard, Frances (1839-1898)

Frances Willard, a graduate of Northwestern Female College in Evanston, was later professor of Aesthetics at Northwestern University. She is known principally as one of the first presidents of the Woman's Christian Temperance Union.

The W.C.T.U. adopted her Declaration of Principles five years before she became its president. One of its provisions read: "We believe in a living wage; in an eight-hour day; in courts of conciliation and arbitration; in justice as opposed to the greed of gain; and in 'peace on earth and goodwill to men.' " Willard's deeply liberal beliefs made her an early and ardent advocate of women's suffrage. She inspired women to demand the right to vote, reaching rural, Bible-believing Christian women no one else had tried to recruit. In the 1870s Willard served as an editor of the *Chicago Evening Post*. Almost single-handedly, she revived the nearly dead women's suffrage movement. With Susan B. Anthony, she founded the National and International Councils of Women. She became president of the World's W.C.T.U. in 1891. When Willard learned to ride a bicycle in 1894, she wrote a book about it. She is buried in Rosehill Cemetery. Her Evanston home, Rest Cottage, is now a museum to her memory and W.C.T.U. causes.

Windy City

The nickname "Windy City" for Chicago dates to 1890. Charles Gibson Dana, editor of the *New York Sun* and former editor of the *Chicago Republican,* coined the phrase in reference to Chicago's promises in the competition to host the World's Columbian Exposition. Dana said, "Pay no attention to the claims of the Windy City." In 1906 would-be reformer Grant Eugene Stevens wrote that the real name for Chicago should be the "Wicked City." The actual wind velocity in Chicago is not unusually high.

Wingfoot Air Express Blimp Crash of 1919

During World War I, the Goodyear Rubber Company could find only one building in the Midwest big enough in which to construct its blimps. This was in Chicago at the White City amusement park on 63rd Street and South Park Avenue. Goodyear's first commercial blimp flew on its maiden voyage to Grant Park on July 21, 1919. The pilot, two mechanics, a publicist for White City and a *Chicago Herald and Examiner* photographer were aboard its ten-passenger open gondola. While

The Water Works in the early 1870s were not intersected by Michigan Avenue but by a short street (Pine) and a parking area. Note how close they were to the lake long before the shore started filling in.

KH collection

flying over the Loop so the photographer could take pictures, the blimp's hydrogen caught fire. When the burning blimp crashed through the skylight of the Illinois Trust and Savings Bank on LaSalle Street, three passengers died. Ten people inside the bank were killed. After the disaster, Goodyear's blimps switched to the more expensive but less volatile helium.

Wolf Point

Wolf Point, west of the south and north branch junction of the Chicago River, retains some semblance of its natural state before civilization found Chicago. Wild ducks swim in the water in front of it and tall plants—the last vestige of the prairie—reach out from nearby banks. Wolves no longer visit the point as they were said to do in the early 1830s. As it has

169

for more than fifty years, the Merchandise Mart squats opposite Wolf Point, joined in the 1970s by its neighbor, the Apparel Mart. Many writers believed that Wolf Point was actually the name for the land on which the Merchandise Mart is located, but research in books like Andreas' *History of Chicago* shows that to be wrong.

World's Columbian Exposition

In the 1880s, the United States decided to try and duplicate the success of the Philadelphia Centennial Exhibition and Philadephia World's Fair of 1876. The year 1892—the 400th anniversary of Christopher Columbus' discovery of America—was selected as an appropriate occasion. Many cities competed fiercely to host the event, but Congress awarded the fair to the burgeoning, boastful and determined city of Chicago. Jackson Park, south along the lake, was chosen as the site. As plans became more elaborate, the opening of the fair was postponed until 1893. Chicago architects John Wellborn Root and Daniel Burnham were selected to design it. Unfortunately, Root contracted pneumonia in 1891 after visiting the swampy site and died. Burnham, in awe of the classic culture, decided to employ classical themes. He allowed the fair's buildings to be copies of classical Greek and Roman structures. Burnham also dismissed Root's dream of a colorful fair and employed whitewash to make it "The White City."

Wright, Frank Lloyd (1867-1959)

Master architect Frank Lloyd Wright once said: "Every great architect is—necessarily—a great poet. He must be a great original interpreter of his time, his day, his age." We lack an outstanding poet who can decisively define what a poet of our age can be. We do have such an architect: Frank Lloyd Wright. His own genius and Louis Sullivan's guidance led Wright away from forms of earlier eras that had shackled other, less gifted architects. He came to realize that columns, rounded arches and classically inspired design were not necessary to create

The World's Columbian Exposition of 1893, shown in this photo, was a beachhead of New York and classic culture on Chicago's shoreline.

KH collection

TIMELINE of CHICAGO HISTORY

1960 (Population: 3,550,404. Metropolitan population is 6,794,461) John F. Kennedy defeats Richard Nixon in presidential election amid charges of vote fraud in Chicago. A police scandal in Summerdale police district features a "babbling burglar" who incriminates a number of police accomplices. Criminologist Orlando Wilson brought in to clean up police department. McCormick Place, a major new convention center, opens on lake. Chicago begins to use nuclear-generated electricity after Dresden Nuclear Power Station opens near Morris, Illinois.

1961 In June, Veeck "evicted" from ownership of White Sox.

1962 Dan Ryan Expressway opens with expectation it will save "fifteen lives and 3,003 crippling injuries" annually. Motorists cautioned to read road signs and study maps carefully when they use it.

beauty. Wright knew the architect did not have to overawe with whiteness or vastness. He used simple need, nature and the materials available, creating his own forms, breaking through to forge a new authority architects had not exhibited since the Greeks invented ways to build. Wright started as an engineering student at the University of Wisconsin in Madison. In 1887 he moved to Chicago, working for Joseph Lyman Silsbee, a prominent Chicago builder of Queen Anne style houses, and a year later he joined the firm of Adler and Sullivan. From Sullivan, whom he called "Der Liebermeister," Wright learned the fundamental architectural principle that form follows function and the ideal that architecture should be organic. His evolving concept of openness and ability to think abstractly inspired the spatial possibilities that became hallmarks of his work. Much of his early and most radical work was done for homes such as the Winslow House in River Forest and buildings such as Unity Temple in Oak Park. Wright took as his model the lines of the Midwest, the flat expanse of the prairie. He attracted students drawn to his innovations and vision. Wright soon felt the prairie alone was not enough to inspire a truly American architecture to replace the transplanted European style, so he turned to the architecture of pre-Columbian Indian cultures. In September of 1909 Wright left his wife, Catherine, and their six children and eloped to Europe with his mistress, Mamah Cheney. By 1911 Wright returned to the United States and Cheney took up residence at "Taliesen," the home Wright built near Spring Green, Wisconsin. The worst tragedy of Wright's life occurred here on August 14, 1914. Cheney had given a lunch for two of her children and three visitors. A new chef, Julian Carlston, who was hallucinating on Wright's "immorality," locked them in the dining room and set fires under the windows. Carlston then murdered with an axe those who tried to escape. Wright married two more times, Miriam Noel in 1923 (divorced 1927), and Olgivanna Milanoff in 1928. Frank Lloyd Wright died April 9, 1959, at age ninety-one.

Yerkes, Charles T. (1839-1905)

Traction magnate Charles T. Yerkes, an expert at bribing the city council and Illinois Assembly, expanded his traction holdings street by street and permit by permit. The profits from his many lines, he claimed, came from the "strapholders," that is, the extra passengers packed into the cars. Another shrewd policy was to let his equipment wear out—to the discomfort of riders—and then sell it to some other unfortunate transit line somewhere. The character Frank Cowperwood in Theodore Dresier's *The Titan* is based on Yerkes. "All in all, he had one of the most colorful lives ever led in Chicago," according to *Chicago and its Makers.*

TIMELINE of CHICAGO HISTORY

1963 In subzero weather at Wrigley Field Bears defeat New York Giants 14 to 10 for National Football championship. U.S. Supreme Court refuses to hear case attempting to stop construction in Harrison-Halsted neighborhood of a campus for University of Illinois. Residents of one of the oldest Italian communities in city displaced.

1964 First of two Marina Towers completed on north bank of river. Designed by Bertrand Goldberg, it represents radical new approach to residential high-rise construction.

1965 Archbishop John Patrick Cody (named Cardinal in 1967) arrives in city. Michael Kutza organizes first Chicago International Film Festival.

1966 Dr. Martin Luther King brings his crusade to city. King moves into West Side apartment and organizes marches to protest racial segregation and civil rights violations in city and suburbs. On July 14, drifter Richard Speck murders seven nurses.

1967 On a cold January morning when fire hydrants are frozen, McCormick Place destroyed by fire. Later in month Chicago paralyzed by heaviest snowfall in history until then: 25 inches. In summer a controversial sculpture by Picasso unveiled in Civic (now Daley) Center Plaza. On October 3, refurbished Auditorium Theater has a grand reopening.

Neighborhood Communities

*A tour of Chicago
is best done one
block at a time—
any block. Chicago
has neighborhoods.
Neighborhoods have
blocks. Blocks have
reasons and histories
and mysteries.*

PART TWO

COMMUNITY AREAS

AS OF 1980 U.S. CENSUS

CHICAGO-O'HARE INTERNATIONAL AIRPORT

LAKE MICHIGAN

COMMUNITY AREA NAMES

1. ROGERS PARK
2. WEST RIDGE
3. UPTOWN
4. LINCOLN SQUARE
5. NORTH CENTER
6. LAKE VIEW
7. LINCOLN PARK
8. NEAR NORTH SIDE
9. EDISON PARK
10. NORWOOD PARK
11. JEFFERSON PARK
12. FOREST GLEN
13. NORTH PARK
14. ALBANY PARK
15. PORTAGE PARK
16. IRVING PARK
17. DUNNING
18. MONTCLARE
19. BELMONT CRAGIN
20. HERMOSA
21. AVONDALE
22. LOGAN SQUARE
23. HUMBOLDT PARK
24. WEST TOWN
25. AUSTIN
26. WEST GARFIELD PARK
27. EAST GARFIELD PARK
28. NEAR WEST SIDE
29. NORTH LAWNDALE
30. SOUTH LAWNDALE
31. LOWER WEST SIDE
32. LOOP
33. NEAR SOUTH SIDE
34. ARMOUR SQUARE
35. DOUGLAS
36. OAKLAND
37. FULLER PARK
38. GRAND BOULEVARD

39. KENWOOD
40. WASHINGTON PARK
41. HYDE PARK
42. WOODLAWN
43. SOUTH SHORE
44. CHATHAM
45. AVALON PARK
46. SOUTH CHICAGO
47. BURNSIDE
48. CALUMET HEIGHTS
49. ROSELAND
50. PULLMAN
51. SOUTH DEERING
52. EAST SIDE
53. WEST PULLMAN
54. RIVERDALE
55. HEGEWISCH
56. GARFIELD RIDGE
57. ARCHER HEIGHTS
58. BRIGHTON PARK
59. McKINLEY PARK
60. BRIDGEPORT
61. NEW CITY
62. WEST ELSDON
63. GAGE PARK
64. CLEARING
65. WEST LAWN
66. CHICAGO LAWN
67. WEST ENGLEWOOD
68. ENGLEWOOD
69. GREATER GRAND CROSSING
70. ASHBURN
71. AUBURN GRESHAM
72. BEVERLY
73. WASHINGTON HEIGHTS
74. MOUNT GREENWOOD
75. MORGAN PARK
76. O'HARE
77. EDGEWATER

Previous page: St. Malachy School playground, adjacent to Henry Horner Homes.

Photo, Cathy Lange

Chicago. . . it's ninety percent its neighborhood communities:
—truck gardens turned into subdivisions
—bungalows a thousand to one over mansions
—long, straight streets with well-worn stores or spiffy shopping centers
—winding avenues and tucked-away hills
—a tavern each block and a church each two
—Thai restaurants and polka dance halls
—stoops and sunken front yards
—iron-grated liquor stores and "amen" storefront churches
—the Gold Coast and River City
—the Robert Taylor and Cabrini-Green homes
—Edgewater and Hyde Park
—North Center and Armour Square
—the "old neighborhood," whichever one it is
—leveled slums turned into garden patches by H'mong tribesmen
—factories converted for living space and called "lofts"
—coal-stove heated houses
—cardboard shacks and chicken-wire single rooms
—retirement homes and high-tech playlots
—Blacks; first, second and third generation Eastern European Americans; boat people from Laos, Cambodia and Ethiopia; French, English and Irish; Germans and Poles; Norwegians and Swedes; American Indians and Southeast Asians; Puerto Ricans and Mexicans; Greeks and Turks; Jews and Arabs; Japanese and Chinese; Russian refugees and descendants of pilgrims
—cemeteries and golf courses

—bookstores and libraries

—Vereins and sokols

—convents and darker corners where crime molds

—railroad yards and factories

—Maxwell Street and Marshall Field's

—car dealerships and city parks

—the projects and Lake Point Tower

These and not just the Loop and North Michigan Avenue are Chicago.

In his Chicago Plan of 1909, Daniel Burnham failed future generations by making no little or big plans for the city's neighborhoods. Politicians—reform candidates as well as corrupt ones—think of the neighborhoods as thickets hiding votes where nothing dynamic happens. Writers from Samuel Paytner Wilson (who called Chicago "a cesspool") to A. J. Liebling (who labeled it "Second City") confuse Chicago with its commercial and entertainment areas. An Illinois governor landed at Midway Airport, drove through a neighborhood neglected by the city, and announced to the press that the residents were not keeping it clean. Newsstand pictorial books distort what the city is about by ignoring the neighborhoods even as their publishers complain the books do not sell.

A tour of Chicago is best done one block at a time—any block. Chicago has neighborhoods. Neighborhoods have blocks. Blocks have reasons and histories and mysteries.

In the 1920s, the boundaries—admittedly arbitrary—of seventy-five designated community areas of Chicago were first described by the Social Science Research Committee of the University of Chicago. Since their pioneering work, two new communities have been added: O'Hare after its land was annexed to the city in the 1950s, and Edgewater that was separated out in 1980 from Uptown's northern half. The official number of delineated neighborhoods in Chicago is seventy-seven. Chicagoans, however, relate day-to-day to probably over a thousand local neighborhoods such as Goose Island, Bucktown, Whiskey Point, Streeterville, Sauganash, Lake View, Back of the Yards, Juneway Terrace, the East Side, the Near North's Su-Hu, River City or—along the lakefront—high-rise buildings such as Lake Point Tower that become neighborhoods in themselves.

178

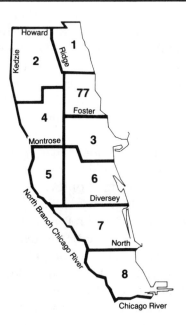

1. Rogers Park
77. Edgewater
2. West Ridge
3. Uptown
4. Lincoln Square
5. North Center
6. Lake View
7. Lincoln Park
8. Near North Side

1. Rogers Park

In the far northeast corner of the city, Rogers Park is trimmed east by Lake Michigan's beautiful shoreline. Beaches and lakefront parks are nestled away from highway view and traffic. Along rock stretches of shore, the lake's tempestuous manifestations or mollified moods are evident. Rogers Park is bordered by Calvary Cemetery (which is in Evanston) on the north, Devon on the south, the lake on the east and Ridge on the west. Loyola University's campus opened here in 1909, after changing its name from St. Ignatius College and moving north from Roosevelt Road. Mundelein College, at the bend in Sheridan Road and the lake, was founded in 1930. Both are in Rogers Park's southeast corner and give it many college town characteristics, especially during exam time. Rogers Park has at least five used bookstores (a good community index), and strong, well-established Jewish, Catholic and Protestant congregations committed to neighborhood improvement. Its origins date to the 1830s when Philip Rogers purchased a 1600-acre tract of land from the government. In 1878, it incorporated as a village. Following a slow ten years and then a five-year growth spurt, Rogers Park was annexed in 1893 to Chicago. Before the "L" reached Rogers Park in 1907, train service was provided by the Chicago and North Western Railroad and later by the Chicago, Milwaukee and St. Paul Railroad (later called the Milwaukee Road) that used the present "L" right-of-way. The "L" tracks were elevated in 1916. Rogers Park has numerous "L" stops and bus routes sharing a large terminal at Howard and Hermitage Streets. An active local historical society has records, photos, oral histories and life stories compiled by residents proud of their history. They will tell you Ridge Boulevard, once the shoreline, was an Indian and later military trail. They will mention the fire that in 1894 destroyed downtown Rogers Park. They will boast of their elaborate (but now closed) Sheridan Road movie palace, the Granada. Rogers Park is an easy neighborhood in which to find a condominium. In the 1970s, many lakefront high-rise apartments went condo. Prior to the conversions, 85 percent of the residents lived in rental apartments. Howard Street and the Juneway Terrace area just north of it are making a slow but dramatic comeback from the early 1970s when families and realtors fled. This revitalization has been led by the Howard-Paulina Development Corporation, established in 1982. Rogers Park's population dropped from 60,787 in 1970 to 55,525 in 1980.

77. Edgewater

Edgewater, along the lake between Rogers Park and Uptown, is numerically out of order on the list of community areas because it was the most recent one designated a distinct area. It was broken off from Uptown in 1980. Edgewater's boundaries are Devon on the north, Ravenswood on the west, Foster on the south and the lake on the east. The community's recorded residential history dates back to 1848, when former Luxembourger Nicholas Kranz built a residence at Clark and Ridge. It was seven miles from downtown Chicago and thus was called

This woodsy view of Rogers Park on a turn-of-the-century photo postcard showed how residents could stroll among trees at Greenview near Greenleaf.

Courtesy, G. Schmalgemeier

180

A PATH IN THE WOODS
RY ST NEAR GREENLEAF AV ROGERS PARK
CHICAGO ILL

BROOKS
PHOTO

273

the Seven Mile House. Immigrants from Luxembourg settled here and founded a parish in the middle of what is now Devon Avenue. A Catholic church, St. Henry's, was moved to the corner of Devon and Ridge. Its cemetery holds the tombstone stories of these pioneers. Edgewater was annexed to Chicago in 1889. The area had a beautiful lakefront and beach a block east of Sheridan Road. A famous hotel, the pink stuccoed Edgewater Beach, capitalized on the beach. The hotel complex with its boardwalk was widely considered the finest resort in the Midwest. When Lake Shore Drive was extended north in the 1950s, the hotel was cut off from its beach and slowly withered away. It was demolished in 1969. "Andersonville" between Bryn Mawr and Foster on Clark is noted for its Swedish restaurants, gift shops, chamber of commerce and bakeries. Not as predominantly Swedish as it once was, Andersonville retains the aura of Sweden and continues the long-honored custom of taking pride in the neighborhood's neatness. Andersonville was named after a local public school. A polyglot mix of nationalities inhabit Edgewater, the latest influx of which are people from South East Asia. Besides the original population of German, Swedish and Irish descendants, Edgewater today includes American Indians, Hispanics, Koreans, Greeks, blacks and Jews. In 1980, Edgewater had a population with 11.2 percent below the poverty level and 28.1 percent with incomes of $30,000 or more. Its population declined from 61,598 in 1970 to 58,561 in 1980.

2. West Ridge

Residents of West Ridge, which borders Rogers Park, often refer to their community as West Rogers Park, because more people have heard of Rogers Park than West Ridge. The communities are quite different. West Ridge's borders are Howard on the north, Peterson to Western down to Bryn Mawr south, Ridge to Devon then south on Ravenswood on the east, and Kedzie south to Devon then to the North Shore Channel of the river to Bryn Mawr on the west. In Philip Rogers, West Ridge shares with Rogers Park a common first settler. Both communities were annexed to Chicago in 1893. The differences, based on geography, go back to the 1870s and 1880s. Rogers Park had developed as a town by then while West Ridge remained a rural suburb. Industry included a brickyard, farms and greenhouses. By 1915 residential construction began in earnest. Occupied by homes and apartments, West Ridge contains a mixture of nationalities: a high number of Jewish residents, as well as Asians and Indians. A recent boon was the redevelopment of the old Edgewater Golf Club into the vast, well-planned Warren Park. The charming Indian Boundary Park at Lunt and Rockwell (opened in 1922) provides a zoo, duck pond and theater. The park's neighbors (some of whom live in the large castle-like apartment complex just east of the park) appreciate these hidden treasures. West of Western Avenue, Devon Avenue shows remnants of having once been a large Jewish shopping district, but now is lined by more Indian restaurants and shops than Jewish ones. As the symbolic item of street apparel along Devon, the sari has replaced the yarmulke. West Ridge's population declined from 65,432 in 1970 to 61,129 in 1980.

3. Uptown
With pockets of both poverty and prosperity, Uptown is not—and never has been—a sterile neighborhood. Like many areas of the city, it has streets where and occasions when its residents and visitors need to be careful for their safety. Uptown's borders are Foster on the north, Irving Park on

TIMELINE of CHICAGO HISTORY

1968 In April, after assassination of Dr. Martin Luther King in Memphis, riots explode on West Side. Stores and residences by the score destroyed and burned. Democratic National convention in August jarred by major anti-establishment and anti-Vietnam War demonstrations in Lincoln Park and on Michigan Avenue. Hubert Humphrey, nominated for president in Chicago amid protests and clashes between police and crowds, is defeated in November by Richard Nixon. Sir Georg Solti named conductor of CSO.

the South, the lake on the east, and Ravenswood Avenue down Montrose then east to Clark Street on the west. Large, architecturally-respected homes are nestled on the east-west streets between Clarendon and Lake Shore Drive, a reminder of the wealth that Uptown once represented. Farther north and west are abandoned buildings, devastated lots and forsaken cars. Perhaps the city's highest concentration of homeless people struggle for survival in Uptown. Although a large number of Uptown residents work to help less fortunate neighbors, the pulse here can beat fast, often tragically. In the 1920s, Uptown boosters predicted the *Broadway Limited* trains of the Pennsylvania Railroad would depart from the Lawrence Avenue terminal rather than from the Loop. They also claimed the Outer Drive would continue northward next to the lake, becoming the superhighway of the Midwest and that the Aragon and Uptown theaters would make Uptown even more "a city within a city" than it was. But overcrowded housing, the Depression, and post-World War II growth of the suburbs sabotaged most of these optimistic predictions. By the 1960s Uptown had become a "port of entry," a euphemism for a problem-plagued neighborhood that draws new immigrants who can't afford to live anywhere else. Uptown has the most diversified population of any Chicago community. Its ethnic groups range from American Indians and Southern Appalachian whites to H'mong tribesmen from Southeast Asia. It also has a sizeable black community. Prior to 1960, Uptown's people had been principally of Jewish, Swedish and Irish descent. The heart of Uptown is made up of four arteries: Broadway and Clark streets and Lawrence and Wilson avenues. In the late 1960s and mid-1970s, Uptown became notorious for its abandoned cars, burnt-out buildings and rough taverns. A major turn-about in the mid-1970s and 1980s has brought improvements that range from a new chain supermarket to a community college. The old Riviera Theater has reopened as a nightclub. In 1976, Truman College (part of the City Colleges of Chicago) opened its classrooms and other facilities in a new structure along the "L" at Wilson and Racine. Since the mid-1970s, part of Uptown has been colonized by thousands of Vietnamese, Laotian, Cambodian and Ethiopian refugees who have created their own enclaves. Two groups with divergent views and agendas—the

Uptown Coalition and the Uptown Chamber of Commerce—have put considerable effort into improving the area. Uptown's population dropped from 74,838 in 1970 to 64,414 in 1980.

4. Lincoln Square

At the "six corners" where Lincoln, Lawrence, and Western avenues intersect, a fine statue of Abraham Lincoln (known as *The Chicago Lincoln*) stands on a marble pedestal keeping watch over Lincoln Square. The area was comprised of such nineteenth century towns and communities as Bowmanville, Ravenswood, Budlong Woods, Winnemac and Summerdale. After a 1978 revitalization redirected through-traffic around the six corners shopping district, this community received a major boost. Lincoln Square's boundaries are Peterson from Ravenswood to Western then down to Bryn Mawr west to the North Branch of the river on the north, Montrose on the south, Ravenswood on the east, and the Chicago River on the west. It has a diverse ethnic shopping area with highly-rated Greek and German restaurants. When the area southwest of the Loop was uprooted in the 1960s to create the Eisenhower Expressway and the University of Illinois at Chicago—Circle Campus, a large part of Greektown moved north to Lincoln Square (although a strip on Halsted Street remains). The music can be loud and the bars and restaurants exuberant. Lincoln Avenue, formerly called Little Fort Road, was the main military highway to Waukegan. The

TIMELINE of CHICAGO HISTORY

1969 Militant underground group calling itself "Weathermen" stages so-called "Days of Rage" in city. Cubs almost win the pennant but wilt in final stretch. On morning of December 4, Black Panthers Fred Hampton and Mark Clark killed by police in raid. State's attorney Edward Hanrahan is indicted for it and acquitted in a sensational trial. First National Bank of Chicago Building opens. One hundred story John Hancock Center on North Michigan Avenue completed.

Budlong Woods, once part of a pickle farm, is pictured here in the late 1920s. This view, at Bryn Mawr and California, looks toward the lake. On the property to the left of the photo now stands St. Hilary Catholic Church. The area was developed after World War II.

Photo, *Chicago and Its Makers*

Bowmanville Hotel became a popular stop-over point on the road in the mid-1800s. Lincoln Avenue today cuts roughly through the middle of the Lincoln Square community. By 1874, it had its first horse-drawn cars and by 1895 its first electric-cars. After the Albany Park branch of the ''L'' was completed, more residential subdivisions were created. The last section of Lincoln Square to be developed was its northwest part, originally a truck farm and pickle factory belonging to Lyman A. Budlong. This is now a subdivision called Budlong Woods. Until 1925 Lincoln Square's name had been Bowmanville. The name is still used for a church and for a cafe in the area. Lincoln Square's population dropped from 47,751 in 1970 to 43,954 in 1980.

5. North Center

This area, in the center of the North Side, is tucked in between Montrose on the north, Diversey Parkway on the south, Ravenswood on the east, and the North Branch of the Chicago River on the west. Two hundred years ago Indians lived along the Chicago River north and south of what is now Foster Avenue. Their villages are charted on a map in Milo Quaife's book, *Chicago Highways: Old and New.* As early as 1869, the Ravenswood Land Company began to promote this area as a residential community. The southwestern section along the North Branch of the River was lined with brickyards. Their workers lived in the community long known as "Bricktown." The neighborhood protested against smoke and fumes from the brickyards, and finally chased them into less populated areas farther north along the river. For sixty-five years (from 1904 to 1968), Riverview, the "World's Largest Amusement Park," occupied the east bank of the river at Western and Belmont. One of Chicago's and North Center's most famous attractions, Riverview dominated the area and its skyline with its popular, scary parachute ride and rollercoasters. Riverview customers filled the buses and streetcars on Belmont and Western. The land where the amusement park stood is a shopping center called Riverview Plaza. A half mile north, Lane Technical High School, at Western and Addison, draws students city wide with scientific and mechanical interests. For most of its history, Lane Tech excluded female students. In the 1970s this policy changed and young women were admitted. North Center is a quiet residential neighborhood with stores and businesses established along the main arteries. The Chicago River, along North Center's west border, has nurtured a band of heavier-industry factories. Western Avenue, through North Center, is one of the city's longest car dealership streets. The population of North Center dropped from 39,410 in 1970 to 35,161 in 1980.

6. Lake View

In the 1860s, Lake View was a quiet suburban farming and summer colony to the north of Chicago, encompassing a much larger area than the present Lake View community. Its boundaries today are Irving Park west to Clark then up to Montrose on the north, Diversey on the south, the lake on the east and Ravenswood on the west. Its principal building boom occurred between 1885 and 1914. Sturdy brick as well as wood two- and three-flats were constructed. Lake View's mostly German and Swedish tradesmen insisted on well-built homes. Over time, other nationalities such as Hungarians, Poles, Slovaks and Italians moved in along Lake View's southern and western edges. Their children and grandchildren, as well as a sizeable population of Hispanics still live here. In the late 1960s, Lake View residents successfully fought the invasion of massive city-backed urban renewal projects. The Lake View Citizen's Council, one of the oldest in the city, is an active community group that watches over housing violations and community problems. Despite high-rises that dot the lakefront west of Lake Shore Drive, Lake View's major asset is still its proximity to the lake. Its largest shopping district is at Belmont, Ashland and Lincoln avenues. Anchored for over sixty years by Wieboldt's Department Store and many smaller stores, Lincoln Avenue north of Wellington teems with German ethnic foodstores, restaurants and music shops. On the east side of Lake View, the construction of high-rise apartments in the New Town area and development of the Century shopping mall at Clark, Diversey, and Broadway have raised property values and rents. New Town, west of the high-rises along the lake, is a young adult and tourist area. New Town and the adjacent Lake Front area is a Chicago rarity: a bastion of independent politics, even in Mayor Washington's era. Just north of New Town is "Wrigleyville," at Clark and Addison, home of the Chicago Cubs and formerly the Chicago Bears. The population of Lake View dropped from 114,943 in 1970 to 97,519 in 1980, in part due to gentrification. The new "gentry" tends to make dens out of what had been additional children's bedrooms. In the same decade, the number of households declined by only nine-tenths of one percent.

7. Lincoln Park

In the 1860s, the community of Lincoln Park—from Diversey on the north, North Avenue on the south, the

Bookstores—new and used—can be an indication of a neighborhood's vitality and literacy. Booksellers Row at 2445 North Lincoln has the best old-fashioned ladders and one of the best reputations of any used bookstore in the Chicago area.

lake on the east and the North Branch of the Chicago River on the west—was next to the City Cemetery. A beautiful lakefront park was developed in the 1870s after the graves were removed. The park was landscaped and a zoo created. The opening of cable car lines in 1885 and 1895 on Clark and Wells streets provided additional impetus for a building boom on "Die Norte Seit," where German immigrants congregated. The wealthy bought up the land closer to the lake after the Ten-Mile Ditch alongside Clark Street (then Green Bay Road) was dug to drain the swampy land. Their fashionable mansions pepper Lincoln Park east of Clark Street, although many high-rise apartments have also been built there. Lincoln Park has long been a favorite area of young professionals. It includes Children's Memorial Hospital (founded 1882), DePaul University (founded in 1898 as St. Vincent's Col-

Division St. E. from State, Chicago, Ill

15731.

These two photo postcards show a Near North Side neighborhood that has changed principally in such details as dress, cars and carriages, gaslamps and fireplugs. Otherwise, these photos could have been taken today.

Courtesy, G. Schmalgemeier

lege), and St. Joseph Hospital. It has some of the city's finest theaters, restaurants, used bookstores, antique stores and clothing shops. Lincoln Park is an "in" place to be single, to party, to go to the movies (the Biograph Theater on Lincoln Avenue where Public Enemy Number One, John Dillinger, was shot in 1934 is now an art film house), to eat out in its many popular restaurants or just stroll, especially with a fancy baby-buggy. However, Lincoln Park's image and reality differ. Its western part retains characteristics left over from the years after the Fire of 1871. Because this region lay outside the city's fire district, workers built shanties here that did not conform to the fire laws. West Lincoln Park has continued to acquire low-income housing and mixed manufacturing. Starting in 1956 in the De Paul Universi-

190

DEARBORN AVE. NORTH FROM MAPLE ST, CHICAGO.

ty area along Armitage Avenue, urban renewal efforts improved property and drove up land values and rents. Substantial land clearing and urban renewal have changed the north side of North Avenue west of Wells Street. The area to the north has seen similar rehabilitation of homes and buildings in the 1980s. This has included: a home for the aged (into the luxurious Sanctuary apartments), the Milwaukee Road Building (into a retirement center), a factory to an athletic club and a seminary (McCormick Theological) into part of DePaul University. Lincoln Park's population decreased by the same percentage (15.2) between 1970 (67,416) and 1980 (57,146) as Lake View's did, with many of the same factors operating.

8. Near North Side

The Near North Side is a quilt of many of the most fascinating parts of the city: North Michigan Avenue, Rush Street, Streeterville, Astor Street, Sandburg Village, the Gold Coast, Olivet, "Little Hell," the Cabrini-Green projects, River

North, Superior-Huron or "Su-Hu" (art gallery row), and Old Town. Its boundaries are North Avenue on the north, the Chicago River on the south, the lake on the east, and the North Branch of the river on the west. North Michigan Avenue (originally Pine Street) developed after the Boulevard Link Bridge connected it in 1920 with Michigan Avenue south of the river. It replaced the Rush Street Bridge that helped make North Rush Street a night club district earlier in this century. The Gold Coast began in the early 1880s when Potter and Bertha Palmer built their castled mansion at 1350 North Lake Shore Drive. Streeterville, east of Michigan Avenue and north of the river, grew around the turn of the century as a gambling and after-hours district run by Captain George Wellington Streeter. Since the 1960s, with an explosion of retail stores and shops on North Michigan Avenue and development of high-rise residential apartments in Streeterville, the Near North Side has skyrocketed economically. In the 1960s, a stark example of the poor being removed from low-priced housing to make way for high-rise, upper-income apartments was construction of Sandburg Village along Clark Street between Division Street and North Avenue. These apartments in the 1970s were turned into condominiums. The greatest renewal effort on the Near North Side, however, occurred in the aftermath of the Fire of 1871, which destroyed nearly this entire section of the city. After the fire, the McCormick Reaper Works (subsequently, International Harvester) left the north bank of the Chicago River for the Southwest Side. Epitomizing urban change over the course of a century, International Harvester (now, Navistar International Corporation) finally moved its corporate headquarters back to a prestigious Michigan Avenue address. Reflecting the fact that the Near North Side has been as much a workplace as living place, the 1980 census showed a slight population decline for the Near North Side from 70,269 in 1970 to 67,167.

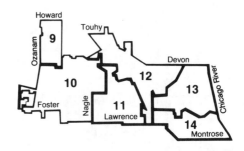

9. Edison Park

Because Christian Ebinger, the first settler of Edison Park on the far Northwest Side of Chicago, was German, the area was first known as "Dutchman's Point." The Ebinger public school in the area is named after his son, Rev. Christian Ebinger, Jr. Its boundaries are: Howard on the north, Devon on the south, Harlem on the east, and the city limits on the west. In the mid-1850s, the town of Canfield was laid out here, but the balloon burst in the Depression of 1857. The name Edison Park (after Thomas A. Edison) was given to this area in 1892. It was annexed along with its 543 residents by Chicago the same year. Before World War II, the population was only 5,000. The post-war boom brought about its present development as a stable and moderately wealthy neighborhood. The area north of Touhy was part of Maine Township until it was annexed in 1922 to Chicago. The first settlers were Germans and Swedes, followed by the English. For generations, the area had no industry and its only major transporation line was the Chicago and North Western Railroad. The growth of O'Hare International Airport and the area adjoining it, through expressways and finally the "L" have made Edison Park less isolated. Its population dropped from 13,241 in 1970 to 12,457 in 1980.

10. Norwood Park

Norwood Park was established as a town between 1869 and 1872, and named after a Henry Ward Beecher

Edison Park at the time of this 1929 photo included only one industrial property, the Edison Press, which was south of the Chicago and North Western tracks. Residents wanted to keep it that way.

Brooks photo. Courtesy, G. Schmalgemeier

novel, *Norwood: A Tale of Village Life in New England.* Its boundaries are the most erratic in Chicago. They jog along the city limits on the north, Foster on the south, Indiana Avenue south to Bryn Mawr west to Nagle on the east, and Canfield on the west. Lemuel P. Swift laid out its winding street patterns after the model created in the 1860s by Frederick Law Olmstead for the western suburb of Riverside. The unusual oval Circle Street resembles a race track. In 1893, the village of Norwood Park was annexed to Chicago. The pre-World War II population was 16,631. The early population of Norwood Park was of English, German, Scandinavian and Polish descent. In the 1920s, large influxes of Germans and Poles moved into the area. The Henry W. Rinker House at Milwaukee and Devon, the oldest house in the area, was built in 1851. Despite protests from its owner, it

194

was declared a city landmark a decade ago. To the disgust and anger of residents who had fought to make it a monument to their heritage, this house was illegally burned down in the middle of the night. Perhaps the most significant event in Norwood Park's history was the 1960 opening of the Kennedy Expressway, which, on its way to O'Hare, cuts through the heart of Norwood Park. Two decades later, when the "L" was completed down the middle of the Kennedy Expressway, Norword Park residents could more easily reach jobs in the Loop or around O'Hare. In 1980, median family income was $27,596. Norwood Park's population dipped from 41,827 in 1970 to 40,459 in 1980.

11. Jefferson Park

John Kinzie Clark opened a trading post during the Indian days of the 1830s in what is now Jefferson Park. One hundred and twenty-five years later, the Northwest (John F. Kennedy) Expressway reached it. The Village of Jefferson Park (named after Thomas Jefferson) was established in 1872 as a market town to serve farmers on the flat prairie around it. After Jefferson Park was annexed by Chicago in 1889, a streetcar line was extended to it. The Northwest Plank Road (Milwaukee Avenue) ran through Jefferson Park. According to local legend, farmers rebelled against its high tolls and, dressed as Indians, attacked the tollroad collection station and chopped down its gates to build a bonfire. They also boycotted the plank road until it was turned into a public highway. If Jefferson Park were a piece in a jigsaw puzzle—and it looks like one—it would be easy to find and put into the map of Chicago, its shape is so unusual. It runs from Devon on the north, Lawrence west to Central then west again on Gunnison to Nagle on the south, the North Branch of the Chicago River to the Milwaukee Road tracks on the east, and up Nagle to Bryn Mawr east to Austin up to Elston on the west. Like much of the Northwest Side, its residents are a mixture of German, Polish, Czech, Scandinavian and Italian descent. In 1887 August Borman opened Borman Shoe Store at 4806 North Milwaukee, where the store remains today, the oldest shoe store in Chicago still operating under its original name. In 1960, portions of the Northwest (later renamed John F. Kennedy) Expressway ran diagonally through Jefferson Park, ending, for better or worse, its relative isolation from the rest of the city. An effort was made to turn part of the Kennedy into a tollway, but residents of Jefferson Park met with Cook County Commissioner Daniel Ryan, reminding him what happened to the earlier tollway and assuring him that descendants of the 1880s "Indians" still lived in Jefferson Park. In 1970, Jefferson Park became the terminus for the rapid transit line. Although the "L" line to O'Hare has since been completed, Jefferson Park remains an important station. Except for the noise from O'Hare jets, it is a quiet residential community. Its population declined from 27,553 in 1970 to 24,583 in 1980.

12. Forest Glen

A number of small far Northwest Side neighborhoods—Sauganash, Edgebrook and Wildwood—comprise Forest Glen. It contains the Caldwell Woods Forest Preserve and an attractive portion of the North Branch of the Chicago River. After the Treaty of Chicago in 1833, the land in this area was awarded to a half-Irish, half-Mohawk Indian, Billy Caldwell, also known as Sauganash. Caldwell's descendants eventually lost the land still listed on plats as "Caldwell's Reserve." Like Jefferson Park, Forest Glen is a jaggedly-shaped community. Its boundaries are: Devon west to the city limits then west to Laramie with a piece jogging diagonally up to Touhy and back to Austin on the north, Gunnison on the south, Devon south along the Chicago, Milwaukee and St. Paul Railroad south to Bryn Mawr then west to Cicero on the south, and another curving line along the North Branch of the Chicago River on the west. Its far northwest point is Touhy and Caldwell avenues. Forest Glen is known as a neighborhood of police captains, as the original home of Jane Byrne and for the unique decorations that adorn its homes at Christmas. In the 1960s, many Chicago city employees, forced by Mayor Daley's insistence on a residency requirement, moved to Forest Glen. Some of the more valuable houses in the city stand here. The impression created by Forest Glen's streets and homes is more like those of adjacent suburbs than city neighborhoods. The large Gothic basilica, Queen of All Saints at 6280 North Sauganash Avenue, dominates the heart of Sauganash. It was the dream and project of Monsignor Francis Dolan, who died in 1984

Circle Drive in Norwood Park, still a substantial Northwest Side neighborhood, was both fashionable and attractive in this pre-World War I photo postcard.

Courtesy, G. Schmalgemeier

at age 86. In 1980 median family income was $31,872. Forest Glen's population dipped from 20,531 in 1970 to 18,991 in 1980.

13. North Park

A Northwest Side community that shares its name with a college, North Park, forms a truncated triangle. It is bordered by Devon and the city limits on the north, the North Branch of the Chicago River on the south, the North Shore Channel on the east, and Cicero on the west. Fifty buildings had been built when the village was laid out in 1855. It was annexed to Chicago in 1893. North Park is an old farming community. North Park College at 3225 West Foster Avenue, founded by the Swedish Evangelical Mission Covenant of America in 1894, attracted Swedes and other Scandinavian immigrants. In the 1970s and 1980s, another school, Northeastern Illinois University at 5500 North St. Louis Avenue, became a university. Felician College at 3800 Peterson Avenue, for a time a Catholic junior college just for young women, is a community and city resource. The Bohemian National Cemetery, which opened over 100 years ago, brought Czech families into the area. They mixed with the Swedes and Germans, who raised vegetables along the south bank of the North Branch of the Chicago River. The northern part of the neighborhood is predominantly Jewish. In 1905, the Chicago Municipal TB Sanitarium at Bryn Mawr Avenue and Pulaski Road was built and served the Chicago area until it closed in the 1960s. It has since been turned into a public park and a school for the handicapped. The population of North Park decreased from 16,732 in 1970 to 15,273 in 1980.

14. Albany Park

Some Chicago communities, once suburbs, grew from the inside out and were then annexed by the city. Not Albany Park. It grew as an accretion to Chicago when railroad, streetcar and bus lines extended northwest from downtown. Albany Park was supposedly named after Albany, New York, the hometown of one of its developers. Its boundaries jog along the North Branch of the Chicago River to Pulaski west to Cicero on the north, Montrose west to Elston then up to Lawrence on the south, the Chicago River on the east, and Cicero on the west. In 1907, the Ravenswood "L" reached Lawrence and Kimball Avenues, bringing an influx of primarily Jewish settlers with it. In 1917, Rabbi Beth Israel founded its first synagogue, the Reform League Temple. According to Melvin Holli and Peter d'Alroy Jones in their book, *Ethnic Chicago,* 23,000 Jewish people lived in Albany Park by 1930. More arrived with the post-World War II migration from the inner-city. After most moved on to northern neighborhoods and suburbs, the Jewish residents who remained by 1975 were principally elderly. Many older Jewish people, who now live in the north suburbs, remember Albany Park as "the old neighborhood." The nationalities that replaced them are a polygot group that includes Hispanics, Koreans, Yogoslavs, Greeks, Iranians, Filipinos, Palestinians, Eastern Indians and Appalachian whites. Albany Park's population decreased from 47,092 in 1970 to 46,075 in 1980.

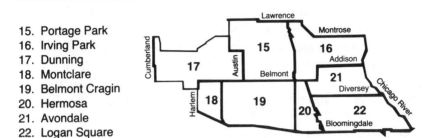

15. Portage Park

For a long time, Portage Park, except for its link via Milwaukee Avenue, was in the middle of nowhere. Its residents preferred it so. After train tracks were laid in the nineteenth century, Portage Parkers went out in the middle of the night and tore them up. No commuter railroad ran to Portage Park. Its name came from the fact that Indians carrying their canoes from the North Branch of the Chicago River to the Des Plaines River traveled through Portage Park. Located on the Milwaukee Plank Road, its tavern was a popular stopping place for early travelers. Portage Park's boundaries are Lawrence on the north, Belmont on the south, the Milwaukee Road tracks on the east, and Austin north to Irving Park west to Narragansett. Its many similar-looking brick bungalows were built in the housing boom following World War I. Portage Park (the city park), at Central and Irving Park, with its large public swimming pool has been a great Northwest Side attraction since the turn of the century. The Sears, Roebuck store at Six Corners (Irving Park, Cicero and Milwaukee) is the commercial and shopping heart of the area. A drainage problem in the area dating back hundreds of years when the area was caught between the Mississippi and the St. Lawrence watersheds was solved in the 1950s by an extensive new drainage system. Much of the post World War II housing construction was done by the Schorsch Brothers Development Corp. Portage Park's population decreased from 63,608 in 1970 to 57,349 in 1980.

16. Irving Park

Bisected today diagonally by the Kennedy Expressway, Irving Park was not always close to transportation. This Northwest Side community's boundaries are Montrose on the north, Addison west to Pulaski then down to Belmont on the south, the North Branch of the Chicago River on the east, and the Chicago and North Western Railroad tracks near Cicero on the west. Before it was annexed to Chicago in 1889, Irving Park was part of the town of Jefferson, which included the communities of Montrose (later called Mayfair), Irving Park and Grayland. Irving Park is cut into north and south sections by the road bearing its name. The Village of Irving Park was laid out in 1869. At the turn of the century after the Chicago and North Western Railroad stopped here, population growth followed. By 1911 it was served by an extension of the "L." Approximately half the buildings in Irving Park are single-family dwellings. According to the 1980 *Local Community Fact Book,* no one ethnic group makes up more than 10 percent of Irving Park, although there has been a recent and significant increase in Hispanics and Asiatics, especially Filipinos. The community's heart has long been the stores along Irving Park Road. Irving Park's population declined from 54,900 in 1970 to 49,489 in 1980.

17. Dunning

Long-time Chicago residents remember Dunning as the original name for the Chicago State Mental Hospital and recall this Northwest Side community as the location of the poor farm and original Chicago-area TB hospital. Andrew Dunning, an early farmer in the area, later became a real estate developer. He planned the settlement next to what later became the state hospital. Although portions of the community had been annexed to the city in 1889, it did not become part of Chicago until 1910. Its boundaries are Harwood Heights on the north, Belmont dropping down between Harlem and Oriole to Wellington on the south, Austin north to Irving then up Narragansett to Montrose on the east, and Pontiac north to Addison over to

Cumberland on the west. The now-antiquated and mostly torn-down Chicago State Hospital contrasts with the modern Chicago-Reed Mental Health Center that has replaced it. Because Dunning had no rapid transit service until the early 1980s when an "L" line was completed, large numbers of Dunning residents worked at these institutions, for local businesses or in the nearby western suburbs. The suburb of Harwood Heights to the north, approximately the same size as Dunning, is the only Chicago suburb completely surrounded by the city. Dunning's population decreased from 43,856 in 1970 to 37,860 in 1980.

18. Montclare

Montclare, one of the smallest Chicago neighborhoods in size, was named for a New Jersey city, Montclair, with a different spelling. This brick bungalow community on the Northwest Side is bounded by Belmont on the north, the Milwaukee Road tracks which are on the south and east, and Harlem on the west. Montclare's 1980 population (10,793) was only 1,100 people more than forty years ago. Examples of the classic Chicago bungalow abound in Montclare. This popular brick house style has its limitations, but Montclare's predominately Italian and Polish residents love their bungalows. These houses are sturdy, relatively maintenance-free and fire-proof. The community attempts to be neat, sturdy, and hassle-free like its bungalows. The Shriner's Children Hospital on Oak Park Avenue and

*T*IMELINE of CHICAGO HISTORY

1970 (Population: 3,369,359. Metropolitan population: 7,085,000) On July 24, a riot breaks out in Grant Park when a rock concert by Sly and the Family Stone never happens.

1971 World's largest shopping center, Woodfield Mall, opens on 191 acre site in northwest suburbs.

1972 Eight million conventioneers and tourists spend over

$850 million in city while attending more than 1,000 conventions. International Monetary Market (IMM), world's first currency futures market, opens.

Rutherford-Sayre Park across the street are well-known Mont-clare landmarks. Light industry lines the railroad tracks. Mont-clare's population dropped from 11,675 in 1970 to 10,793 in 1980.

19. Belmont Cragin

"Cragin" in the name of this Northwest Side area comes from an early neighborhood fixture, the Cragin Manufacturing Company. What's in a name? The area around Armitage and Grand Avenues was once known as "Whiskey Point." One explanation for this name offered by Peter Vukosavich in the 1980 *Local Community Fact Book* was that a tavern here was bought from Indians for a bottle of whiskey. A forty-five-year-old description of this neighborhood rings true today: "Most of the streets in the Cragin area are unusually attractive to the eye. Open spaces abound, the streets are broad and generally clean, grass strips are well kept, and there are many trees. Even the alleys, with neat rows of little garages, are attractive in many blocks." Its boundaries are Belmont on the north, the Milwaukee Road tracks on the south and west, and the Chicago and North Western Railroad tracks on the east. Among Belmont Cragin's well known landmarks are Riis Park, Hanson Park, Steinmetz High School, Weber High School, Notre Dame High School and Prosser Vocational School. Belmont Cragin is the oldest settlement in this part of the Northwest Side. Other neighborhoods that began to grow in this community during the 1880s were Galewood, Hanson Park and Belmont Park. Ethnic groups in Belmont Cragin include Poles, Germans and Italians. The Brickyard, 6465 W. Diversey, an imaginative shopping center, was opened in 1977. Belmont Cragin decreased in population from 57,399 in 1970 to 53,371 in 1980.

20. Hermosa

Hermosa was first subdivided in 1870. Its boundaries are Belmont on the north, the Milwaukee Road tracks on the south and east, and the Chicago and North Western Railroad on the west. Early Scotch settlers called the section north of

Fullerton and east of Kilbourn Avenue Kelvyn Grove after the eighth Lord of Kelvyn (now known as Kelvyn Park). Hermosa lies opposite Belmont Cragin from Montclare in the heart of the Northwest Side. The name, "Hermosa," means "attractive" and was given to the conglomeration of neighborhoods when they were annexed to Chicago in 1889. Like several other Chicago community areas, railroad tracks and embankments block off Hermosa from surrounding areas. In the 1960s and 1970s, the railroad right-of-way posed a threat to Hermosa's isolation when city planners proposed it as the site of a cross-town expressway, unsuccessfully pushed by Mayor Daley. Many pre-World War I bungalows, considered superior in materials and workmanship to those constructed between the wars, are still standing in Hermosa. Its population decreased slightly from 19,838 in 1970 to 19,547 in 1980.

21. Avondale

Like several Northwest Side communities, Avondale owes its initial growth to the laying of the Milwaukee Plank Road in 1848. During the spring these areas were swampy and impassable. The plank road solved this problem but created two others. First, it was bumpy and its logs often warped. Riding over the plank road could be miserable. Second, it was a toll

---

TIMELINE of CHICAGO HISTORY

1973 Tallest building in world, the 110 story Sears Tower, topped out on May 3. Chicago Board of Options Exchange opens trading in stock market futures.

1974 Three aldermen, including city council leader Thomas Keane,

convicted of tax fraud and put in jail. *Chicago Today* newspaper dies September 13. Standard Oil Building opens.

1975 In April, Mayor Daley elected to sixth term. Annual September tug-of-war over

too little money for public schools results in eleven day teachers' strike. On June 19, Sam "Momo" Giancana shot in head seven times while cooking sausages in his Oak Park basement. Veeck buys White Sox for second time.

road and many residents resented paying the fee. After Avondale was annexed to Chicago in 1889, its citizens were among
those who rioted to protest the tolls. The first church in the area,
Allen Church, was founded in 1880 by 20 black families, who
lived east of Milwaukee. Avondale's boundaries are Addison on
the north, Diversey on the south, the North Branch of the Chicago River on the east, and the Milwaukee Road tracks north
to Belmont back east to Pulaski on the west. Its main shopping
district lies along Milwaukee, Diversey and Belmont. Except for
the nearby roar of the Kennedy Expressway, Avondale has remained by and large a quiet community. Its population dipped
from 35,806 in 1970 to 33,527 in 1980.

22. Logan Square

A surprising fact about Logan Square is that it
had a larger population in 1980 than Evanston, Oak Park or any
other Chicago suburb. After Austin, Lake View and West Town,
it is the fourth largest city community. It was named after Civil
War General John A. Logan. Logan Square's boundaries are Diversey on the north, the Milwaukee Road tracks on the south
and west, and the North Branch of the Chicago River on the east.
Logan Square was first populated by Germans, Norwegians, Russian Jews, Poles and most recently by an influx of Hispanics. Industrial areas are at both ends of Logan Square, along the railroad
tracks and the North Branch of the Chicago River. The Kennedy
Expressway cuts through its eastern boundary. For years, Logan
Square was the terminus of the northwest "L." Logan Boulevard,
which cuts east-west through it, is a fine, broad parkway lined
with mansions built in the 1890s by merchant prince families,
bankers, and manufacturers of the Northwest Side. Every spring
some of these homes are opened for one of the better city
housewalks. Milwaukee Avenue—a crowded, bustling commercial street—cuts northwest through Logan Square at Kedzie. Kedzie Avenue, Logan Boulevard and Milwaukee Avenue meet at
Logan Square and form a rare Chicago area rotary. The population of this community decreased from 88,555 in 1970 to 84,768
in 1980.

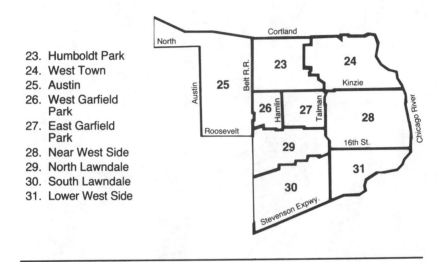

23. Humboldt Park
24. West Town
25. Austin
26. West Garfield Park
27. East Garfield Park
28. Near West Side
29. North Lawndale
30. South Lawndale
31. Lower West Side

23. Humboldt Park

Sharing its name with the large city park adjoining it to the east, Humboldt Park extends from the Milwaukee Road tracks on the north, the Chicago and North Western Railroad on the south and west, and from California north to Chicago west to Sacramento and up Kedzie on the east. It was named for German naturalist, Alexander von Humboldt. In the 1870s Henry Greenebaum, the "Father of Humboldt Park," developed this area. It grew in spurts after the establishment of the West Side Park Board in 1869 (the year it was annexed to the city), the Fire of 1871 and extension of streetcar lines in the 1880s and 1890s. The north central section where the two major railroad lines meet was originally known as Pacific Junction. To the east was Simon's Subdivision. Humboldt Park contained a variety of nationalities: Italians, Russians and Germans (many Jewish). It is now predominantly Hispanic. Its south side has turned increasingly black. Although the black population increased by 12,000 (from 19.6 percent to 35.6 percent between 1970 and 1980), the total population dipped from 71,726 in 1970 to 70,879 in 1980.

Students in the Fifth City Preschool at 3415 West 5th Avenue are the bright hope of the East Garfield Park community.

Photo, Ovie Carter. Courtesy, the *Chicago Tribune*

24. West Town

The earliest history of West Town goes back almost to the founding of Chicago. Its first spurt of growth occurred in the late 1840s when both the Southwest Plank Road (Ogden Avenue) and Northwest Plank Road (Milwaukee Avenue) were opened. The Galena and Chicago Union Railroad, which was opened in 1848, ran along West Town's southern border at Kinzie Street. West Town's boundaries extend from the Milwaukee Road tracks on the north, the Chicago and North Western Railroad on the south, the North Branch of the Chicago River on the east, and north on California over to Kedzie on the west. In 1910, West Town had a population of 219,889. If it had been incorporated as a city that year, West Town would have been—after Louisville—the twenty-fifth largest U.S. city. It has lost inhabitants every decade since. The area was plagued by arson-set fires in the 1970s, a situation that greatly improved in the 1980s. Parts of West Town, such as Wicker Park and Bucktown, are being slowly repopulated and rehabilitated. More than 50 percent Hispanic, West Town voters, in a special 1986 election, chose their first Latino representative to the city council. West Town's population dropped from 124,800 in 1970 to 94,428 in 1980.

25. Austin

The most populous Chicago community (138,026) in 1980, Austin is also largest in area. It was named after hardware company representative Henry W. Austin, who developed the area with wide tree-shaded streets. He donated four acres to the township for a town hall and built a railroad terminal at Central Avenue. Austin's boundaries are the Milwaukee Road tracks on the north, Roosevelt Road on the south, the Chicago and North Western Railroad to Jackson Boulevard back to Kolmar on the east, and Austin to North over to Harlem on the west. In 1888 an early industrial area in Austin along the Chicago and North Western Railroad was destroyed by fire. Besides the extensive railroad yards, industries that have been located in Austin include: Zenith, Brach Candy, Mars Candy and Revere Copper and Brass. Brick two-flats and bungalows served moderate to upper income people from nationalities and ethnic groups such as the English, Scots, Irish and Jews. These groups have moved through on their way to suburban living. A 19th century bastion of temperance, Austin followed the spirit of its namesake, Henry Austin. As a state legislator, he introduced an 1872 Illinois temperance bill. Although part of Austin was annexed in 1889 to Chicago, most of it did not become part of the city until a decade later. Austin underwent swift racial change—its black population grew from 0.09 percent in 1960 to 32.5 percent in 1970 and 73.8 percent by 1980. The Eisenhower Expressway cuts across the southern part of Austin and the Lake Street "L"across its center. In the last census, it was one of thirteen city communities that increased in population. Its total number of households decreased, however, in this period from 42,931 to 41,617.

26. West Garfield Park

West Garfield Park has struggled for survival in the last two decades. Its borders are the Chicago and North Western Railroad on the north and west, Taylor Street on the south, and Hamlin on the east. Many buildings are abandoned and boarded up and vacant lots have replaced apartment buildings. It is 98.8 percent black. Although sections have been black for generations, the major influx of blacks began in the 1950s. Change started in the 1920s and 1930s as the predominantly first and second generation Irish saw an immigration wave of Russian Jews. It was best known for its commercial heart at Madison and Pulaski (then Crawford Avenue). The area in the last century was the site of the Gentlemen's Trotting and Racing Club racetrack. The Paradise Theater, a famous movie palace and the Paradise Ballroom were the pride of the neighborhood from the 1920s on. Many local residents found work at Sears, Roebuck and Company on Arthington and Homan. The area is missing homes and apartment buildings, especially north of Madison Street. Despite their disappearance, further overcrowding prevented the population from dropping even more than it has. West Garfield Park's population decreased from 48,464 in 1970 to 33,865 in 1980.

27. East Garfield Park

Slightly older than adjoining West Garfield Park, East Garfield Park shares comparable statistics with it. It was devastated by rioting in spring, 1968, especially along Madison Street, and has never been rebuilt. Its borders are the Chicago and North Western Railroad on the north and on the east, Taylor west to Kedzie up to Arthington west to Hamlin on the south, and Hamlin on the west. It is served by both the Lake Street "L" and Congress "A" train that runs in the median of the Eisenhower Expressway. It was 99 percent black in 1980. The median rent in 1980 was $155 a month. The four-and-a-half acre Garfield Park Conservatory at 300 North Central Park Boulevard at Lake Street is open 9 a.m. to 5 p.m. every day. Some argue East Garfield Park will return, citing the beauty of the Conservatory. Its future depends on federal, state and city redevelopment funds, as well as a return of businesses and supermarkets. The 138-unit Martin Luther King Jr. Plaza at Madison and Kedzie and the Ike Simms Village Complex are both practical responses to the enormous housing problem of the area. Fifth City—the area around Madison, California and the diagonal Fifth Avenue—has seen several very encouraging, indigenous projects and programs. These have included: one of the best and most creative preschools in Chicago, Fifth City Business Careers, the Fifth City Industrial Promotions Corporation and even a Fifth City Supermarket. East Garfield Park dropped in population from 52,185 in 1970 to 31,580 in 1980.

28. Near West Side

In October of 1872, when 214,000 people struggled to live here, the Near West Side had its highest population. In the wake of the Fire of 1871, half the population of Chicago was crowded here. By 1910, the densest population of the city—75,000 per square mile—was contained between Roosevelt and Cermak Roads, and Halsted Avenue to the river. To grasp exactly what this meant, one should read the text and maps of the *Hull House Papers* (1895) that vividly document overcrowding, sweat shops, and dire poverty. The Near West Side's population was 189,745 in 1910, making it after West Town the second most populous Chicago community. Since 1920, substan-

TIMELINE of CHICAGO HISTORY

1976 On December 20, Mayor Daley dies of heart attack in his doctor's North Michigan Avenue office. Water Tower Place shopping center opens. Saul Bellow wins the Nobel Prize in Literature.

1977 On February 11, an "L" train plunges over side of its tracks on curve at Lake and Wabash streets, killing eleven people. Another Bridgeport resident, Michael Bilandic, elected mayor in special election.

1978 After one hundred years of publication, world-famous *Chicago Daily News* dies on March 4. Police work ends macabre murder spree of John Wayne Gacy.

tial decreases in population have occurred every decade. Urban decay and westward spreading blight have hit the Near West Side and other older city communities hard. Twenty percent of its housing units are part of such public housing projects as the 1,665-unit Henry Horner Homes, the 1,218-unit Abbott Homes and the 834-unit Robert Brooks Homes. The medical complex around Cook County Hospital along the southern edge of the Near West Side keeps its arteries pulsing with vitality. The medical center district includes Cook County Hospital (the city hospital before 1905), Rush-Presbyterian-St. Luke's Hospital, the University of Illinois Medical Center and the V. A. West Side Hospital. The Congress "A" and "B" trains serve the area. The "B" line heads south along Paulina and then turns west along 21st Street. West Taylor Street, with its string of Italian beef stands, stores and restaurants, has remained wonderfully intact. East of this area stood the old Taylor-Halsted Italian neighborhood that in the 1960s was guillotined to make room for the University of Illinois at Chicago-Circle campus. The Near West Side's boundaries are the Chicago and North Western Railroad on the north, 16th Street on the south, the South Branch of the Chicago River on the east, and Talman Avenue on the west. In 1980 Near West Side had 57,305 residents, down from 78,703 in 1970. The majority were black, with Hispanics constituting the second largest group.

29. North Lawndale

Subject of a 1985 *Tribune* series, "The Urban Millstone," life in North Lawndale (which is often referred to simply as Lawndale) was documented with grim interviews. The series painted a bleak picture of a community short on hope. Some North Lawndale residents protested the series' tone and argued the community is trying to improve itself. Its boundaries

A careful look at this 1900 photo of 12th Street (Roosevelt Road) and Kedzie Avenue shows a small medical complex: The store is a pharmacy; the sign advertises a dentist and the window lettering shows doctor's offices.
Courtesy, G. Schmalgemeier

PHARMACY

Dr. W.H. WALSH
DENTIST

DRUG

are Taylor and Arthington on the north, the Burlington Northern Railroad on the south, the Chicago and North Western Railroad on the east, and the Belt Railway of Chicago on the west. The population increased after 1902 when the Douglas Park "L" was extended to Crawford (now Pulaski). Most early arrivals were Bohemian (many moving west from Pilsen) and Polish. A wave of Russian Jews followed. In 1930 the population reached 112,000. Many North Lawndale residents worked at the Sears, Roebuck headquarters at Homan and Arthington or for other mail-order houses along the "L" route. The number of residents now is less than half of what it was fifty to sixty years ago. It is 96.5 percent black. Among the organizations actively working to make Lawndale more liveable are: The Lawndale People's Planning and Action Conference; the Lawndale Local Development Corporation and the Pyramidwest Development Corporation, which sponsored the $7 million federally-subsidized apartment complex, Lawndale Terrace; and the Lawndale Shopping Center at Roosevelt and Kedzie. North Lawndale suffered a 35 percent drop in population from 1970 (94,775) to 1980 (61,534).

30. South Lawndale (Little Village)

Before World War II, a quarter of the residents of South Lawndale were foreign born. Nationalities living here were Czech, Polish, Yugoslavian, German and Austrian. In 1986, over 50 percent of the population was Hispanic. South Lawndale's boundaries are the Burlington Northern Railroad on the east and on the north (to 19th Street), the Stevenson Expressway on the south, and the Belt Railway of Chicago on the west. The Criminal Courts Building, Cook County Jail, the House of Corrections, Washburne Trade School and Lawndale Park are located here. Its major retail district is 26th Street from Kedzie to Karlov Avenues. The Pyramidwest Development Corporation has attempted to develop a not-yet-successful industrial park on the site of the former International Harvester plant across California from the Cook County Court House. A good chance exists that city planners in the future will support a local effort to

Mural at 18th Street and Ashland Avenue: an example of neighborhood fine art.

Photo, Cathy Lange

change South Lawndale's name to Little Village. South Lawndale's population rose from 62,895 in 1970 to 75,204 in 1980—slightly more than in 1930.

31. Lower West Side

The Lower West Side, in the crook of the South Branch of the Chicago River, encompasses three neighborhoods: Pilsen, Heart of Chicago and a smaller one, known as Little Tuscany. The Lower West Side, the core of Chicago's Mexican-American community, runs west to 2500 (the Burlington Northern Railroad) and to 16th Street on the north. Pilsen on the east was a port of entry in the 1890s for Czechs and was named by them for Pilsen back in the old country. It serves the same role for Mexican immigrants, who next move off to homes that are usually in Heart of Chicago, centered at 18th and Leavitt, or in Little Village (South Lawndale) farther west. The murals on the walls—many of them now faded—emphasize the bright convictions and the art of the Mexican-American community. A mural on the southwest corner of May and 18th streets is a copy of Diego Rivera's *Homenaje* originally done for Rockefeller Center in New York City. A sizeable artists' community is also thriving alongside of the Mexican-Americans in Pilsen. Many artists' studios and lofts open each fall in a popular walk. The area west of Ashland contains one of Chicago's more quaint sections of nineteenth-century Chicago-style cottages. William J. Adelman's book, *Pilsen and the West Side* (Revised 1983)—an excellent tour guide to the Lower West Side's history—describes the 1885 and 1886 organizing and eight-hour-day strikes at the McCormick Harvesting Company plant at Blue Island (then Black Road) and Western Avenue. These strikes led to the tragic May 4, 1886, Haymarket rally and deaths. A film crew recently looking to shoot a movie about 1890s Chicago was delighted to find how much this neighborhood replicated turn of the century Chicago. More than 59 percent of its structures were originally single family dwellings. Most of the rest are two or three flats. It has few large apartment buildings. The principal growth occurred between 1857 and the World's Columbian Exposition of 1893. The street level grade was raised eight to ten feet to install sewers and water mains. For the houses already built, new entrances up to the second floors were constructed and front lawns, at the original grade, appear sunken. The Lower West Side is an animated neighborhood. Neighborhoods such as Blue Island, Harrison Park and Addams Park in this area are "stoop" neighborhoods. People socialize on their front porches and stairs as they have done for decades. Only the southwest corner of the Lower West Side along Oakley Avenue, known as Little Tuscany, is non-Hispanic. The center of this Italian neighborhood is St. Michael's Italian Catholic church at 2323 West 24th Place. Along the South Branch of the river is a mixture of heavy industry and boatyards. The population of the Lower West Side increased very slightly from 44,498 in 1970 to 44,951 in 1980.

32. Loop
33. Near South Side
34. Armour Square
35. Douglas
36. Oakland
37. Fuller Park

32. The Loop

The Loop, as a community area, is bordered by the Chicago River on the north and the South Branch on the west, by Roosevelt Road on the south, and the lake on the east. As a residential area, it was already well established before the Fire of 1871. The Loop was settled from the river south. In the 1840s, land south of Madison was pasture. The Loop north of Harrison Street (except for the block between Wabash and Michigan) was destroyed by the Chicago Fire. It was quickly rebuilt, but the private residences, especially the fine ones lining Michigan Avenue, were not rebuilt. In the 1890s, with construction of the then radically new skyscrapers, Henry Blake Fuller compared the streets between them to canyons and called the people who worked and occasionally lived in the tall buildings "cliff-dwellers." At the turn of the century, census reports showed an unusually high number of "actresses" in the Loop. These women were prostitutes in the three or four red light districts between Jackson and Taylor and along Fifth Avenue (a name later changed to Wells to improve its reputation). The Loop contains the main downtown business district with much of Chicago's distinctive skyline. In an explosion of real estate development, more than one hundred new high-rise structures have been built in the Loop area since 1955. Along Halsted Street to the west of downtown are the remnants of Greek Town. In the last two decades, as many of the cheap hotels along Van Buren, South Dearborn and West Madison streets have been torn down, the transients who lived in the chicken-wire flophouses and SRO (single room occupancy) hotels have been forced to seek shelter elsewhere or on the streets. The newest residential patterns in the city—lofts, condominiums, hotels and high-rise apartments—are emerging in the Loop's environs. The Presidential Towers, 400 East Randolph, Dearborn Park apartments, the Printer's Row historic district and River City have all developed and brought residents back to the area within the last decade. The Loop's population grew from 4,933 in 1970 to 6,462 in 1980, but this number seems to rise with every new loft conversion.

33. Near South Side

The Near South Side extends from Roosevelt Road on the north, 26th Street on the south, the lake on the east, and the South Branch of the Chicago River to 18th then down Clark on the west. In 1812, the land that now extends from Prairie Avenue east (at about 1800 south) was the site of the Fort Dearborn Massacre. The fort contingent, led by Captain Nathan Heald and Captain William Wells, marched this far south before being attacked by the Indians. At the turn of the century, the Near South Side was the most storied part of the city. It contained both the red-light Levee District and blue-stocking Prairie Avenue. Parts of "Mansion Row" on Prairie Avenue, such as the Glessner House at 18th Street, have been restored, but it is difficult to recreate a fashionable street lined with thirty of the largest, most expensive mansions in the city. The Levee is of course completely demolished. Only the Lexington Hotel, once Capone's headquarters, at State Street and Cermak Road still stands. It is being restored. The buildings that housed Capone's Four Deuces at 2222 South Wabash Avenue and the Everleigh Club brothel at 2131-3 South Dearborn are gone. McCormick Place, the Mc-Cormick Center Hotel, and the R. R. Donnelley & Sons Company printing plant make up a commercial complex at Cermak between Calumet and the IC tracks. Public housing now stands where the Levee once did, west of State and north of Cermak. In 1980 the median contract rent on the Near South Side was $89 per month, second lowest in the city. The Near South Side's population dropped from 8,767 in 1970 to 7,243 in 1980.

34. Armour Square

Armour Square was named after the park with the same name just north of Comiskey Park at 35th and Shields Avenue. The original White Sox ballpark was farther south, at Pershing and Wentworth. After the White Sox left, it was used by the American Giants of the Negro League. The Armour Square community is a north-south corridor that lies roughly between 18th Street on the north, Pershing Road on the south, Clark Street on the east, and Stewart north to the South Branch of the Chicago River on the west. Always a workingman's residential area, Armour Square has seen Irish, Germans, Swedes, Italians, Yugoslavians, Chinese (since 1912) and blacks pass through it. Chinatown is now along Wentworth Avenue on Armour Square's north side. It was developed after the Chinese businessmen's association, On Leong Tong, used a firm with a non-Chinese name to purchase ten-year leases on the buildings. Though adjacent to public and substandard housing, Chicago's Chinatown has managed to maintain itself as a lively neighborhood that attracts tens of thousands of tourists to its string of restaurants and shops every year. Italians, a declining number of blacks and a growing number of Mexicans live in the area. The number of residents dropped from 13,058 in 1970 to 12,475 in 1980.

35. Douglas

Douglas, south along the lake, is one of the city's oldest communities. It runs from 26th Street on the north, Pershing Road on the south, the lake south to 35th Street down Vincennes on the east, and Federal on the west. It bears the name of its first developer and most famous citizen, Senator Stephen

Streeter Hospital, pictured here in a 1910 ad, was on the Near South Side. Like many others, it was swallowed up in a continuing history of hospital consolidations. Room, board and nursing then—according to another 1910 hospital ad—cost $1.75 to $4 a day. Note the role of physicians.

1910 Blue Book

A. Douglas, who owned seventy-five acres next to the lake between 33rd and 35th streets. "The Little Giant," who ran against Abraham Lincoln for senator and then for president of the United States, is buried here. His monument, visible from Lake Shore Drive, is at the east end of 35th Street. Camp Douglas, a Civil War prison camp where several thousand Confederate prisoners died, was just north of where his monument and tomb now stand. The original University of Chicago (unconnected to the present school) was located here from the 1850s to the 1880s. Douglas is the site of Prairie Shores and Lake Meadows, two large experimental integrated housing developments built in the 1960s. Noteworthy institutions in Douglas include: Michael Reese Hospital, Mercy Hospital, Illinois Institute of Technology, Illinois

College of Optometry, Dunbar Vocational High and De La Salle Institute, attended by Mayor Richard J. Daley. Illinois Institute of Technology (State Street between 31st and 35th streets) was created after World War II by the merger of the Armour and Lewis institutes. Its campus is noted for its Mies van der Rohe-designed architecture. The area is marked by extensive vacant lands around Michael Reese and I.I.T. These institutions helped instigate the "urban renewal" that began in the late 1940s to clear away surrounding residences and buildings. The Stateway Chicago Housing Authority project is in the far southwest corner of Douglas. The Douglas area is predominantly black. Its population decreased almost 14 percent from 41,276 in 1970 to 35,700 in 1980.

36. Oakland

Oakland, a South Side lakefront community with twice as many families below the poverty level (1979) as above it, had the lowest median contract rent in the city ($87 per month) in 1980. Much of the housing is very old and was shabby from the beginning. Neighborhood groups want to build new housing to renew the area. Oakland was originally a section of Hyde Park (its southern neighbor), and was annexed along with Hyde Park to Chicago in 1889. Earlier, it had been known as Cleaverville, after Charles Cleaver who in 1853 opened a soap factory here and built homes in the surrounding area for his workers. Oakland's boundaries are 35th Street on the north, 43rd Street on the south, the lake on the east, and Cottage Grove to Pershing up Vincennes on the west. The first Japanese community in Chicago developed on Lake Park Avenue between 35th and 39th streets. Among public housing projects in Oakland are the pre-World War II Ida B. Wells homes. In that era, 31 percent of Oakland's residences lacked private toilets or baths. Julia Abrahamson in her 1959 book, *A Neighborhood Finds Itself,* repeats the point several times that nothing much could happen in Oakland or Woodlawn until strong local community organizations were developed to monitor housing violations, community problems and neighborhood planning. The Woodlawn Organization (TWO) has garnered more headlines, but the Kenwood-Oakland Community Organization at 1236 East 46th Street has become a force respected in the community as well as citywide. Its community development division has become active in the last few years. The 1980 population was 16,748—1,500 less than 1970, but 2,000 more than 1940. Oakland is one city community where even impoverished residents have a view of the lake.

37. Fuller Park
Fuller Park, a mid-south community west of the Dan Ryan Expressway, adjoins the southern limit of the half-mile wide Armour Square corridor. Its boundaries are Pershing Road on the north, 55th Street (Garfield Boulevard) on the south, the METRA (formerly Rock Island) tracks past the Dan Ryan Expressway on the east, and the Conrail tracks on the west. Fuller Park, which gives the area its name, lies south. Starting in the mid-1800s, Fuller Park became the site of railroad shops, roundhouses and machine shops. In addition, there were plants and foundries, providing generations of local residents with jobs. By the 1860s and 1870s it was a hub of the railroad industry, with the Rock Island's car and locomotive works and other engine houses there. Fuller Park grew from railroad shanties along the tracks. Almost all the older structures here predate 1895. In the late 1950s and 1960s, construction of the Dan Ryan Expressway cut away a third of its homes and population. Fuller Park has the second smallest population of any community in the city and is 98.7 percent black. It is the kind of inner-city neighborhood that desperately needs federal funds for basic community services and rehabilitation. Federal stinginess is what ails Fuller Park, according to many residents. In the meantime, community groups like Friends of Fuller Park are doing what they can through trauma medicine to keep Fuller Park liveable. A start will hopefully come with development of a new shopping center across the Dan Ryan Expressway at Garfield Boulevard (5500 south). It could mean some needed jobs as well as better local shopping. Fuller Park's population declined from 7,372 in 1970 to 5,832 in 1980.

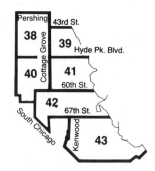

38. Grand Boulevard
39. Kenwood
40. Washington Park
41. Hyde Park
42. Woodlawn
43. South Shore

38. Grand Boulevard

Grand Boulevard is named after a street that no longer exists. The street became South Parkway, but is now Dr. Martin Luther King Dr. Grand Boulevard is an area hoping to feel favorable effects from the city's new "Boulevard Restoration" project, which has started in its boundaries. Grand Boulevard extends from Pershing Road on the north, to 51st Street on the south, Cottage Grove on the east, and the METRA (formerly Rock Island) tracks on the west. Blacks have lived here since the 1890s. Grand Boulevard has been predominantly black since 1950. Many of its residents live in a massive series of high-rise public housing projects, the Robert Taylor Homes, that run along State Street. On its east side is the expansive north and south boulevards, Dr. Martin Luther King Drive, Drexel and Cottage Grove, with some of the finest old turn-of-the-century homes in Chicago. Some of these are single family residences while many others are used for professional offices and boarding houses. In 1929, the Michigan Boulevard Apartments at 47th Street and Michigan Avenue were a model housing project financed for $2,750,000 with assistance from Chicago's greatest philanthropist, Julius Rosenwald. The apartments are a landmark on the National Register of Historic Places. In the early 1980s, a $15 million rehabilitation of the apartment complex gave them new life, attractiveness and vitality. If the Michigan Boulevard Apartments' low-rise design had been copied for later projects, instead of the high-rise pattern that was adopted, most housing experts agree, the city and public housing residents would be in a far better situation. Two historic sites near Grand Boulevard's southern boundary are Provident Hospital, a black hospital where the first open heart surgery was performed, and the Du Sable Museum of African-American History at 740 East 56th Place, which has done much to present and preserve the black heritage of Chicago and the U.S. This was the neighborhood James T. Farrell immortalized in his *Studs Lonigan* trilogy. Farrell attended Corpus Christi grammar school at 4910 South Grand (now Martin Luther King Jr.). The Urban League at 4510 S. Michigan Avenue and the Grand Boulevard Community 76 Organization are other excellent and locally available resources of this community. Grand Boulevard's population plummeted from 80,150 in 1970 to 53,741 in 1980.

39. Kenwood

Kenwood shares characteristics with both struggling Oakland to its north and cosmopolitan Hyde Park to its south. It runs from 43rd Street on the north, to Hyde Park Boulevard on the south, and from the lake on the east to Cottage Grove on the west. It was named after Dr. John A Kennicott, a settler who built a house south of 43rd Street in 1856. By the 1870s a horse-railway line operated down Cottage Grove to 55th Street. By 1890, Kenwood was a fashionable suburb. In the 1940s, blacks began moving out of the "Black Belt" west of Cottage Grove and into Kenwood. By 1960, it was almost all black. Kenwood is still predominantly black but many have moved away. A branch of the "L" once extended east to the lake and 42nd Place. Like other South Side lakefront communities, larger homes were converted over the years into boarding houses and kitchenette apartments. Some of these (including the 20-room Julius Rosenwald house) have been restored to their original condition, upgrading the buildings and the neighborhood. The legendary 47th Street runs down the middle of Kenwood. In his 1948 book, *47th Street,* Frank Marshall Davis wrote of it, saying "the sound track injects shots of the hottest jazz in the straight black arm of 47th Street." The headquarters of Operation PUSH

Grand Boulevard, in the middle of the South Side, was portrayed as a fashionable carriage way on this 1909 photo postcard. It would have its name changed to South Parkway and now is Martin Luther King Jr. Drive.

Courtesy, G. Schmalgemeier

(People United to Save Humanity) is at 930 East 50th Street. The diverse nature of the northern and southern halves of Kenwood can be seen in the two major community organizations: the Hyde Park Community Conference at 1376 East 53rd Street and the Kenwood-Oakland Community Organization at 1236 East 46th Street. One of the most encouraging housing developments in the area occurred in 1971. The Harper Square complex was built between Lake Park and Dorchester and 48th and 49th streets, defying the high-rise housing mentality. Kenwood's population went down from 26,908 in 1970 to 21,974 in 1980.

40. Washington Park

Washington Park, long an economically-troubled, mid-South Side community, shared its name with a city park and in the 1800s, with a local race track. The track opened in 1884 at 61st and 63rd streets, and Cottage Grove and South Park avenues. On Derby Day, club member Chicagoans rode out to Washington Park in decorated "Tally Ho" coaches and hansom cabs. The track was closed in 1905 after Illinois passed an anti-betting law. The community extends from 51st Street on the north, 63rd Street on the south, Cottage Grove on the east, and the Dan Ryan Expressway on the west. A Catholic church, St. Anne's, at Wentworth and Garfield Boulevard served Irish Catholics. In 1971 its name was changed to St. Charles Lwanga Parish "to reflect its identity as a black institution," Dominic Pacyga and Ellen Skerrett point out in their *Chicago: City of Neighborhoods*. St. Charles Lwanga was an African Catholic martyr. The neighborhood park, Washington Park, covers almost the whole eastern half of the community. The park contains the famous *Fountain of Time* sculpture by Lorado Taft, a work slowly eroding. Rich Chicagoans no longer "Tally Ho" out to this area. If they did, they might realize it should become a long-term place to invest capital. Washington Park should benefit from a new fifteen-store shopping center planned at Garfield Boulevard and the Dan Ryan Expressway and from the late 1980s "Boulevard Restoration" project. Washington Park's population dropped 30 percent from 1970 (46,024) to 1980 (31,935).

41. Hyde Park

Hyde Park, a very special South Side enclave along the lakefront, is the University of Chicago's neighborhood. Hyde Park's diversity includes: The Museum of Science and Industry, the gothic quadrangles of the University, its Oriental Institute, excellent used-bookstores (such as Powell's and Joseph O'Gara's, which successfully fought eviction in 1985 when hundreds of Hyde Park residents signed petitions to save it), theaters, Old Glory Marching Societies, the 57th Street Fair, fine restaurants, art galleries, natural food stores, independent politics, music and dance of all varieties and enough discussions, lectures and intellectual events to enlighten the world. But it is also an historic community area that began as a pastoral, wealthy, summer residence suburb. It has had problems and community organizations attempting to solve them since the turn of the century. Hyde Park was founded in the 1850s by Paul Cornell and incorporated as a town in 1861. By 1889, when it was annexed to Chicago, this suburb included an area several times its present size and had 130,000 residents. The Hyde Park community extends from Hyde Park Boulevard (51st Street) on the north, 60th Street on the south, the lake on the east, and Cottage Grove on the west. Both horse car and railroad came to Hyde Park in 1856, the steam dummy in 1868, the cable car in 1887, and the trolley in 1906. In 1892 the University of Chicago, Hyde Park's great anchor, was founded on the northern side of the Midway Plaisance between Washington Park and Jackson Park (the location of the World's Columbian Exposition). Hyde Park was where Clarence Darrow and a plethora of Nobel Prize winners have hung their hats. At the turn of the century, it had the Hyde Park Betterment League and Hyde Park Protective Association (an anti-saloon organization). Problems other than saloons plagued Hyde Park. The Hyde Park-Kenwood Community Conference was started in 1949 by the 57th Street Meeting of Friends to respond to neighborhood deterioration and to promote integration—bold goals for any community. These were achieved, but not the way the organization envisioned and at a heavy price to many who lived and worked here. Starting in the 1950s under Mayor Kennelly, but principally under Mayor Daley, the city worked with the University to clear almost 1,000 acres of homes and com-

TIMELINE of CHICAGO HISTORY

1979 When record snowstorm hits Chicago, Mayor Bilandic maintains all is well, losing credibility throughout city. He alienates inner city residents by advocating elevated lines not stop in their neighborhoods. Bilandic and Democratic machine suffer historic defeat when they lose at polls to Jane Byrne.

1980 (Population: 3,005,072. Metropolitan population: 7,057,853) An old Chicago manufacturer of slot and pinball machines launches a new video game called "Pac-Man."

mercial buildings in Hyde Park. These included not only slums, but also an art community. This infamous operation inspired the bitter motto, "Urban renewal means Negro removal." The South East Chicago Commission, organized in 1952, was supported by the university and played a willing hand in this massive undertaking. Community programs focus on housing, business development and crime. Its population decreased from 33,559 in 1970 to 31,198 in 1980.

42. Woodlawn

Woodlawn, south of Hyde Park, is a community where (since 1960) deterioration, neglect and fire have emptied or destroyed more than 50 percent of its housing units. Homes and investments have turned to ashes and trash. This happened despite determined and energetic efforts by the community led by TWO (The Woodlawn Organization) and more recently WECAN (Woodlawn East Community and Neighbors). TWO (originally, the Temporary Woodlawn Organization) was organized in 1960 and has been a strong, active and controversial organization. It was organized by Saul Alinsky's Industrial Areas Foundation. WECAN, at 1541 E. 65th Street, began as a completely volunteer community organization. One of its many accomplishments was to bring into Woodlawn an outreach branch of the City Colleges, a city-wide first. Still, Woodlawn is an area of abandoned and burned apartment buildings and will need a ferocious amount of work to be saved as a community. It was done before. Originally part of the vast South Side swamp, the land was first claimed by Dutch truck farmers. Their scattered farmhouses were eventually surrounded by rooming houses, boarding hotels and apartment buildings. Woodlawn is bounded on the north by the Midway Plaisance created in the 1890s for the World's Columbian Exposition. This was the midway where Little Egypt danced. Woodlawn's other boundaries are 67th Street on the south, the lake on the east, and Dr. Martin Luther King Drive on the west. Sixty-third Street, for generations the last stop on the Jackson Park "L" line, is Woodlawn's main street. The Depression, World War II crowding and rapid racial turnover hurt Woodlawn severely. Its buildings deteriorated before people's eyes. TWO's first battles in the 1960s were to get the mainly white merchants in the area to stop cheating their customers. TWO fought blight, land acquisitions by the University of Chicago and often city hall. It became especially adept at obtaining federal funds without going through Mayor Daley. It has been aligned with street gangs and fought slum landlords. Speaking of TWO's successes, Arthur Brazier wrote in 1969: "They happened because people in Woodlawn developed a near obsession for self-determination. They came about because the church cared and risked its reputation to step out and initiate action. They happened because some liberal subsystems of the establishment supported what was happening in Woodlawn. TWO was not without its failures—failures that hurt but did not crush the organization." Woodlawn most needs residential restoration, a fact that the 65th Development Corporation understands. This group, founded by a crossing guard, an assistant pastor, and several Woodlawn housewives and widows, in the mid-1980s obtained the funds by dipping into resources reserved for rehabbing deteriorated buildings after the Reagan Administration said the government could not afford to help. A golf course, harbor and park are in Jackson Park, site of the World's Columbian Exposition. In 1980, Woodlawn's population was 36,323, a 32 percent drop from the 1970 number of 53,814.

*T*IMELINE of CHICAGO HISTORY

1981 On May 25, Sears Tower scaled by "Spider" Dan Goodwin. When he later climbs the Hancock Center, Chicago firemen turn a hose on him.

1982 Chicago's often reviled weather proves why on January 10 with record of 26 degrees below zero and wind-chill index of 81 below. Marshall Field and Company acquired by British firm BAT in friendly takeover. John Cardinal Cody, embroiled in controversy over his personal finances, dies on April 25. On July 10, Joseph Cardinal Bernardin appointed Archbishop of Chicago. Cyanide poison added to Extra-Strength Tylenol capsules on store shelves kills seven Chicago area residents.

43. South Shore

In the 1960s, South Shore learned the harsh lesson that a strong self-esteem is not enough to hold a community together. Many South Shore residents saw it as an elite enclave. When the protective bonds of such a community—no matter how prestigious and secure they appear—break, chaos can follow. The exclusive and private South Shore Country Club (incorporated 1906) along the lake betwen 67th and 71st streets and long-segregated Rainbow Beach could not keep South Shore from racial change that swept across it from adjoining Washington Park. Rather, what these institutions stood for probably helped feed the panic that ensued. South Shore changed racially from the 1960 census (9.6 percent black) to 1980 (95 percent black). The last decade has seen some stabilization and at least some movement back to the attractive community South Shore had long been. In the early 1880s, a water works was built next to Rainbow Park, spurring growth around it. In 1881, the Illinois Central Gulf Railroad opened a stop at 71st Street and Jeffery Avenue to supply the water works pumping station with coal. In 1930, a history of South Shore began: "Wrested from the heart of a vast jungle of swamps and thickets, that part of the South Shore between Stony Island Avenue, Lake Michigan, 67th and 87th Streets, in a few brief years became the most rapidly growing section of Chicagoland. Now the home of health and plenty, culture and refinement, ten miles southeast of the Loop, lies this beautiful corner of domestic felicity." South Shore's boundaries are 67th Street on the north, 79th Street on the south, the lake on the east, and the Illinois Central Gulf Railroad on the west. There is virtually no industry in South Shore. High-rise apartments line the lakefront and lower rental units lie farther west. After closing in 1971, South Shore Country Club's main building, beach and golf course facilities reopened as a beautiful public park. The hope of the area comes not only from its assets, such as the lake, the parks and solid housing, but also from the work of the South Shore Commission. As in no other community in Chicago, the name of a local bank—The South Shore Bank at 71st and Jeffery—constantly surfaces as being involved with solving the community's problems. South Shore's population went down from 80,660 in 1970 to 77,743 in 1980.

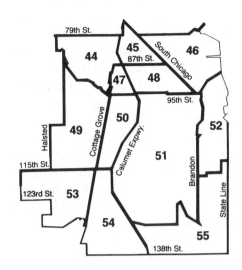

44. Chatham
45. Avalon Park
46. South Chicago
47. Burnside
48. Calumet Heights
49. Roseland
50. Pullman
51. South Deering
52. East Side
53. West Pullman
54. Riverdale
55. Hegewisch

44. Chatham

Chatham, in the very center of the black South Side, has a very positive image. One good test is the phone book listings because, in a neighborhood with a good reputation, local stores and businesses will take its name as part of their own. The Chicago phone book contains forty listings starting with the word "Chatham." These range alphabetically from Chatham Avalon Nursery School to Chatham Wigs. In October, 1986, a four-year rehabilitation of its Chatham Center, 753 E. 79th Street, restored the multi-use shopping and recreation center to its original (1937) grandeur. An oddly shaped community, Chatham runs from 79th Street on the north, Burnside diagonally up to Holland Road along the south, Dauphin to 87th and the New York, Chicago & St. Louis Railroad on the east and Parnell on the west. Chatham has a fascinating early history. In 1837, due to the owner's failure to pay $1,500 in taxes on an eighty-eight acre tract at 88th and Cottage, the city foreclosed the mortgage. However, the wrong mortgage was foreclosed, a fact not discovered until forty years later. In 1939 the case was finally resolved when the Illinois Supreme Court decided the heir, writer Janet Ayer Fairbank, deserved title to the original land but still owed the $1,500 plus 10 percent interest compounded semi-annually from 1837. The bill came to $34,755,600—but she settled the debt for $30,000. The earliest structures in Chatham were corncribs built by the Illinois Central Railroad from 75th to 95th streets. By the 1880s, communities had developed in the area: Avalon Highlands, southeast of 79th and Cottage Grove; Chatham Fields, between 79th and 83rd streets and Cottage Grove; and the Garden Homes, between Indiana Avenue and State Street and 87th and 89th streets. Chatham had 9,774 residents in 1920, a number that reached 36,228 by 1930. With median home values around $40,000, Chatham is a proud black middle and upper-middle class community. The Chatham Park Village Cooperative—from 83rd to 84th streets and from Evans to St. Lawrence avenues—is one of the largest such cooperative housing projects in the country, having converted from rental units. Chatham's population dropped from 47,287 in 1970 to 40,725 in 1980.

45. Avalon Park

Avalon Park, in the center of the South Side and to the west of Chatham, shares many of that community's characteristics. Both changed racially in the 1960s and have similar percentages in most statistical rankings. Avalon Park has a slightly higher average income and median years of schooling. A big difference is home ownership. Chatham is 37.8 percent owner-occupied; Avalon Park is 71.3 percent. Early Avalon Park was such a deep swamp (except for the ridge that is now Stony Island Avenue) that homes here were built on posts. In 1900, the 79th Street sewer was completed and the swamp drained. Avalon Park is bounded by 76th Street on the north, 87th Street on the south, South Chicago Avenue on the east, and the Illinois Central Gulf tracks on the west. In 1890, Avalon Park, for which the community is named, at 83rd Street and Woodlawn Avenue was called Mud Lake. The neighborhood developed before the 1893 World's Columbian Exposition. Avalon Park was originally known as Pennyville, after its subdivider Mr. Penny. By the 1920s, residential construction was in full-swing. In 1980, Avalon

Park was 96.1 percent black. It faces the bleak problem of area job losses as a result of the steel mills and other firms closing. Avalon Park's population dropped from 14,412 in 1970 to 13,792 in 1980.

46. South Chicago

South Chicago, on Lake Michigan at the mouth of the Calumet River, has been staggered in the last decade by deep unemployment due to loss of jobs at U.S. Steel South Works and companies associated with it. This steeltown has had problems since the turn of the century, but none to compare to the recent loss of employment. In the 1820s, South Chicago and the Calumet River were considered as a possible lake terminus for the Illinois and Michigan Canal (ultimately built to utilize the Chicago River). This determined where the heart of Chicago would be. Illinois state legislator Gurdon Saltonstall Hubbard argued that a canal starting so close to Indiana would benefit that state more than Illinois. South Chicago extends from 79th Street on the north, 95th Street on the south, the Calumet River on the east, and South Chicago Avenue on the west. During the early 1850s, the Lake Shore and Michigan Railroad opened a station and boarding house for railroad workers in South Chicago. It was given the name, "Ainsworth," and acquired a post office, churches and a school. Its name was changed to South Chicago the same year (1871) as the Chicago Fire. The 1860s, 1870s and 1880s saw manufacturing plants, lumber yards, and grain elevators come into the area. In 1880, establishment of the North Chicago Rolling Mills South Works brought Irish, English, Welsh, Swedish, Polish and German workers who settled in South Chicago. Many of its churches and structures are distinctly Eastern European. It is a working-class neighborhood somewhat reminiscent of Pittsburgh without the hills. The Chicago Skyway runs along the southwest side of the community. South Chicago in the 1980 census was almost half black and has nearly as many Hispanics. Local neighborhoods include The Bush (named after bushes along the beaches a century ago), South Works and Millgate (named after the steel mills). The population went up from 45,655 in 1970 to 46,422 in 1980.

47. Burnside

Burnside, a small wedge in the middle of the South Side, is the smallest and least populous city community. It underwent swift racial change from 1970 (2.9 percent black) to 1980 (88.6 percent black). The most interesting statistic in the change is that the median school years of residents increased from 9.4 to 12.2 years. Subdivided in 1887 and named for Civil War General Ambrose E. Burnside (whose name was inverted and bestowed on sideburns), Burnside forms a rough triangle whose base is 95th Street and sides are the Conrail tracks on the east and Illinois Central Gulf tracks on the west. Like many other communities, Burnside grew with the railroads. In the 1880s, the Illinois Central roundhouse and repair shop works at 95th Street and Cottage Grove Avenue brought Poles, Hungarians, and Italians, who built brick and frame two-flats. Many early settlers were male immigrants who lived in shanties and boarding houses until they could save enough money to bring the rest of their families from Poland, Italy or Hungary. Mexicans—many of whom were employed in the steel industry—moved into the area during the 1950s and 1960s but moved out in the 1970s. Their percentage dropped from 7.9 percent to 2.5 percent. Burnside's population did grow from 3,181 in 1970 to 3,942 in 1980.

48. Calumet Heights

Calumet Heights, centered at Stony Island and 91st Street, is best known for its two communities: Stony Island Heights and Pill Hill. The "Heights" is a brick, middle-income community that has a suburban feel to it. Pill Hill, centered at 92nd and Jeffery, has a far wealthier, better-side-of-the-tracks appearance with split-level, sprawling homes that compare with

The electrified Chicago South Shore & South Bend Railroad—America's last interurban—cuts across Chicago's Southeast Side neighborhoods and through northern Indiana. In this photo, it is leaving the Illinois Central Gulf tracks at Torrence and Kensington for the South Shore right of way.

Courtesy, William M. Scott

those in Beverly or Winnetka. Calumet Heights is bounded by 87th Street on the north, 95th Street on the south, South Chicago Avenue on the east, and the Conrail tracks on the west. In the 1880s, the community began along a famous geological ridge known as Stony Island. This ridge jutted out of Lake Chicago ten thousand years ago. Geologists say this is the only place in the city where Niagara limestone is exposed. A quarry at Stony Island and 92nd Street revealed the more recent geological history of Chicago, that is, within the last 100,000 years. The ridge and railroads on three sides isolate Calumet Heights. For decades it stayed a rural community. Its many single-family houses were put up in the 1920s and 1930s. It did not develop substantially until after World War II, when its population increased from 7,343 in 1940 to 19,352 by 1960. With a median home value (in 1980) of $43,600, it sits between Burnside ($30,200) and South Chicago ($32,400). Calumet Heights' population rose just slightly from 20,123 in 1970 to 20,505 in 1980.

49. Roseland

Roseland on the far South Side, is going to need help—a lot of it—in pulling itself up by its bootstraps. It is afflicted by the dire problems of unemployment, crime, lack of mortgage money, and business failures. Settled by Dutch farmers and George Pullman's workers not wanting to live in his company town in the 1880s and 1890s, this community is bounded by the METRA (formerly Rock Island) tracks past Highway 20 on the north, 115th Street on the south, Cottage Grove on the east, and Halsted north to 103rd east to Stewart on the west. Roseland was originally a Dutch truck farm community called Hope. The Dutch are usually associated with tulips, but early settlers of Hope preferred roses. Ten years after its founding, the residents changed its name to Roseland for the flowers they grew beside the vegetables in their front yards. A dominant factor in Roseland's growth, as with many communities, was the railroads. By the 1880s, seven trunk lines passed through Roseland, connecting Chicago with the east and south. The railroads brought industry, jobs and immigrants. Roseland was featured in Edna Ferber's Pulitzer Prize-winning 1924 novel *So Big*. Roseland is the commercial district for the area surrounding it.

Before World War II, the black section of Roseland, Lilydale, had 1,000 residents. Blacks made up 55 percent of Roseland's residents in 1970, and 97.5 percent by 1980. In the early 1980s, Roseland suffered deep unemployment when Pullman Standard and Wisconsin Steel along with related industries closed or cut back. The Roseland Business Development Council is working to counteract the loss of business in the area. Roseland's population increased from 62,512 in 1970 to 64,372 in 1980.

50. Pullman

For a century, Pullman Palace or Pullman-Standard railroad cars rolled out of the plants on the north side of the town and community of Pullman. The last railroad car was produced in 1981. It was 100 years after train-car magnate George Pullman built the town of Pullman, designed to be a morally-uplifting and highly-controlled community for his employees. It was laid out by S.S. Beman to meet its workers' every need, possessing a library, church (rented to various denominations) and a hotel named after Pullman's daughter, Florence. In 1889 the residents voted to annex themselves to Chicago, a decision angering its autocratic founder. George Pullman greeted the 1894 workers' strike with the intransigent statement: "There is nothing to negotiate." The federal government and the U.S. Attorney General—a former railroad lawyer—took Pullman's side, breaking the strike with the use of federal troops. In 1898 by order of the Illinois Supreme Court, the Pullman Company was divested of ownership of the town. The Pullman community of 1986—bounded by 95th Street on the north, 115th Street on the south, Stony Island on the east, and Cottage Grove on the west—is not, however, synonymous with George Pullman's model industrial town, which was smaller. The area's northern section, principally industrial and full of vacant railroad yards, saw some post-World War II residential growth. Pullman has thrived as a well-located, relatively inexpensive rental neighborhood. Today, the old Pullman town is a popular tourist attraction. The Florence Hotel has been delightfully restored. It now houses a restaurant and bar (George never allowed liquor in his town), but 111th Street is no longer called Florence Avenue. The Sherwin Williams Paint Co. at 549 East 115th Street is located where former Pullman Company buildings stood. Median rents are around $170 a month. Pullman's population dropped slightly from 10,893 in 1970 to 10,341 in 1980.

51. South Deering

South Deering, a large community encompassing Lake Calumet Harbor and much of the winding Calumet River, has a proud, but difficult and troubled history. For over one hundred years, it was principally a one-industry community—steel, although the harbor and nearby refineries offered work. During economic hard times, this has meant heavy stagnation and unemployment. During good times, it often means racial tension and conflict as new groups move in to get the jobs. South Deering has seen good and bad economic times in decade after decade. In the 1980s, it has faced its biggest challenge, the loss of its major employer, Wisconsin Steel. The community of South Deering is bounded by 95th Street on the north, 130th Street on the south, the Calumet River on the east, and the Calumet Expressway on the west. Several industries moved to this area crisscrossed by railroads in the early 1870s when the federal government developed the Calumet River and a channel to connect lakes Calumet and Michigan. The Calumet Canal and Dock Company turned Lake Calumet into the substantial, protected harbor that Lake Michigan vessels had never had. By 1875, the area had its first steel mill, the Joseph H. Brown Iron and Steel Company, and its first settlement, Ironton. While many communities declined in population during the late 1930s, South Deering's grew. The reason was largely construction during 1937 and 1938 of the Trumbull Homes built by the WPA and leased to the Chicago Housing Authority. They contained 454 units and would be the site in the 1950s of a difficult conflict over integration. On August 5, 1953, the Donald Howard family, the first blacks, moved into Trumbull Homes. Racial agitation continued to flare up around the Chicago Housing Authority project for a decade afterwards. South Deering is a highly industrialized region with grain elevators, railroad yards, and some heavy industry. A mixture of nationalities work in its mills, on the docks, and in the factories and oil refineries. The community will need help for the rest of the century with problems of toxic wastes, unemployment and housing. Median rent in 1980 was $140. Although South Deering's population changed from 15.9 percent to 54.8 percent black, its total figure remained level going from 19,405 in 1970 to 19,400 in 1980.

52. East Side

The East Side, reached by the Indiana Avenue exit off the Calumet Skyway, is a community many Chicagoans scarcely believe exists. Few have visited it. Most hear of it only in connection with its former alderman Edward Vrdolyak, chairman of the Cook County Democratic Party. It is bordered by 118th Street on the south, the Indiana state line on the east, and the Calumet River on the north and west. Before construction of the Chicago Skyway, the East Side was a difficult drive or a lengthy streetcar ride from downtown Chicago. Industrial development began by the 1880s and drew German, Swedish, Italian and Yugoslavian immigrants. Many East Side industries—foundries, coal yards, grain elevators, breweries, steel mills and oil refineries—have either been shut down or scaled back. Its residents, fighting heavy unemployment, retain deep pride in their homes, churches and community. The steel mills, oil refineries and other businesses have created odors and other pollutants that residents tolerated for years but have risen up against recently. Many tell you they would accept more pollution if it meant more jobs for the area. The residents are first and second-generation Eastern Europeans. The population of the East Side decreased from 24,649 in 1970 to 21,331 in 1980.

53. West Pullman

West Pullman, which is actually southwest rather than west of Pullman, is facing some serious problems that seem unique to the 1980s. According to a 1986 Woodstock Institute study, it is one of the South Chicago neighborhoods being systematically denied residential mortgage money. Without it, there can be very little stability. The same year, 1986, a test of residents who live near the Dutch Boy Paints factory at 12000 S. Peoria Street revealed that 309 persons suffered from various forms of lead poisoning. The factory, which had burned down the year before, was considered equivalent to a toxic dump with the amounts of lead and asbestos it harbored. This community, ironically, is just north of one of the oldest sites in the Chicago area known to have been inhabited by man. Along the banks of the Calumet River south of West Pullman archeologists excavated the Anker Site, where hundreds of years ago prehistoric Indians lived and traded. A gorget or shell mask was discovered that represented the expression of a fine individual artist as well as trading skills of Chicago area residents five hundred years ago. West Pullman, in the 1880s, was one of several communities that developed as an alternative to George Pullman's company town, northwest of it. By 1881 when some workers were moving into the highly-touted Pullman, others decided to build their own homes in this undeveloped area then called Kensington (now West Pullman) at 115th Street and Cottage Grove Avenue. Its residents grew from a mere 250 in 1880 to 1,278 by 1883. A second community called Gano developed between 115th Street and 119th Street and from State Street to Wentworth Avenue. West Pullman actually lies west of Hegewisch. West Pullman is bordered by 115th Street on the north, the city limits on the south, the Illinois Central Gulf Railroad on the east, and Ashland Avenue on the west. An area between 119th and 121st streets, where the Conrail and the Illinois Central Gulf tracks meet, developed into a heavy industry site over the years. The community has a high percentage of home ownership along with heavy unemployment and a lack of available mortgage money. Those problems, like the lead and the asbestos, can provide their own timebomb if the broader community does not get involved. This relatively populous community is served by the Calumet Expressway. Between 1970 and 1980 census, West Pullman changed from 16.5 percent to 90.6 percent black. Its population increased from 40,318 in 1970 to 44, 904 in 1980.

54. Riverdale

Riverdale, a community south of Pullman and west of the Calumet Expressway, started off in the 1880s as a sewer farm for Pullman. The people of Riverdale settled far to the south, but the north has continued to harbor a sewage treatment plant for the Metropolitan Sanitary District. Suddenly, the residents realize the problem is more than its odor. A 1986 Illi-

The old ways in Hegewisch: Young Polish folk dancers at St. Florian Church, 131st Street and Houston Avenue.

Photo, Kim Tonry

nois Public Health Department study for the Illinois Environmental Protection Agency indicated a higher death rate among white men in six Southeast Side communities than those in the other parts of Chicago. The Calumet sewage treatment plant in Riverdale as well as 31 landfills in the area became chief suspects. The leader of Riverdale's Citizens United to Reclaim the Environment (CURE) complained, "We have become the garbage dump of the city. It is as though nobody cares." This community on the southern limits of Chicago has the same name as a suburb southwest of it. It is bounded by 115th Street on the north, 138th Street and the Calumet River on the south, the Calumet Expressway on the east, and the Illinois Central Gulf tracks on the west. Farming and lumbering were the main occupations of its early native American, German and Dutch settlers. The vast truck farms in this area gave rise to food-processing plants. Blacks began to move here in the 1950s and 1960s. Much land in the center of the community is vacant. The section farthest north contains railroad yards. The Calumet Expressway runs along the west bank of Lake Calumet. Riverdale is also served by METRA trains over the Illinois Central Gulf Railroad tracks. Its population dropped from 15,018 in 1970 to 13,539 in 1980.

55. Hegewisch

Hegewisch, 15 miles from the Loop, is the community in the far southeast corner of the city. On a visit here in 1986, Mayor Washington did what many another Chicagoan might do, he mispronounced it "Hegwitch." It is named for Achilles Hegewisch, a president of the United States Rolling Stock Company that lies about fifteen miles to its west. Hegewisch wanted to build a company town like George Pullman's. In 1883, to erect a plant, his company purchased 100 acres at 135th Street and Brandon Avenue. With a group of investors, Hegewisch then bought 1,500 acres north and northwest of the plant site for a town. Parts were subdivided for residences and businesses by 1883 and 1884. While it never attained the dimensions and fame of Pullman's company town, Achilles Hegewisch did manage to leave the town with his name. East Side residents feeling ignored by the rest of Chicago often say, "You ought to hear the people from Hegewisch complain." Its boundaries are 118th Street on the north, the city limits on the south, the Indiana state line and Wolf Lake on the east, and the Beaubien Forest Preserve on the west. In 1980 the median rent was $151 a month and its population was almost 3 percent black. Of the relatively poor state of housing, the 1940 book *The Forty-Four Cities in the City of Chicago* said, "A number of features offset the rather bad quality of the dwellings. The blocks are not overly crowded with structures; there is a satisfying amount of grass and trees; and the places of employment of most of the residents are nearby." Hegewisch might have fared better if the long-planned canal between Lake Mud and Wolf Lake (the Illinois half of which would have been in Hegewisch) had been built. The area is fighting its problems, but it shares along with neighboring communities those of unemployment, toxic wastes and lack of mortgage money. Area residents add lack of police protection to that list. Hegewisch's population rose from 11,346 in 1970 to 11,572 in 1980.

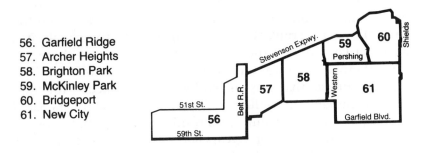

56. Garfield Ridge

Garfield Ridge, on the far Southwest Side, is bounded by the village of Forest View on the north, 59th Street on the south, Midway Airport on the east and Summit on the west. The name was bestowed on it by developer Fred Bartlett. In the 1870s and 1880s, a large portion of this community was the farm of "Long John" Wentworth, an early mayor of Chicago. Until a few years ago, Wentworth's farm house stood at the corner of Archer Road and Harlem Avenue. The population of Garfield Ridge spurted from 12,900 in 1950 to 40,449 by 1960. The growth happened before completion of the Stevenson (first called the Southwest Expressway), joining this community to the rest of Chicago. The area's industry and prosperity were hurt by the loss of the heavy use of Midway Airport. Those who built businesses and motels based on it were damaged the most, but a turnover to lighter industry and diversified retail establishments developed steadily. The 316-unit Le Claire Courts at 44th Street and Cicero Avenue brought the first racial integration into Garfield Ridge. Its black population increased from one in 1950 to 2,686 by 1960. Garfield Ridge's population decreased from 42,998 in 1970 to 37,935 in 1980.

57. Archer Heights

It is difficult to find the heights in Archer Heights, although there is a slight elevation near St. Richard

Church at 50th Street and Kostner Avenue. Archer Heights is easy to find. Its borders are the Stevenson Expressway on the north, the Grand Trunk Western Railroad on the south and along the Santa Fe yards on the east, and Forest View on the west. Its northern section was part of Mud Lake and a portion of the Chicago Portage that was cursed by early voyageurs, fur trappers and Indians. In 1900 Archer Heights, noted for its Santa Fe railroad yards, had almost no residents. By 1940, the population reached 8,202. Forty years later, it was 9,708. Homes are mostly scattered. Considerable vacant land exists. The Archer Express provides the area's only public transportation to the Loop. Large, greasy hamburgers with grilled onions are known in Archer Heights as "Big Babies" and the similarly prepared hotdogs as "Fat Freddies." The largest ethnic group is Polish, but unlike older Polish neighborhoods, most are second and third generation Americans. Other nationalities include Lithuanians, Czechoslovakians, Russian Jews and Mexicans. Archer Heights' population declined from 11,134 in 1970 to 9,708 in 1980.

58. Brighton Park

Brighton Park, on the Southwest Side just south of the Stevenson Expressway, had its day in the world spotlight on Oct. 5, 1979, when Pope John Paul II celebrated Mass in the parking lot of Five Holy Martyrs Catholic Church. The Poles, the dominant ethnic group of the community, were particularly proud and led the movement to rename 43rd Street between Western Avenue and Kedzie Avenue, Pope John Paul II Drive. Brighton Park, bounded on the north by the expressway extends to 49th Street on the south, to Artesian on the east and to the Santa Fe tracks (3600) on the west. It is an old community separated from Archer Heights on the west by the yards of the Santa Fe railroad and to the east by the Baltimore & Ohio Chicago Terminal Railroad near Western Avenue. Brighton Trotting Park, founded by "Long John" Wentworth in the mid-1800s, was located in the triangle formed by Archer Avenue and Pershing (then Egan) Road. Until closed after passage of the 1905 Anti-Betting Law, this race park stood east of the current Brighton Park neighborhood. Around the turn of the century, gypsies camped in the area at 47th and Western Avenue. Other nationalities who have immigrated to Brighton Park are French, Poles, Italians, Slovaks, Irish and Germans. The railroads, beginning at the turn of the century, brought considerable industry to Brighton Park. It has lost much of its heavy industry including International Harvester and the Crane Co., but has gained a broader role as a truck and train shipping area with the development of the piggyback operation in the Santa Fe yards. The area grew most between 1910 and 1920 when the population jumped from 8,474 to 33,019. Brighton Park's population dropped from 35,167 in 1970 to 30,770 in 1980.

59. McKinley Park

McKinley Park, along the south side of the Stevenson Expressway between Brighton Park and Bridgeport, belies the image of Chicago as "a city of villages." The size, diversity and industry of communities such as McKinley Park make them more comparable to U.S. cities than to villages. Its other boundaries are Pershing Road on the south, the South Fork of the Chicago River (Bubbly Creek) on the east, and the Baltimore & Ohio Chicago Terminal Railroad tracks on the west. In the mid-1880s, the banks of the Chicago River, both on the North and South Branches, were home to a major industry: brick-making. It required cheap, strong labor. There were almost thirty brickyards during that era of McKinley Park. Its population peaked during World War I when the stockyards attained their highest meat production. In 1835, the northern portion from 21st to 31st streets and from Ashland to Western Avenue was mapped out as a subdivision called Canalport. This was a shanty town where people grew cabbage and worked in the slaughterhouses along the river. They took home (for free) leftovers such as hearts, kidneys, livers. The area stabilized with the development of McKinley Park. Mayor "Long John" Wentworth owned the land where the park is and Damen Avenue on old maps is noted as "Long John Street." The area was the "American" section of Packingtown because of the high percentage of Irish and other English-speaking residents. The grand- and great-grandchildren of many early settlers still live in McKinley Park. Around 1900, McKinley Park was the site of one of the first planned industrial parks in America called the Central Manufacturing District. William Wrigley built his gum factory in it and it is still here. It looks to the development of the "L" to become a highly affordable residential community connected closely to the Loop and the rest of Chicago. Its population decreased 15 percent from 1970 (15,632) to 1980 (13,248).

60. Bridgeport

Bridgeport, on the Near Southwest Side, was the lifelong home of Mayor Richard J. Daley and many Irish before and after him. It also included some Poles, Lithuanians, Italians and Chinese, but few, very few, black Chicagoans. It held a political dynasty from 1933 until 1979, since every Chicago mayor was from Bridgeport: Edward J. Kelly, Martin Kennelly, Richard J. Daley and Michael Bilandic. The community got its name from the fact that there was a low bridge near the South Fork in the 1840s and heavily-loaded canal boats had to unload items from the decks and carry them around it. Bridgeport extends from the Stevenson Expressway north to Pershing Road on the south, and from the Conrail tracks on the east to Bubbly Creek (a small fork of the Chicago River) on the west. In the 1830s and early 1840s, its original settlers were Irish canalers. These squatters built their shanties on federal land— the canal banks—near the source of fresh water. Bridgeport was a city suburb until 1863. In the 1850s, it was alleged that Bridgeport residents had illegally voted in a Chicago mayoral election. Industries included the canal, the meatpacking houses (in 1865 consolidated into the Union Stock Yards), a limestone quarry at Halsted and 29th Street, brickyards, and Illinois Steel (built in 1870 at Archer and Ashland avenues). These have all disappeared except the quarry. The Union Stock Yards lasted until 1971. Bridgeport residents subsequently became merchants, saloonkeepers, teachers, clergymen—but more than anything else—politicians, policemen and city employees. Political patronage has long flourished here. The northeast corner of Bridgeport abuts Chinatown and, beginning in the 1970s, Chinese-Americans have begun to move into Bridgeport. In two census tracts, the figure for "non-whites" in Bridgeport jumped from 2.9 percent in each in 1970 to 10.9 percent in one census and 25.2 percent in the other by 1980. Bridgeport's population decreased from 35,167 in 1970 to 30,923 in 1980, half of what it was in 1920.

61. New City

New City, the site for over 100 years of the Union Stock Yards, was known at the turn of the century as Packingtown and more recently as The Back of the Yards. The community area includes Canaryville, east of Halsted. Now closed and cleared away, the yards were a mile square of animals waiting to be slaughtered. They extended from Pershing Road to 47th Street and between Halsted and Ashland and made up the heart of New City. New City's borders are Pershing Road on the north, Garfield Boulevard (5500 south) on the south, the Penn Central Railroad on the east, and Western Avenue on the west. The source of the jobs, commerce and stench in the area from 1865 to 1971 was officially known as the Union Stock Yards and Transit Company. A character in *The Jungle* tried to describe life here: "The people come in hordes; and old Durham had squeezed them tighter and tighter, speeding them up and grinding them to pieces, and sending for new ones. The Poles who had come by the tens of thousands, had been driven to the wall by the Lithu-

TIMELINE of CHICAGO HISTORY

1985 Bears win divisional football championship. Arlington Park Race Track burns to the ground.

1986 Bill Veeck dies. Bears win Super Bowl.

On June 30, investor group led by *Sun-Times* publisher Robert Page buys newspaper from Murdoch organization. Chicago peace activist, labor leader and writer Sidney Lens

dies. Refurbished Chicago Theater opens.

1987 Chicago celebrates its 150th birthday on March 4.

anians, and now the Lithuanians were giving way to the Slovaks. Who there was poorer and more miserable than the Slovaks, Grandmother Majauszkiene had no idea, but the packers would find them, never fear.'' In 1920, at the height of the stockyards' productivity, New City had 92,659 residents. In 1940, Albert Dickens wrote of this area: ''Historical precedent and far-sighted planning have combined to make the Near Southwest Side an efficient, well-organized industrial development; while a notable absence of planning has produced a multitude of scattered and disorganized residential clusters and strips, many of which are blighted and in decay.'' In 1939, Saul Alinsky and Joseph Meegan started the Back of the Yards Council to unify these clusters and improve neighborhood conditions. Enjoying support from area churches, this controversial organization was largely successful in achieving its goals. None of these, however, dealt with long or short range integration. Blacks moving into the area eventually formed their own community group, the Organization for New City. In 1986, Robert Slayton wrote about New City in his *Back of the Yards: The Making of a Local Democracy.* He differentiated not only among the nationalities who live in New City, but also among the nationalities of the various parishes. The book appropriately starts with a particularly vivid description of the pungent odor that long dominated the Back of the Yards. The quote comes from a nun newly assigned to the Back of the Yards area some years ago. An effort to develop the empty spaces left by the loss of the yards has focused on light industry. The site at one point was proposed as an optional one for the 1992 World's Fair. The former yards area has been attractively cleared. The community of New City east of the stockyard area (between Halsted and the railroad tracks to the east), known as Canaryville, at one time was called ''The Village.'' It is a storied place of many first, second and third-generation Irish-Americans. James T. Farrell wrote several short stories about the area including ''Calico Shoes.'' New City's population dropped from 60,817 in 1970 to 55,860 in 1980.

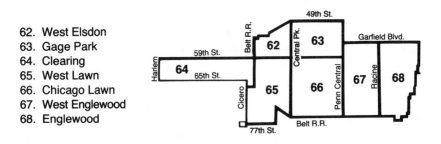

62. West Elsdon

West Elsdon, in the heart of the Southwest Side, is one of many city communities defined by railroad tracks. Its center is 55th and Pulaski. West Elsdon boundaries are the Belt Railway of Chicago on the north, 59th Street on the south, the Grand Trunk Western Railroad on the east, and the Belt Railway of Chicago on the west. It includes many streets whose names all begin with the letter "K." In 1940, Homer Hoyt said of West Elsdon: "There is still room for expansion in West Elsdon, but the boom days are gone—probably forever." The population was 3,241. It has since then quadrupled. West Elsdon should benefit from construction of the Southwest "L" line to Midway Airport. Since it is near Midway, an airport terminus for the "L" would help end its isolation from the Loop and the rest of Chicago. On the other hand, it might also be all of Chicago that benefits. One of the authors once had occasion to interview a group of garbage collectors who worked in this area. They spoke almost reverentially of the cleanliness and neatness of West Elsdon's residents. The alleys, they said, were spotless. Not infrequently the residents met them with garbage in hand when they made their rounds. And, even then, it was often double-bagged. The garbage collectors, on their part, never missed a pick-up, no matter what the weather. They were, they said, not only conscientious, but also afraid of the ire of the residents if a pick-up were missed. The 1980 census found the median rent here was $238 a month. West Elsdon's population decreased from 14,059 in 1970 to 12,797 in 1980.

63. Gage Park

Gage Park, centered at California and 55th, is named for George W. Gage, whose family first settled this area in the 1840s. George Gage was a member of the South Side Park Commission in the late 1860s, when it was developing the expansive park system for the South Side of Chicago. The community of Gage Park lies solidly in the middle of the Southwest Side. Its boundaries are 49th Street (Grand Trunk Western Railroad) on the north, 59th Street on the south, Western Avenue (Conrail) on the east and the Grand Trunk Western Railroad on the west. It is a neat and clean community of second- and third-generation Americans, many of whose parents and grandparents came from Eastern Europe. Over 80 percent of its residents, however, were born in Illinois. The population grew from a scant 214 in 1910 to 31,535 in 1930. The institution that well represents local residents' strong belief in thrift is Talman Federal Savings and Loan at Kedzie and 55th. It was started by Czechs in 1905. It has grown and its offices are now in a dozen suburbs as well as in downstate communities such as Peoria and Pekin. In the 1970s, Gage Park gained notoriety for its racial intransigence. Local residents met with stiff resistance efforts to achieve school integration by busing black children into a Gage Park school. The 1980 population was 24,445 (of whom only 163 were black) down from 26,698 in 1970.

64. Clearing

The name "Clearing" for this Southwest Side community that includes the southern portion of Midway Airport, derives from railroad terminology for a "clearing yard," where incoming trains are broken down or outgoing trains are assembled. The man who planned such a yard in this area was Chicago Great Western Railroad President Alpheus B. Stickney. The yard failed in 1894 and was dubbed "Stickney's Folly." Clearing today runs from 59th Street on the north, 65th Street on the south, the Belt Railway of Chicago on the east, and Harlem on the west. Clearing, an area three miles wide and three quarters of a mile from north to south, in many ways is an insulated neighborhood. When Clearing annexed to Chicago in 1915, it was a German and Dutch truck-farm community. The first business in the area, George Hill's hardware store at 63rd and Central, still prospers here. The railroads and Midway Airport both aided its commercial development. The vast Clearing International District lies where "Stickney's Folly" had been. Of the 6,000 workers in the district, only 325 lived here. According to the Clearing Industrial Association, approximately 175 companies are in the area. The group sponsored a pilot project begun in 1984 called, "Buy a Business, Sell a Business." Young people in the area who want to go into business meet owners who want to retire. The publicly-funded program resulted in five businesses being sold and staying in the area in the first two years. Clearing's population was 24,911 in 1970 and 22,584 in 1980.

65. West Lawn

West Lawn, on the Southwest Side, is the home of Ford City Shopping Center and of Daley College at 7500 S. Pulaski. It ranges from 59th Street on the north to 75th Street on the south and from the Grand Trunk Western tracks at 3600 West on the east to the city limits at Cicero on the west. Laid out at the beginning of the Depression, West Lawn barely grew at first. It was on the flight path between Municipal Airport (Midway) and Areo Club Field at 83rd and Cicero and little else. The area, some of it improved by the WPA, was not built up. Many of the single-family bungalows that were here had tax and mortgage liens on them. Because tax assessments in that era would have been too great, homes were then built on unpaved streets, rather than on paved ones. World War II turned it around, as Chrysler Corp. built airplane engines in a plant where Ford City now is. After the war, a new automobile manufacturer used the plant in an abortive effort to build and market a zesty, supermodern car, the Tucker Automobile. During the Korean War the Ford Motor Co. built jet engines in the plant. The site, starting in 1960, became the Southwest Side's largest shopping area— Ford City Shopping Center. The plant and shopping center brought both jobs and residents to West Lawn. Daley College (formerly Bogan College and later, Southwest College) is now

'OOD'S PAGEANT OF PROGRESS

TO LOOP

Right in the Heart of **ENGLEWOOD**

Englewood was where the trains, the interurban and the CTA trains met in the 1920s.

Courtesy, G. Schmalgemeier

at 75th and Pulaski, near the shopping complex. In 1980 West Lawn's population was 24,748, down almost 3,000 from 1970 (27,644).

66. Chicago Lawn

Chicago Lawn, the heart of the Southwest Side area, is better known as Marquette Park after both its biggest neighborhood and the city park that it embraces. The community of Chicago Lawn is bordered by Gage Park at 59th Street on the north, Ashburn at 75th Street on the south, and by the Conrail tracks that run along Gage Park on the east and the Grand Trunk Western tracks that run along West Lawn on the west. Its focal point is the mile-wide Marquette Park that lies between California and Central Park and from Marquette Road (6700 south) and 71st Street. With its fieldhouse, lagoons and golf course, Marquette Park is one of the better Chicago parks. An enclave of Lithuanian-Americans surrounds it. *The Jungle* describes Chicago-Lithuanian life in Chicago Lawn's early days. The Lithuanians have been unique in their ability to keep their cultural traditions and language alive as Marquette Park's Lithuanian churches, programs and cultural events testify. At the southwest corner of Marquette Road and California Avenue stands a monument that has had special meaning to area residents for more than 50 years. It is a memorial to Stephen Darius and Stanley Girenas, two Lithuanian fliers who crashed over Germany in their 1933 effort to set a speed record flying from the United States to Lithuania. While Lithuanian-Americans dominate in numbers and culture, the shops, restaurants and homes of other nationalities are also a significant part of Chicago Lawn. The area received national attention in the 1960s and again in the 1970s for the actions there of the Ku Klux Klan and the American Nazi Party. Both garnered local support and inflamed racial hatred in the area. Some vocal Marquette Park parents attempted to retain school segregation by demonstrating against black children bused to Gage Park High School. The more recent response by church and area groups has attempted to allay neighborhood frustrations by focusing on community strengths rather than its fears. On the northern border live a sizeable number of Chicagoans of Middle Eastern extraction. Chicago Lawn's population in 1980 was 46,568, some 2,000 less than it had in 1970 (48,435).

67. West Englewood

West Englewood, which is centered at 63rd and Ashland, probably has a better future than immediate past. It has all the indications of a troubled community: a high infant mortality rate (26.4 per 1,000 in 1986), a vast number of abandoned houses and a low amount of mortgages and home improvement dollars invested in it. West Englewood is 64th on the list of 77 communities in the amount of mortgages and home improvement dollars invested in it. It also has the element most essential for the hope of a rebound, a hard-working community organization: West Englewood Community Organization (WECO), formed by the churches of the area. WECO is an organization beginning to be respected for its goals and accomplishments in the neighborhood. The community's borders are Garfield Boulevard on the north, 73rd Street on the south, Racine on the east, and the Conrail tracks on the west. West Englewood, especially south of 63rd Street, has decent housing of mostly two-story brick structures, tree-lined streets and little industry. From 1877 to 1911, a western section of West Englewood was owned by Hetty Green, the richest woman in the United States. She was known as "The Witch of Wall Street." Despite her $100 million fortune, Hetty dressed in rags to receive free medical care. In 1911 a "cabbage field" she owned was subdivided and sold, earning her another fortune. Hetty Green had other land in Chicago Lawn and also a 450-acre section at 63rd and Western Avenue.

68. Englewood

The future of Englewood, at the geographic center of the South Side, could well determine what will happen to the rest of the South Side. Because of its location, its cross streets (63rd and Halsted) and the "L," it has long been the hub of the region. In the 1920s, it had four railroad stations and boasted "All trains stop here." The interurbans met the "L" at 63rd and Halsted. For years, Englewood was also the Greyhound bus stop serving the entire South Side. It was known for several generations as the "largest outlying business district" in the United States. The name comes from Englewood, New Jersey, which got it from a forest in England where Robin Hood-era outlaws hid out. The community area extends from Garfield Boulevard (55th Street) on the north, 75th Street on the south, the METRA (formerly Rock Island) tracks on the east, and Racine on the west. It was first built up in 1852 after the Michigan, Southern & Northern Indiana Railroad (later, the New York Central) tracks were laid through this area. Shortly afterwards a nexus of eight railroad lines, known as Grand Junction, connected Englewood with downtown Chicago. The northeast corner of 63rd and Halsted was popular for its communal artesian well. Englewood became part of the city in 1889. In the 1890s, the pride of Englewood was the Cook County Normal School, the official Chicago teacher's college, run by Colonel Francis Parker. The area peaked during World War II. Gone is its dominance of the South Side as a commercial center, which resulted from its spot at the hub of transportation. A multimillion dollar urban renewal plan for Englewood announced in 1980 by Jane Byrne never got off the drawing board. Englewood, however, is a community where indigenous organizations are forming and helping. One such group formed in 1980 was Black Men United Against Rape, which later changed its name to Deacons of Christ. It has about 70 members and does not tolerate rape or other neighborhood crimes. "If we see someone breaking in," Rev. John Porter, a local pastor, said, "We'll catch him, whomp him good and hope to God he doesn't die. The way we see it, they're stealing from mother's cupboard." His church also dished out 25,000 plates of neckbones, corn bread and sweet potato pie in a recent year. Englewood's population plummeted nearly 35 percent from 1970 (89,713) to 1980 (59,075).

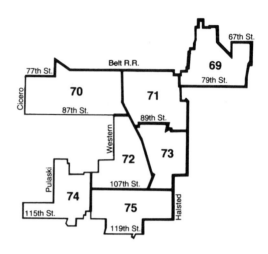

69. Greater Grand Crossing

Greater Grand Crossing, centered at 63rd Street and King Drive, is divided by the Dan Ryan Expressway. Greater Grand Crossing has the shape of an irregular triangle. The boundaries reach 61st Street on the north, then jog to 67th Street to 79th Street on the south, Woodlawn on the east, and Wallace jogging to Wentworth on the west. On April 25, 1853, Greater Grand Crossing was the site of a major wreck between trains on the Michigan Central and the Michigan Southern railroads. Eighteen people were killed and many more injured. This tragedy led to a local regulation mandating all trains make complete stops before crossing other railroad tracks—a practice soon adopted nationwide. Paul Cornell, the builder of Hyde Park, also developed Greater Grand Crossing. With many apartment buildings, it is principally residential. In its northeast corner is Oak Woods Cemetery with the graves of Confederate soldiers who perished at Camp Douglas as well as prominent Chicagoans, such as former Mayor William "Big Bill" Thompson. Census figures indicate sections with income below the poverty level in 1980 ranged from 5.9 percent to 33.4 percent. Its infant mortality rate in 1986 was a tragic 27.5 per 1,000. A community organization (the Greater Grand Crossing Organizing Committee), however, was one of six in the city singled out by the Campaign for Human Development in 1985 and given a grant to continue its work. Greater Grand Crossing's population went down from 54,414 in 1970 to 45,218 in 1980.

70. Ashburn

Ashburn, a Southwest Side community that runs east and west along the northern border of Evergreen Park, is a residential area with long straight streets of bungalows. Ashburn extends from the Conrail tracks on the east, the Belt Railway of Chicago on the north, to the city limits at Cicero Avenue on the west. It is named after Ashburn Field, an airfield at its west end that dated to pre-World War I days. In the first part of this century, Ashburn was the least populated Chicago neighborhood. It had only 730 residents in 196 dwellings. After World War II, its seams burst. Brick bungalows sprang up as industry was attracted to the area. Ashburn borders Burbank, Hometown, two cemeteries, Evergreen Park, Beverly, the Dan Ryan Woods, West Lawn and Chicago Lawn. It houses William J. Bogan High School (3939 W. 79th Street), where some of the school's parents successfully stopped a 1960s Board of Education proposal to integrate the school with black honor students. It was later successfully integrated without a major incident. An indication of its prosperity and well-being is the fact that it ranked 26th of 77 community areas in getting mortgage and home improvement money according to the 1986 Woodstock Institute study. Ashburn's population dipped from 47,161 in 1970 to 40,477 in 1980.

71. Auburn-Gresham

Auburn-Gresham, south of Englewood and West Englewood, and east of Ashburn, reflects the black racial makeup of its northern neighbors rather than the white community to the west. A portion of it is in the same ward as Ashburn. As a result, when a black attempted to run for alderman, she had to vie for the votes of the very residents who once blocked integration of Bogan High School. The boundaries are the Belt Railway of Chicago on the north, Stewart and Parnell on the east, 89th Street to 91st Street on the south, and the Baltimore & Ohio Chicago Terminal Railroad on the west. The Dan Ryan Woods forest preserve borders Auburn-Gresham's west side. The community's center is the corner of Ashland Avenue and 79th Street. The Highland Theater once stood on this corner for many years, surrounded by small shops. With the "L" a short bus ride away at 63rd and Ashland, transportation to the Loop was easy. The theater and stores are closed now, leaving the many churches along Ashland as Auburn-Gresham's focal point. These churches starting at 77th Street include: Evangelist Hope Church, Truth Missionary Baptist Church, True Church of Holiness, Chicago Assembly Hall of Jehovah's Witnesses, Holy Memorial Miracle Temple, Apostolic Little Rock Church and Faith Revival Center Church, Inc. It is a community in the bottom third (57th) in getting mortgage and home improvement money, according to the 1986 Woodstock Institute study. The 1980 population was 65,132, down by 3,000 from 1970 (68,854). Its black population grew rapidly from 68.7 percent in 1970 to 98.4 percent in 1980.

72. Beverly

Beverly, in the hilly far South Side section of Chicago, is one of the city's most prominent community areas. Its deep conviction is that it has a lot going for it. Attractive and neat, it has winding, tree-lined streets, perky businesses and many Historic Landmark homes. It also can claim probably the most active community organization in Chicago, the Beverly Area Planning Association (with a large, paid staff) and an art tradition that goes back before the turn of the century. Beverly starts at 87th Street on the north and extends to 107th Street on the south. It follows the Conrail tracks south to Vincennes Avenue on the east and jogs from Western to California to Kedzie on the west. It is ringed by country clubs and public golf courses, the Evergreen Shopping Plaza at 95th and Western, the Dan Ryan Woods on the north and the Conrail tracks on the east. Beverly is an insulated community, except on its south where it merges into

Morgan Park. Beverly residents consider their community special and always have. It began to grow along the Blue Island ridge as early as the 1840s after travelers reached the safe-during-high-water Vincennes Trail. Geographically, Beverly is the highest area of Chicago. Prosperous Chicagoans who wanted to leave downtown built mansions in Beverly. One notable mansion, "The Castle," at 10244 South Longwood Drive is a copy of an Irish castle. Constructed to attract people to move and build here, it is now used by the Beverly Unitarian Church. Beverly has homes designed by Frank Lloyd Wright and his disciple, Walter Burley Griffin. For Chicagoans accustomed to the city's flatness, Beverly's hills are charming. It is very much a residential community. In 1940 a commentator said, "The predominance of single-family homes in Beverly is so great that a bar graph of the distribution of residential structures by type makes the single family detached house stand out like the Field Building in a cemetery." The Beverly Area Planning Association battled to keep the railroad and helped fight and win a crucial anti-solicitation suit against a local realtor. A large percentage of residents are of upper-middle class and of Irish descent. METRA (formerly Rock Island) stops at 107th, 103rd, 99th, 95th and 91st streets and provides Beverly residents with fast transportation to the Loop. Beverly's population was 26,771 in 1970 and 23,360 in 1980.

73. Washington Heights

Washington Heights, to the east of Beverly, is a community divided diagonally by the Old Vincennes Trace (now Vincennes Avenue) and the METRA (formerly Rock Island) tracks. Washington Heights is centered approximately at Racine and 95th. It is separated from neighboring communities by a ring of railroad tracks. These are the east-west bend of the METRA tracks at 89th and 90th streets north, the Conrail tracks on the west and the Chicago and Western Indiana Railroad on the east. South between 103rd and 107th streets, Washington Heights abuts Morgan Park and Roseland. Beverly was once part of the village of Washington Heights (subsequently annexed to Chicago in 1890). Washington Heights is a hodgepodge of communities, including Fernwood on the southwest and Brainard around the park at Loomis and 91st Street on the north. To the east, is the old center of Washington Heights. The Vincennes Trace, or Trail, was the focus of Washington Heights' early development. It had been a cattle trail and this put a damper on early exclusive residential growth. Brick bungalows are popular in this residential community. The neighborhoods of Washington Heights vary considerably, with the most stable being in the far northwest corner, across the tracks from the Dan Ryan Woods. On the list for getting mortgage money and home improvement funds, it is 47th between South Shore and Humboldt Park, according to the 1986 Woodstock Institute report. Washington Heights' population stayed stable from 1970 (36,540) to 1980 (36,453).

74. Mount Greenwood

Mount Greenwood, the community farthest southwest in the city, is best known for its cemeteries. It is one of the city's newest neighborhoods, in terms of both development and the date of its annexation. Its pre-World War I population was only 1,077 but as the streetcar lines extended into it to serve the cemeteries, the population started to grow. The 1980 population was 20,084. It adjoins Beverly at Ridge Country Club between 103rd and 106th streets (about 3000 west). Mount Greenwood zigzags in and out on its four sides, extending to Crawford on the west, 116th Street on the south and where Ridge Country Club connects with the city on the east. Diversions developed around the cemeteries, including a plethora of saloons, the Worth race track and a greyhound race track. A rendering plant opened at the turn of the century. Mount Greenwood in-

The Irish Castle on the northwest corner of 103rd Street and Longwood Drive was built in 1886 by Robert Givins to be a landmark as well as a home. More than 100 years later, it has ceased being a residence and serves as a Unitarian church.

Photo, Mati Maldre

corporated in 1907 to protect its wide-open identity, although gradually its character evolved into a sedate residential neighborhood. In 1927, after a heated referendum, it voted to be annexed by Chicago. Mount Greenwood has kept a suburban atmosphere. It takes its name from a cemetery, the first of many located here. It's proud of its name, and many businesses and churches use "Mount Greenwood" as part of their names. Mount Greenwood's population decreased from 23,186 in 1970 to 20,084 in 1980.

75. Morgan Park

Morgan Park, which lies south of Beverly, is closely and deliberately identified with it. The two community areas and neighborhoods share similar geography, interests and facilities. The Beverly Art Center is in the heart of Morgan Park at 2324 W. 111th Street. Morgan Park extends from 107th Street on the north to 119th Street on the south, and from Halsted (107th to 115th) and Ashland (115th to 119th) on the east to California on the west. On its western border are three cemeteries: Mount Greenwood, Mount Olivet and Mount Hope. The area around 108th and Longwood Drive was once known as "Horse Thief Hollow." A gang of rough-and-ready characters used this heavily-forested ravine to stash and corral horses swiped from the open prairies around the young city. Like Beverly, Morgan Park has tree-lined and winding residential streets. It also grew up along the Blue Island-Vincennes Trail ridge. In the 1870s, three educational institutions were founded here: Mount Vernon Military (now Morgan Park) Academy in 1873, the Chicago Female College in 1873 and the Baptist Theological Seminary in 1877. The latter's president, William Rainey Harper, merged it in 1892 into his new school, the University of Chicago. In 1890, 1914 and 1915, different parts of Morgan Park were annexed to Chicago. A sizeable black community was in Morgan Park before World War I, although for many years that area had few city services such as water or sewers. This very active community (through the Beverly Area Planning Association) solicited 20,000 local signatures and conducted a successful lobbying and media campaign in the early 1980s to persuade Mayor Washington not to close the Morgan Park police station. Its population dropped from 31,016 in 1970 to 29,315 in 1980.

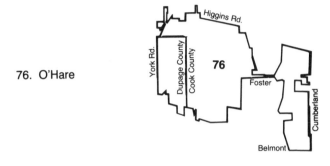

76. O'Hare

76. O'Hare

Before O'Hare International Airport was opened to scheduled airline traffic, this flat, vacant area had only farms and cemeteries. In June of 1942, Douglas Aircraft Company built a plant here, twelve miles northwest of the Loop. The factory at its peak employed 22,000 people. A small airport, Orchard Field, attached to the aircraft plant was known by the call letters ORD. This abbreviation still appears on all O'Hare luggage-tags and documents. In 1949, the site was acquired by the city, but it was not formally annexed until 1956. A thirty-three foot strip of land along Higgins Road was also annexed to make O'Hare contiguous to the city. When the Illinois Supreme Court questioned these annexations, Chicago traded the Higgins strip to the Village of Rosemont for a 185-foot strip along Foster Avenue. In the 1950s, the city annexed a second strip between Peterson Avenue on the north, Belmont on the south, Cumberland Avenue on the east and the Des Plaines River on the west, consolidating its claim to O'Hare. In 1960, only 763 people lived on these 900 acres, although because of an error they were not counted in the census that year. The residences east of the airport are a mixture of single homes, condominiums and apartments. It is an area where lenders in 1986 were more willing to loan money per residential unit than anywhere in Chicago except the Loop, the Near North Side and Lincoln Park. The 1980 population of O'Hare, the neighborhood, was 11,189, up from 6,342 in 1970.

Looking Ahead Through The '90s

Here is the newest and the latest in Chicago's story.

PART THREE

Introduction

We have expanded *Hands On Chicago* to include the 1990s. What an interesting challenge it has proved to be: to look at history as it just happened!

Chicago is a good news town. Local readers and listeners as well as those from around the world find what happens in the great metropolis on Lake Michigan fascinating. A dateline with Chicago in it, they know, promises something extra to a story, whether it's about a strange flood in old tunnels under the Loop, the latest crime, the accomplishments of Chicago's sports heroes or something we are doing to help end school problems or racial segregation.

Hands On Chicago, first published in 1987 on the occasion of Chicago's 150th birthday, was written with an earnest respect for the city, its history and its institutions. It was designed to help make Chicago a more understandable, more workable and more lovable place. It did this by publishing handy, meaningful information about the city. It has attempted to take the reader beyond the facade, behind the glib facts and trivia to Chicago's substance. The book's coverage is not limited to the Loop or gentrified territories, but presents all the communities of Chicago: rich and poor, African-American, Hispanic, ethnic and mixed.

Hands On Chicago has been well received and is a popular seller years after it was first issued. Book dealers and publishers find this extraordinary because such volumes, even the very popular ones, tend to have a shelf life of no more than two or three years. *Hands On Chicago,* after seven years, continued to be in demand and the latest printing had sold out completely. A decision has had to be made either to reprint it one more time or to make it more useful by expanding and updating it. The authors and the publisher agreed to add to it, including a section for Chicago's residents, visitors and observers on the newest and the latest in Chicago's story.

The problem in compiling the material became not what to include, but all we could not. In the years since Chicago celebrated its 150th birthday, it has continued the fast pace of change found in a young city, one that is both dramatic and dynamic.

The temptation was to scramble to update all of the city's sports, politics, crime, new buildings and news events. We have instead selected representative developments with a focus on those occurring during the 1990s.

Michael Jordan and the stadium his popularity helped create is certainly a most representative event that looks toward the future of sports in the city.

The material we have added to this book lists the new buildings that make up the city's skyline, but we have included only those downtown Chicago high-rises completed in the 1990s. Chicago has many structures that are part of the class of the 1990s. Their very newness as well as their size and architectural innovations help tell the story of this dynamic city.

In putting the expanded material in this book the authors have selected two representative events from the cultural and economic development of the city: the creation of the new Harold Washington Public Library and the resumption of railroad-car manufacturing at Pullman 50 years after the historic plant closed.

We have written of changes and inventions, of heroes and political figures, of sports champions and a tragic fire, of a flood and panhandlers in the Loop. We have written of Chicago and the 1990s.

In putting together *Hands On Chicago,* we focused on the city's past. In expanding it, we have looked to Chicago's present and its future.

CHICAGO PUBLIC HOUSING: A NEW VISION

The plans to construct public housing in Chicago in the late 1940s were formulated by City Council members who knowingly bunched together high-rise public housing sites. The poor were to be stacked on top of one another and isolated from the rest of the city around them. Cynical aldermen found this short-sighted and finally disastrous plan an acceptable means of keeping the poor out of their own largely-white wards.

By the early 1970s, a federal judge ended aldermanic veto power over public housing sites. He also ordered the Chicago Housing Authority to develop a scattered-site housing program and work to integrate the segregated units that had been built.

Twenty years later, a new start has been made, inspired by civic groups and other individuals committed to more viable public housing, a start spearheaded by Chicago Housing Authority Chairman Vincent Lane (appointed head of the CHA in 1988; he resigned day-to-day management in 1992 but remains on the CHA board). Under Lane, a successful real estate developer who specialized in housing for people of low and moderate incomes, a true revolution in housing for the poor seems to have begun.

If there was a single point at which the situation reached its nadir, it was the slaying in October 1992 of ten-year-old Dantrell Davis. He was shot by a sniper in the Cabrini-Green Homes as he walked to school with his mother. Forces clamoring for change in Chicago's public housing, when confronted with the terrible spectacle of Dantrell's meaningless murder, collectively cried "Enough!"

Public housing in Chicago in 1992 housed 86,000 people in eighteen developments, ten of which are high rises. They are mean, tough and dangerous places to live.

"There are no children here," one mother told reporter Alex Kotlowitz, who wrote a book bearing that title.

Public housing residents whom we interviewed about living in Chicago Housing Authority housing gave one main reason for wanting to live in public housing—safety from fire. An even more basic reason is that public housing is all poor people can afford.

The city has little decent low income housing, however, for either subsidized or working families. Developing such housing is one of the noblest efforts that non-profit groups are working toward in the city. The Chicago Rehab Network, a coalition of housing advocates and non-profit developers, is creating a quiet revolution in the city for those who require low-income housing.

The city itself, however, offers little one way or the other for the working poor. Its promises in the past to allocate part of such developments as Prairie Shores and Carl Sandburg for poor people were not kept.

The Chicago Housing Authority, under Lane, did move in a positive direction. His efforts were praised by former Housing and Urban Development Secretary Jack Kemp as "progressive"; by *The Chicago Tribune* as "a new light shining at the CHA"; and by *The Wall Street Journal* as "a bold experiment" geared "to end the isolation of the poor." *U.S. News and World Report* named him "a national hero."

Lane moved to refurbish and renovate two lakefront high rises known as Lake Parc Place. "People said, 'You'll never get middle-class people to move in next to these welfare people,' " Lane told *Fortune*. "I say three things. They will if it's safe, if it's clean, and if there's some kind of economic incentive." Half of this project was rented to subsidized families and the other half to working families. Lake Parc was a success, and has a waiting list with 2,000 names.

Lane's revitalization plans for other established, but crime-ridden Chicago Housing Authority developments were even more ambitious. They started with Operation Clean Sweep, a controversial crackdown and apartment-by-apartment sweep of Cabrini-Green.

The Chicago Housing Authority successfully tapped into its Housing and Urban Development funding to tear down some of its worst high rises, to renovate the neighborhoods around Cabrini-Green, and to provide $10 million more worth of social services to its clients. Other Chicago Housing Authority developments are slated for similar upgrading.

Largely as a result of the impact of Lane's efforts and the senseless killing of Dantrell Davis, the future is beginning to look a little more promising for the people who call the Chicago Housing Authority home.

CHICAGO'S ECONOMY: RUST, RUST, GO AWAY

The business pages of Chicago's newspapers in recent years have contained running counts of worker layoffs, companies going out of business and firms relocating out of the area. These phenomena caused the Midwest to become known as "The Rust Belt."

Once in a while, a dramatic glimmer of hope appears. No case highlighted this better than when, on April 27, 1993, a new railroad passenger car rolled off the production line at the Pullman Standard Plant on the Southeast Side of Chicago. It was the first one built there since World War II!

The first Highline passenger rail car made its debut amid festive ceremony. The car, presented to Metra Rail System chairman Jeffrey Ladd, was part of a 313-car Metra order with the Morrison-Knudsen Corporation, the company which took over the Pullman Standard Plant. The $379 million contract called for the manufacture of 173 new cars and the rebuilding of 140 older models.

The rail car manufacturer, which started renovating the old Pullman plant in 1992, has an additional contract worth $100 million to manufacture fifty rail cars for Amtrak, with an option for fifty more.

Railroad cars were first built in Chicago in the 1860s when mogul George Pullman created the plush luxury cars that bore his name. He developed the Pullman area around Lake Calumet as both a manufacturing site and company town in the 1880s. Pullman rail cars continued to be built there throughout the first half of this century, although in steadily dwindling numbers. The company was last at its full manufacturing capacity during World War II. Since then, as transportation patterns changed, the demand for railroad passenger cars largely evaporated, and those built were often manufactured in other countries.

Manufacture of passenger railroad cars at the Pullman plant is expected to continue to grow well into the next century, even more so if proposed plans for high-speed railroads develop.

Newspapers might soon find the need to run a "Jobs Returning" feature, even if such a feature is short and infrequent—at the beginning.

LOOP FLOOD
OF 1992

Every city weathers its share of bizarre events, but that adjective surely describes the flood that paralyzed the Chicago Loop beginning on April 13, 1992.

In dollar claim amounts, insurance underwriters reported the Loop flood as ranking as the ninth worst national disaster of 1992. But, as Mayor Daley later insisted, no one was killed or seriously injured. City employees shouldered the blame and some were either fired or reprimanded. Other individuals got work out of the flood, notably tunnel construction expert John Kenny of Kenny Construction, who became an overnight media celebrity in his hard hat and yellow waders. While total losses can never be tabulated, general estimates exceed $1 billion—with initial claims ranging from the $30 plant a Merchandise Mart florist lost to the $6.8 million damage DePaul University estimated it suffered.

The news media in Chicago tried to romanticize the Loop flood, or at least put a dramatic spin on the strange occurrence. This odd story had one truly suspenseful time element: Would the hole from the Chicago River into the vast, but largely forgotten, complex of tunnels underneath the Loop ever be plugged?

The flood started early on that Monday morning, and most people, at first, could not tell what was happening. The only external sign was a small eddying whirlpool in the North Branch of the Chicago River. The whirlpool was plainly visible swirling in the blue-green water near some pilings beside the bridge over the river at Kinzie Street.

By noon, with the basements of major buildings in the Loop flooded, businesses had to shut down. A giddy feeling pervaded workers freed for the day as they scrambled to find ways home. The subway was flooded and closed. The Chicago Transit Authority suspended collection of fares on the "L" and buses in the Loop and gave free rides to all.

The Kinzie Street site soon became the backdrop for a virtual twenty-four-hour-a-day live television broadcast as reporters attempted to make sense out of the story. An increasingly large number of heavy trucks, cranes and earthmoving vehicles, along with other equipment, soon clogged the streets around the site. In contrast to the normal action of a flood, the Chicago River itself was not rising—its level was going down.

The extensive, mainly forgotten complex of tunnels beneath the Loop quickly became the topic of conversation citywide. As everyone soon concluded, the unwitting culprits were workers from the Chicago Dredge and Lock Company. While installing new pilings to protect the Kinzie bridge over the river, the workers had inadvertently punched pilings through one tunnel wall. They claimed the city had not properly informed them how close the tunnels were to their job site.

The tunnel system rapidly filled with draining river water, then in turn the basements of thirty older Loop buildings became filled with it. Theories of ways to plug the hole proliferated, and a few were tried. One was a huge inflatable bladder. For a few days, even the best attempts failed to stuff the hole or halt the rush of river water into the Loop basements.

Mike Royko got a solicitous call at the *Tribune* inquiring how the situation was affecting him. He told the caller with his usual tongue-in-cheek that the water was almost up to his fourth floor office.

The old tunnels, used for half a century to deliver coal and haul away ashes, had outlets into many older Loop buildings. River water filled basements and sub-basements of prominent Loop buildings, including: LaSalle National Bank, City Hall, the Merchandise Mart, the Chicago Board of Trade (which was forced to halt trading), Marshall Field & Co., Carson Pirie Scott & Co., the Pittsfield Building, the old Wieboldts building, and De-Paul University at Jackson and Wabash.

Marshall Field's State Street store was closed for a week, Carson Pirie Scott & Co. for two. The latter subsequently rehabilitated its basement area, using insurance funds to do so.

As expected, heads rolled. The principal city scapegoat was acting transportation department Commissioner John La Plante. He was forced to resign. A lifelong city worker, he had earlier been responsible for designing the plan to straighten the infamous "S" curve on Lake Shore Drive at the river. La Plante, after being terminated, got a new position as vice president and chief traffic engineer with a firm that held a fat contract to do projects for the city.

Some Loop buildings were closed for weeks by the after-effects of the flood. Their tenants were often hurt by a lack of insurance. One such businessman, whose shop was located on the seventh floor of a Loop building, exclaimed, "I didn't take out flood insurance. It was a safe bet the lake wasn't going to come in my window!"

MAYOR DALEY: LIKE FATHER, LIKE SON

Richard M. Daley
(born April 24, 1942)

Mayor Daley—Chicago has had one off and on since 1955. So linked are the two words in local parlance that when the late Mayor Washington was once greeted by a Ukranian Village resident as "Mayordaley Washington," her gaffe was a source of amusement.

Mayor Richard J. Daley was the mayor from 1955 until his death in December 1976.

His son, Mayor Richard M. Daley, was elected in 1989 to fill out the remainder of the late Harold Washington's second term. The longer Richard M. Daley served in office, the more similarities between him and his famous father seemed to appear.

He was elected by a wide margin to his own first full term as mayor of Chicago on April 2, 1991. Daley, the son, served as an Illinois state senator (from 1972 to 1980), held a county office (state's attorney) from 1980 on, and lost his first bid for mayor in 1983.

The longer Richard M. Daley served in office, the more similarities between him and his famous father seemed to appear.

Richard J. Daley had also served in the Illinois State Senate (in 1936), lost in a political race (for sheriff), and held a county office (clerk). Both Daley the elder and Daley the son lost an election before being elected mayor.

Daley, the elder, wanted and desperately fought for a multimillion dollar transportation project (the proposed Crosstown Expressway was to run north and south directly through the West Side of the city), but his plan was never realized. Daley, the son, dreamed of building a third major regional airport (to handle the air traffic overflow from O'Hare International and Midway Airports) on a controversial site in the Southeast Side of Chicago that would have displaced many residents. The Third Airport, too, failed to achieve popular acceptance, funding or reality.

Both father and son were embarrassed by a uniquely Chicago-style affliction: political proteges investigated, indicted, and some convicted of corruption. Among political cronies of Richard J. Daley who went to jail was powerful 31st Ward Alderman Thomas Keane (known for remarking, "Daley wanted power, and I wanted to make money, and we both succeeded"). When Keane was convicted of rigging insider land sales in 1974, his wife Adeline won an easy victory to fill his council seat.

Richard M. Daley's list, while shorter, featured City Clerk Walter Kozubowski, whom Daley had retained on the Democratic Party ballot despite rumors that the clerk faced a federal investigation and possible indictment. Kozubowski pleaded guilty in the spring of 1993 to felony charges that he paid six employees for little or no work over 12 years.

Both Richard J. and Richard M. Daley used unique speaking and communicating styles. Their often malaprop-laden idiom, twisted syntax and linguistic fumbling were displayed at press conferences. "They want to take the politics out of poverty, and politics should never be in poverty," Daley the elder once told a committee in Washington. His son, reflecting on the consequences of the Great Loop Flood of 1992, snapped at a reporter, "We did a very good job on the tragedy. No one was injured or killed. The evacuation of the downtown area was an example for the federal government to follow."

Both Daleys were to-the-bone Chicagoans with an honest feel and concern at times for the people of the city.

PANHANDLERS IN THE LOOP

In the 1990s Chicago has seen an unexpected change in its downtown area. This was a marked increase in the number of panhandlers holding out paper cups and offering a plea phrased in such words as "Have a nice day" or simply "Hello."

These individuals, in *Chicago Tribune* interviews, spoke of their lives and homelessness, the response of middle-class passersby, the facts of day-to-day survival, mental problems, the lack of alternatives, and the little ways they have found to help them make it.

Many of these panhandlers spoke of attempting to avoid homeless shelters.

"I've tried the shelters," said one woman. "I have a list of them. They give me no security. Sometimes, I stay by the river."

The hopelessness of one man was expressed in his words, "I've been through a hell of a life, and then I turn around and have to die."

Another said, "I know it's going to get better. I keep my Bible with me. I know it. That's why I have a smile on my face."

Most spoke of making between $20 and $30 a day by panhandling.

A man on the Randolph Street Bridge said, "I'm not a thief, that's one thing for sure. I'm a panhandler, a hustler, call it what you want, I don't like calling it begging."

Michael on the Wabash Avenue Bridge, asked where he spent the night, explained, "There are three dumpsters near here for recycling. One of them is for newspapers. That is where I have been sleeping nights."

An older man added, "I grew up in the Depression, and we had more than they do now. At least you could eat."

One new promising way for panhandlers to make money is by selling *Streetwise*. It is a one-dollar-a-copy newspaper published to create a way for the homeless to earn money. The vendor keeps a portion of the money for each paper sold. Editorially, issues so far have always had something to say. On most corners in the Loop, you hear the singsong of an enterprising vendor calling, "Empower the homeless! Get your *Streetwise!*"

PAXTON HOTEL FIRE

Rarely in Chicago's history have firefighters played as crucial a role as they did in the Paxton Hotel Fire on March 16, 1993.

Firefighters did not save the Paxton itself, a single room occupancy (or S.R.O.) hotel at 1432 North LaSalle Street. As flames raced through it, abetted by strong winds, the structure was quickly engulfed. Residents opened windows to escape, thereby creating more drafts to feed the fire.

The Paxton Hotel was filled to near capacity with 130 residents, a mixture of students and older people on fixed incomes. Average rent at the Paxton was $280 a month. To keep rents low enough for such individuals to afford rooms in S.R.O. hotels, city fire codes did not require the installation of expensive safety features such as sprinkler systems.

When the first fire trucks arrived at a little after 4 a.m., firefighters glimpsed people perched on window ledges and literally hanging out windows on the higher floors. Many residents had jumped to safety, some being injured in the process. These people lay on the ground.

Firefighters raised their ladders to save as many of the unfortunate residents as possible. In vivid scenes captured by television mini-cam crews, the heroics of Chicago's fire department were dramatically underscored. Firefighters, their faces smothered in bellowing smoke, reached in windows and grabbed residents out of their rooms. In other scenes, firefighters held victims precariously and carried or guided them down the ladders to safety. Shot after shot showed them risking their lives in efforts to save people. A fire official at the scene estimated at least twenty-seven residents were rescued this way.

One Paxton resident, a member of the Jesse White Tumbling Team, used his acrobatic skills to save his son and himself while jumping out a window.

Not all were rescued. Twenty persons perished, some found in their beds, others in charred hallways; one luckless person died in a closet. Authorities found it difficult to uncover all the bodies in the collapsed, burned-out structure.

The Paxton Hotel Fire is a story of sadness, loss and death among people who were beginning to survive in Chicago. But it will also be remembered as a scene of resourcefulness and heroism by residents and, especially, by the firefighters of Chicago's Fire Department.

PEOPLE MOVER AT O'HARE

O'Hare International Airport has a new toy and Chicago residents and visitors can have a look into the future, at least into the future of public transportation.

The airport's futuristic new mechanism is known as a "people mover:" a system of tracks and automated cars (no driver on board) on a 2.7 mile line connecting the long-term parking area and terminals.

This high-tech mini-"L" line started in May 1993 to carry passengers after design problems caused a two-year delay on the $127 million project.

For Chicagoans, used to loud, rickety "L" cars and human-error problems on the subway and elevated system of the city, the people mover is astonishing. It runs on huge, nitrogen-filled Michelin tires with treads twelve inches across. A button on the car can put the rider in touch with the control center and a car will stop automatically if it gets too close to a car in front of it.

The speed the people mover cars can attain is twenty-six miles an hour and the entire trip between the parking lot and Terminal One is 7.5 minutes.

Construction and operation of this project was underwritten by the airlines that use the airport and the fare is free.

The hope, at least, is that the congestion that often exists at O'Hare at points of arrival and departure will become a thing of the past as people realize the future is a free ride.

SCHOOL REFORM

Chicago faced the 1990s with a bold blueprint for what is commonly called "school reform." Whether one dubs it reform, change or outright revolution, this new plan represented a major shift in the way that local public schools were controlled and operated.

Movement for change started in the wake of a bitter Chicago Board of Education-Chicago Teachers' Union strike in September 1987, one that stopped Chicago public schools from opening on time. The reform movement was spurred by the deep problems of the schools as exemplified by a widely-cited comment made by then Secretary of Education William Bennett on November 7, 1987: "Chicago's schools are the worst in the nation. You've got close to educational meltdown here."

The groundswell for change also followed a devastating series by the *Chicago Tribune* staff, who uncovered more strong evidence showing that the city's public schools were among the worst in the country.

A broad coalition of concerned groups came together to do something about the state of education in Chicago. Differing widely in the places from which their members came and in the agendas they held, this coalition nevertheless reached a rough consensus. Agreement tended to center around the notions that: 1) Local public schools needed more autonomous power to set up particular programs and control budgets; 2) School principals needed more substantial authority and bigger staffs; 3) Lower-income receiving public schools needed a movement toward parity and equity in distribution of funding; 4) Non-performing teachers needed to respond to pressure to do better, or else be forced to leave; and 5) An oversight commission was needed to promote reform thoroughly.

Teachers' union local president Jackie Vaughn has said that real school reform will happen when schools have supplies, academic freedom, and money.

Led by business leaders and educators, the coalition turned itself into a movement able to get Senate Bill 1840 enacted. Those who wanted change converged on state legislators in Springfield. They sported yellow "Don't Come Home Without It [reform]!" buttons, and, with the help of concerned lawmakers and a number of civic-minded foundations, achieved their goal.

The historic legislation mandated a number of things: a) Local school councils would be created, made up of members elected by the students' parents, members of each community, and representatives from each public school's own staff; b) These local school councils would have the power to hire and fire school principals; c) Local school council board members would create ambitious three-year plans to address improvements in student academic achievement, attendance levels and overall performance; d) Local school councils would budget, be collective bargaining agents, and work with the bureaucrats from the central Pershing Road offices of the Chicago Board of Education.

This ambitious agenda for radical, from-the-roots up reform met with varying degrees of compliance. Especially in the first elections, voter turnout was high although certain public schools had few candidates or parents choose to run for places on the local school council. Others, witnessing a variety of pressure groups vie for the powerful positions, saw extraordinary results. It seemed to stir the schools' souls. Some local school councils decided that, if they had the power, they should exercise it—and there and then fired their principals whether they were performing well or not!

No one promised immediate or dramatic improvements in reading or math scores, and the reform plan passed the legislature because it did not require additional funding by the state.

School reform in Chicago was not the creation of an entirely new educational system, nor was it merely the bringing of new personnel into classrooms. It was the empowering of a new group of people—people closer to the students themselves—to make tough judgments about educational goals, successes, and hopes. If the plan fell short of full-blown reform, it was at least a fresh hope.

SKYLINE ADDITIONS IN THE 1990S

The 1990s have witnessed a bumper crop of the commodity Chicago is world-famous for: architecturally-fascinating buildings. Here are some of the buildings completed in this decade and a few subjective thoughts about them:

1) The 311 South Wacker Building. Sixty-five stories. 1,281,000 square feet. Completed in 1990.

The world's tallest reinforced concrete structure. Did you know that?

2) Two Prudential Plaza. 180 North Stetson Ave., next to the Prudential Building. Sixty-four floors. 941,000 square feet. Completed in 1990.

An impressive Art Deco piece of Chicago's skyline.

3) The 181 West Madison Building. Fifty floors. 1,100,000 square feet. Completed in 1990.

A beautiful building with a stepped-back design that pays homage to Eliel Saarinen's Second Place entry in the 1922 Tribune Tower Architectural Competition.

4) The Chicago Title and Trust Center. 161 North Clark Street. Fifty floors. 980,000 square feet. Completed in 1992.

Supposed to be matched with a second tower, but not soon because there is so much vacant office space on the market. Contrasts sensibly with the James R. Thompson State of Illinois Building across Clark Street.

5) The 77 West Wacker Drive Building.
Fifty floors. 940,000 square feet. Completed in 1992.

Stately, classical structure that has become part of the city's river row of innovative buildings.

6) The 120 North LaSalle Building.
Forty floors. 380,000 square feet. Completed in 1991.

One of the most creative, imaginatively-designed buildings in the Loop both at street level and as a skyscraper.

7) City Place. 676 North Michigan Avenue.
Forty floors. 140,000 square feet. Completed in 1990.

Chicago's latest, upwardly-designed shopping mall. The apartment section was designed by a separate architectural firm.

8) Morton International Building. 100
N. Riverside. Thirty-six floors. 760,000 square feet. Completed in 1990.

The architectural firm of Perkins & Will did an extraordinary job of integrating the design of this building within the context of the river.

9) The One North Franklin Building.
Thirty-six floors. 615,000 square feet. Completed in 1991.

Favorable location, but this building ran hard into the big problem of the 1990s, a low occupancy rate.

10) The 515 North State Building. Thirty
floors. 225,000 square feet. Completed in 1990.

This building with a very imaginative cutout in the top houses the American Medical Association. It is on North State Street in an area with potential, parking and consequent good oc-cupancy rate.

11) The 633 St. Clair Place Building.

Twenty-eight floors. 535,000 square feet. Completed in 1991.

Handsome steel and glass addition to the Streeterville neighborhood. To say that it started off with much more space than tenants is an understatement.

12) The Chicago Bar Association Building.

321 South Plymouth Court. Sixteen floors. 102,000 square feet. Completed in 1990.

Hidden on South Plymouth Court (between State and Dearborn), this simple design is highlighted by an exciting statue on its facade.

13) The Rookery.

209 South LaSalle St. Twelve floors. 272,000 square feet. Renovation and reopening completed in 1990.

This newly renovated structure is almost everyone's choice as one of the most exciting buildings (and certainly, lobbies) ever designed by Chicago architects.

14) The 820 West Jackson Building.

Nine floors. 182,000 square feet. Completed in 1990.

Started the 1990s with a low occupancy rate and enticingly low rental rates.

STATE STREET:
A NEW LOOK

The return of State Street to being an actual street, not some half-mall, half-CTA bus corridor, is viewed by some as a return to its nature, in the sense that form follows function.

State and Madison, from the turn of the century on, was universally referred to as the "world's busiest intersection." State Street was always known as the throbbing heart of Chicago's Loop, which was itself the focus of the city of Chicago's businesses and commerce.

Frank Sinatra crooned, "On State Street/that great street/they do things they don't do on Broadway!" Once there were ten different department stores on State Street. The world-renowned window displays of Marshall Field and Carson Pirie Scott, especially at Christmas, were and still are a mecca for children.

State Street had it all, from the premier example of commercial architecture, Louis Sullivan's world-famous Carson Pirie Scott & Company; to the historic Art Deco Chicago Theater palace; to an auction house where you could pull up a chair almost any time of the day; to the incomparable Boston Store. There was also Wieboldts, where tigers were once on display; the architecturally interesting Sears Roebuck & Company store; a range of pawnshops; and even a string of burlesque houses, although these tended to be just south of the loop made by the "L" tracks.

Underneath mighty State Street runs the arterial North-South subway line, shuttling people to and from this bustling commercial strip. Buses, for most of the century, lined up where cable and streetcars once did on State Street, headed north and south into Chicago's myriad neighborhoods.

The hurlyburly of thriving businesses, which centered on State Street, brought to the street itself a particular aura. "State Street" became a byword for an almost unlimited potential for financial, business and commercial success.

By the 1960s, a time of social change and turmoil, the storied greatness of State Street had largely waned, and its flagship businesses were struggling. The more fashionable retail establishments—including a branch of Marshall Field & Company in the white-marbled temple to shopping, Water Tower Place—opened on North Michigan Avenue, an area soon crowded with other prestigious vendors such as Saks Fifth Avenue, Nieman Marcus, Niketown and eventually that most New-York-like icon, Bloomingdale's.

The downtown stretch of State Street by 1970 resembled a boxer who had lost his punch. A miracle, or at least some striking act of magic, was needed to revive State Street. City planners and chieftains of the State Street Council, a merchants' association, thought they had found their lost magic formula in the notion to ban all automobiles from State Street and thus create a Loop version of a typical mall.

The State Street Mall, completed in 1979, never quite worked. The design actually tended to isolate State Street from the rest of the Loop and, therefore, from Chicago. Some felt a major reason why the mall failed was its widened sidewalks. The expanses of walking area made the shopping area feel empty, even when it was not.

Still groping for a solution to State Street's problems, planners finally decided to deep-six the mall design, explore the use of trolleys, look at allowing cars to use the street again and give State Street a new overall feel and look—one more befitting the 1990s.

Louis Sullivan would most likely approve the new game plan for State Street, but he would probably be even more radical in the quest to find a form which appropriately reflects and expresses this quintessential Chicago street's manifold and crucial functions in the downtown life of the city.

UNITED CENTER: THE HOUSE THAT MICHAEL BUILT

New astronomical discoveries are not so rare in our day as scientists scan the heavens with improved equipment.

Such a discovery was made in the mid-1980s in Chicago. Not just a star, but a supernova was reported in Chicago—and his name was Michael Jordan (born 1963).

The young basketball player carried his team, the Chicago Bulls, first to respectability and then to world championships. His nickname "Air Jordan" came from his seeming ability to fly toward the basket on his way to a show-stopping dunk and a certain two points.

Michael Jordan, who perennially won league scoring championships (his average points per game an astonishing 30.1!) and often the Most Valuable Player award, came with talent, a driven work ethic, magic, competitiveness, intensity and a great smile. He proved to be a basketball player who belonged to the world, but most especially to Chicago.

But Michael Jordan became more than a superb competitive athlete, a winner. He proved an immense money-maker for anything and everybody even remotely connected with him. Vendors of Bulls t-shirts, caps, posters and makers of shoes ("Air Jordans," of course), the soft drink Coca-Cola, and automobiles—all benefitted from their association with him. To "be like Mike" was the refrain of the day.

His memorial, like Babe Ruth's, will be a stadium, the United Center. The Jordan phenomenon became so lucrative that the name of the house that Michael built could be sold and it was—to United Airlines!

The United Center stands as a monument to a man, to two successful sports franchises (it houses the Chicago Blackhawks hockey team, too) and to success at making money. The United Center also hosts a variety of concerts, ice shows, sports exhibitions and other functions.

Neighborhood residents displaced by construction of the new stadium organized and negotiated with its developers. To some extent they were satisfied that their needs were at least taken into consideration.

More accommodations were made within the stadium itself. Restroom space is three times larger than that in the Chicago Stadium, with an emphasis on increasing facilities for women. Twice the number of concession stands were created.

Persons with disabilities found the building well adapted to their special needs with two hundred seats available for them as well as special concession stands.

Playing action has been enhanced with an eight-sided color video scoreboard with replay capabilities to help the audience relive important moments.

In contrast to the funding of the second Comiskey Park (underwritten by State financed bonds), the developers of the United Center describe it as "a privately-financed, state-of-the-art, multiuse facility which will take Chicago sports and entertainment into the 21st Century."

Chicago, on the other hand, will most likely treasure the United Center for a generation or more to come as "The House that Michael Built."

HAROLD WASHINGTON LIBRARY CENTER: READERS ARE LEADERS

Chicago's late Mayor Harold Washington, a controversial but much loved politician, seemed to gain respect the longer he served in office and the more things he accomplished. From many who gave him praise only grudgingly, Mayor Washington won it with his energy, zest, penchant for florid oratory mixed with street slang, and honest caring for the future of the city. Many hoped these qualities would be forever embodied in the new public library named after him.

Mayor Washington was a lifelong voracious reader with an interest in almost every topic. When he flew somewhere on a trip, a bag of books was always with him and every book was devoured. The knowledge, wisdom and experience Mayor Washington got from books underlay a large measure of the esteem that people had for him.

Washington had a vision that reading could do something special for the city he loved so much. He took an avid interest in the plans for building a new public library, from its design and construction to selection of the proper site.

But within two years of being built, the Harold Washington Library Center—far from moving the city dramatically forward—was undergoing dramatic cuts in services. The building and its potential earned good grades initially. It was designed by architect Thomas H. Beebe who won praise for his previous work at the Sulzer Regional Library at 4455 N. Lincoln Avenue.

Of its Classical design, Paul Gapp, the late Pulitzer-Prize-winning *Chicago Tribune* architecture critic, said, "The library fails as an immense Neo-Classical object on the streetscape." Gapp called it "a disappointingly leaden exercise."

However, Gapp also saw the library as functionally a triumph, commenting, "As a clearly organized and handsome collection of interior spaces, the new Harold Washington Library Center appears to be an unqualified function success."

The new structure—which opened October 7, 1991—stands a half block south of the Loop on State Street at Congress. It is a ten-story building containing almost five million books, magazines and microfilm archives.

The library's facilities include many things that Chicagoans had not dreamed of, all looking toward the future. These include a preservation laboratory to save rare books that are falling apart; a beautiful auditorium for lectures, films, and events seating 400; a drive-up window; and an impressive display of artwork by more than fifty artists.

The service cutbacks—ordered because the state of Illinois cut funding to the city and its libraries—included closing both the Municipal Reference Library and the Clarence Darrow Library at the County Jail, trimming the operating hours at local branch libraries throughout the city, and shuttering the Harold Washington Library Center itself on Mondays.

The Chicago Public Library system was also forced to cut its acquisitions and its maintenance staff, and was left with no money to purchase new equipment or furniture.

Working under such conditions forced many capable, dedicated and talented employees to seek more productive environments in which to work.

Even as some of the cuts were modified, if not fully restored, the Chicago Public Library system's overall image had suffered, both professionally and in the eyes of its many patrons.

Harold Washington, honestly, would have cried—not only as mayor, but even as a kid wanting to check a book out of the library.

Index

Index

Index

Index

Index

Index